LIBRARY AND INFORMATION RESOURCE MANAGEMENT

LIBRARY AND INFORMATION RESOURCE MANAGEMENT

Arul Jothi
M.Sc., M.Ed.
Principal, Arcot Sri Mahalakshmi Women's Teacher Training Institute,
Villapakkam, Vellore Dist.-632521 T.N.

Dr. D.L. Balaji
B.Com., M.A., M.Phil., D.Lit.
Correspondent, Arcot Sri Mahalakshmi Educational Institutions,
Villapakkam, Vellore Dist.-632521 T.N.

Pramod Kumar Singh
Deptt. of Library Science,
Vinoba Bhave University,
Hazaribagh

CENTRUM PRESS
NEW DELHI-110002 (INDIA)

CENTRUM PRESS
H.O.: 4360/4, Ansari Road, Daryaganj,
New Delhi-110 002 (India)
Ph.: 23278000, 23261597
B.O.: No. 1015, Ist Main Road, BSK IIIrd Stage
IIIrd Phase, IIIrd Block,
Bangalore - 560 085 (India)
Tel.: 080-41723429
Visit us at: www.centrumpress.com

Library and Information Resource Management

First Edition, 2009

PRINTED IN INDIA

Printed at Balaji Offset, Delhi

Contents

Preface

Library management refers to the issues involved in managing a library. There were days when libraries were considered as a storehouse of books. Today Libraries are much more than that. Libraries are now looked upon as information centers, where information is gathered, stored and disseminated to its members. With the ever-increasing sea of information, this modern function of the library is becoming very complex and tedious to handle manually. The librarian has to devote most of his time to handing such functions of the library. He does not get time to guide the people to the right books for their information needs. Library Automation System is designed to meet the needs of all information seekers. Academic researchers can search the world's library collections using a seamlessly integrated client. For the librarian, Library Automation System provides simple interfaces to catalog new books, manage patrons, create reports and control budgets and acquisitions.

As information services become more complex in nature and more technologically sophisticated, managers need to keep pace with innovations and thinking in the field to offer the most professional service with the resources they have. Information resource management (IRM) is an idea whose time has come. While the notion has existed for more than a decade, recent developments in the world of information processing have made the concept and the philosophy underlying it not only viable but imperative. Interpreted literally, IRM suggests that data or information should be recognized as an entity independent of the technology that manipulates it. Further, it is seen as representing worth to its possessor. As such, it is recognized as a significant organizational resource in much the same way as people, machines, and capital are considered to be corporate resources. There are various factors that contribute to an enabled environment for optimum utilisation of information resources. These include the digital form of information resources, which are inherently sharable, consortia as a concept to bring people and materials together and unified portals as technology to bring together disparate and heterogeneous resources for sharing and access. Explores the capabilities of emerging technologies that support sharing electronic resources in a heterogeneous and distributed consortia environment.

It is hoped that this book shall provide the reader all there is to know about quality management in libraries and shall prove to be a worthy addition to any librarian's bookshelf. Students of library and information science would also find this book a concise and precise reference tool.

— *Pramod Kumar Singh*

UNIT-I

Library and Information Society

Library: Meaning, Definition

A library is a collection of information, sources, resources, books, and services, and the structure in which it is housed: it is organized for use and maintained by a public body, an institution, or a private individual.

In the more traditional sense, a library is a collection of books.

The term can mean the collection, the building that houses such a collection, or both.

Public and institutional collections and services may be intended for use by people who choose not to—or cannot afford to—purchase an extensive collection themselves, who need material no individual can reasonably be expected to have, or who require professional assistance with their research.

However, with the collection of media other than books for storing information, many libraries are now also repositories and access points for maps, prints, or other documents and various storage media such as microform (microfilm/microfiche), audio tapes, CDs, cassettes, videotapes, and DVDs. Libraries may also provide public facilities to access CD-ROMs, subscription databases, and the Internet.

Thus, modern libraries are increasingly being redefined as places to get unrestricted access to information in many formats and from many sources. In addition to providing materials, they also provide the services of specialists, librarians, who are experts at finding and organizing information and at interpreting information needs.

More recently, libraries are understood as extending beyond the physical walls of a building, by including material accessible by electronic means, and by providing the assistance of librarians in navigating and analyzing tremendous amounts of knowledge with a variety of digital tools.

The term "library" has itself acquired a secondary meaning: "a collection of useful material for common use," and in this sense is used in fields such as computer science, mathematics and statistics, electronics and biology.

Early History

Antiquity: The first two libraries were composed for the most part, of published records, a particular type of library called archives. Archaeological findings from the ancient city-states of Sumer have revealed temple rooms full of clay tablets in cuneiform script. These archives were made up almost completely of the records of commercial transactions or inventories, with only a few documents touching theological matters, historical records or legends. Things were much the same in the government and temple records on papyrus of Ancient Egypt.

The earliest discovered private archives were kept at Ugarit; besides correspondence and inventories, texts of myths may have been standardized practice-texts for teaching new scribes. There is also evidence of libraries at Nippur about 1900 B.C. and those at Nineveh about 700 B.C. showing a library classification system.

Over 30,000 clay tablets from the Library of Ashurbanipal have been discovered at Ninevah, providing archaeologists with an amazing wealth of Mesopotamian literary, religious and administrative work. Among the findings were the Enuma Elish, also known as *the Epic of Creation,* which depicts a traditional Babylonian view of creation, the Epic of Gilgamesh, a large selection of "omen texts" including *Enuma Anu Enlil* which "contained omens dealing with the moon, its visibility, eclipses, and conjunction with planets and fixed stars, the sun, its corona, spots, and eclipses, the weather, namely lightning, thunder, and clouds, and the planets and their visibility, appearance, and stations.", and astronomic/astrological texts, as well as standard lists used by scribes and scholars such as word lists, bilingual vocabularies, lists of signs and synonyms, and lists of medical diagnoses.

Libraries in Persian Empire

During the Achaemenid Persian Empire (558–330 BC) the religious and scientific books of Persia since Zoroaster, were archived in the libraries of "Ganj-i-hapigan" in Takht-i-Suleiman and "Dez-i-Napesht" in Persepolis. These books were probably in the fields of philosophy, astronomy, alchemy and medical sciences, the fields in which Magus of Persia were master in. After the invasion of Persia by Alexander the Great all these books were burned. It has been mentioned in the book Arda Viraf that:

> *"He came to Persia with severe cruelty and war and devastation... and destroyed the metropolis and empire, and made them desolate... all the avesta and zand, written upon prepared cow-skins and with gold ink, was deposited in the archives... he burned them up."*

Libraries in the Hellenic world and Rome

Private or personal libraries made up of non-fiction and fiction books (as opposed to the state or institutional records kept in archives) appeared in classical Greece in the 5th century BC. The celebrated book collectors of Hellenistic Antiquity were listed in the late second century in *Deipnosophistae:*

> *Polycrates of Samos and Pisistratus who was tyrant of Athens, and Euclides who was himself also an Athenian and Nicorrates of Samos and even the kings of Pergamos, and Euripides the poet and Aristotle the philosopher, and Nelius his librarian; from whom they say our countryman Ptolemæus, surnamed Philadelphus, bought them all, and transported them, with all those which*

he had collected at Athens and at Rhodes to his own beautiful Alexandria.

All these libraries were Greek; the cultivated Hellenized diners in *Deipnosophistae* pass over the libraries of Rome in silence. By the time of Augustus there were public libraries near the forums of Rome: there were libraries in the Porticus Octaviae near the Theatre of Marcellus, in the temple of Apollo Palatinus, and in the Biblioteca Ulpiana in the Forum of Trajan. The state archives were kept in a structure on the slope between the Roman Forum and the Capitoline Hill.

Private libraries appeared during the late republic: Seneca inveighed against libraries fitted out for show by non-reading owners who scarcely read their titles in the course of a lifetime, but displayed the scrolls in bookcases (*armaria*) of citrus wood inlaid with ivory that ran right to the ceiling: "by now, like bathrooms and hot water, a library is got up as standard equipment for a fine house (*domus*). Libraries were amenities suited to a villa, such as Cicero's at Tusculum, Maecenas's several villas, or Livy the Younger's, all described in surviving letters.

At the Villa of the Papyri at Herculaneum, apparently the villa of Caesar's father-in-law, the Greek library has been partly preserved in volcanic ash; archaeologists speculate that a Latin library, kept separate from the Greek one, may await discovery at the site.

In the West, the first public libraries were established under the Roman Empire as each succeeding emperor strove to open one or many which outshone that of his predecessor. Unlike the Greek libraries, readers had direct access to the scrolls, which were kept on shelves built into the walls of a large room. Reading or copying was normally done in the room itself. The surviving records give only a few instances of lending features. As a rule Roman public libraries were bilingual: they had a Latin room and a Greek room. Most of the large Roman baths were also cultural centers, built from the start with a library, with the usual two room arrangement for Greek and Latin texts.

Libraries were filled with parchment scrolls as at Library of Pergamum and on papyrus scrolls as at Alexandria: export of prepared writing materials was a staple of commerce. There were a few institutional or royal libraries which were open to an educated public (like the Library of Alexandria, once the largest library in the ancient world), but on the whole collections were private. In those rare cases where it was possible for a scholar to consult library books there seems to have been no direct access to the stacks. In all recorded cases the books were kept in a relatively small room where the staff went to get them for the readers, who had to consult them in an adjoining hall or covered walkway.

In the sixth century, at the very close of the Classical period, the great libraries of the Mediterranean world remained those of Constantinople and Alexandria. Cassiodorus, minister to Theodoric, established a monastery at Vivarium in the heel of Italy with a library where he attempted to bring Greek learning to Latin readers and preserve texts both sacred and secular for future generations. As its unofficial librarian, Cassiodorus not only collected as many manuscripts as he could, he also wrote treatises aimed at instructing his monks in the proper uses of reading and methods for copying texts accurately. In the end, however, the library at Vivarium was dispersed and lost within a century.

Through Origen and especially the scholarly presbyter Pamphilus of Caesarea, an avid collector of books of Scripture, the theological school of Caesarea won a reputation for having the most extensive ecclesiastical library of the time, containing more than 30,000 manuscripts: Gregory Nazianzus, Basil the Great, Jerome and others came to study there.

With education firmly in Christian hands, however, many of the works of classical antiquity were no longer considered useful. Old texts were washed off the valuable parchment and papyrus, which were reused, forming palimpsests. As scrolls gave way to the new book-form, the codex, which was universally used for Christian literature, old manuscript scrolls were cut apart and used to stiffen leather bindings.

Ancient Chinese Libraries

Little is known about early Chinese libraries, save what is written about the imperial library which began with the Qin Dynasty. One of the curators of the imperial library in the Han Dynasty is believed to have been the first to establish a library classification system and the first book notation system. At this time the library catalog was written on scrolls of fine silk and stored in silk bags.

Islamic Libraries

In Persia many libraries were established by the Zoroastrian elite and the Persian Kings. Among the first ones was a royal library in Isfahan. One of the most important public libraries established around 667 AD in south-western Iran was the Library of Gundishapur. It was a part of a bigger scientific complex located at the Academy of Gundishapur. Upon the rise of Islam, libraries in newly Islamic lands knew a brief period of expansion in the Middle East, North Africa, Sicily and Spain. Like the Christian libraries, they mostly contained books which were made of paper, and took a codex or modern form instead of scrolls; they could be found in mosques, private homes, and universities. In Aleppo, for example the largest and probably the oldest mosque library, the Sufiya, located at the city's Grand Umayyad Mosque, contained a large book collection of which 10,000 volumes were reportedly bequeathed by the city's most famous ruler, Prince Sayf al-Dawla. Some mosques sponsored public libraries. Ibn al-Nadim's bibliography *Fihrist* demonstrates the devotion of medieval Muslim scholars to books and reliable sources; it contains a description of thousands of books circulating in the Islamic world circa 1000, including an entire section for books about the doctrines of other religions. Unfortunately, modern Islamic libraries for the most part do not hold these antique books; many were lost, destroyed by Mongols, or removed to European libraries and museums during the colonial period.

By the 8th century first Iranians and then Arabs had imported the craft of papermaking from China, with a paper mill already at work in Baghdad in 794. By the 9th century completely public libraries started to appear in many Islamic cities. They were called "halls of Science" or *dar al-'ilm*. They were each endowed by Islamic sects with the purpose of representing their tenets as well as promoting the dissemination of secular knowledge.

The 9th century Abbasid Caliph al-Mutawakkil of Iraq, even ordered the construction of a 'zawiyat qurra *literally an enclosure for readers which was `lavishly furnished and equipped.'* In Shiraz Adhud al-Daula (d. 983) set up a library, described by the medieval historian, al-Muqaddasi, as`*a complex of buildings surrounded by gardens with lakes and waterways. The buildings were topped with domes, and comprised an upper and a lower story with a total, according to the chief official, of 360 rooms.... In each department, catalogues were placed on a shelf... the rooms were furnished with carpets...'*. The libraries often employed translators and copyists in large numbers, in order to render into Arabic the bulk of the available Persian, Greek, Roman and Sanskrit non-fiction and the classics of literature. This flowering of Islamic learning ceased centuries later when learning began declining in the Islamic world, after many of these libraries were destroyed by Mongol invasions. Others were victim of wars and religious strife in the Islamic world. However, a few examples of these medieval libraries, such as the libraries of Chinguetti in West Africa, remain intact and relatively unchanged even today. Another ancient library from this period which is still operational and expanding is the Central Library of Astan Quds Razavi in the Iranian city of Mashhad, which has been operating for more than six centuries.

A number of distinct features of the modern library were introduced in the Islamic world, where libraries not only served as a collection of manuscripts as was the case in ancient libraries, but also as a public library and lending library, a centre for the instruction and spread of sciences and ideas, a place for meetings and discussions, and sometimes as a lodging for scholars or boarding school for pupils. The concept of the library catalogue was also introduced in medieval Islamic libraries, where books were organized into specific genres and categories.

The contents of these Islamic libraries were copied by Christian monks in Muslim/Christian border areas, particularly Spain and Sicily. From there they eventually made their way into other parts of Christian Europe. These copies joined works that had been preserved directly by Christian monks from Greek and Roman originals, as well as copies Western Christian monks made of Byzantine works. The resulting conglomerate libraries are the basis of every modern library today.

Medieval Christian Libraries

With the retrenchment of literacy in the Roman west during the fourth and fifth centuries, fewer private libraries were maintained, and those in unfortified villas proved to be among their most combustible contents.

In the Early Middle Ages, after the fall of the Western Roman Empire and before the rise of the large Western Christian monastery libraries beginning at Montecassino, libraries were found in scattered places in the Christian Middle East.

Medieval library design reflected the fact that these manuscripts —created via the labour-intensive process of hand copying— were valuable possessions. Library architecture developed in response to the need for security. Librarians often chained books to lecterns, armaria (wooden chests), or shelves, in well-lit rooms. Despite this protectiveness, many libraries were willing to lend their books if provided with security deposits (usually money or a book of equal value). Monastic libraries lent and borrowed books from each other frequently and lending policy was often theologically grounded. For example, the Franciscan monasteries loaned books to each other without a security deposit since according to their vow of poverty only the entire order could own property. In 1212 the council of Paris condemned those monasteries that still forbade loaning books, reminding them that lending is "one of the chief works of mercy."

Lending meant more than just having another work to read to librarians; while the work was in their possession, it could be copied, thus enriching the library's own collecion. The book lent as a counter effort was often copied in the same way, so both libraries ended up having an additional title. The early libraries located in monastic cloisters and associated with scriptoria were collections of lecterns with books chained to them.

Shelves built above and between back-to-back lecterns were the beginning of bookpresses. The chain was attached at the fore-edge of a book rather than to its spine. Book presses came to be arranged in carrels (perpendicular to the walls and therefore to the windows) in order to maximize lighting, with low bookcases in front of the windows. This *stall system* (fixed bookcases perpendicular to exterior walls pierced by closely spaced windows) was characteristic of English institutional libraries. In Continental libraries, bookcases were arranged parallel to and against the walls. This *wall system* was first introduced on a large scale in Spain's El Escorial.

Early Modern Libraries

Johannes Gutenberg's movable type innovation in the 1400s revolutionized bookmaking. From the 15th century in central and northern Italy, the assiduously assembled libraries of humanists and their enlightened patrons provided a nucleus around which an "academy" of scholars congregated in each Italian city of consequence. Cosimo de Medici in Florence established his own collection, which formed the basis of the Laurentian Library. In Rome, the papal collections were brought together by Pope Nicholas V, in separate Greek and Latin libraries, and housed by Pope Sixtus IV, who consigned the Bibliotheca Apostolica Vaticana to the care of his librarian, the humanist Bartolomeo Platina in February 1475.

In the 16th century Sixtus V bisected Bramante's Cortile del Belvedere with a cross-wing to house the Apostolic Library in suitable magnificence. The sixteenth and seventeenth centuries saw other privately-endowed libraries assembled in Rome: the Vallicelliana, formed from the books of Saint Filippo Neri, with other distinguished libraries such as that of Cesare Baronio, the Biblioteca Angelica founded by the Augustinian Angelo Rocca, which was the only truly public library in Counter-Reformation Rome; the Biblioteca Alessandrina with which

Pope Alexander VII endowed the University of Rome; the Biblioteca Casanatense of the Cardinal Girolamo Casanate; and finally the Biblioteca Corsiniana founded by the bibliophile Clement XII Corsini and his nephew Cardinal Neri Corsini, still housed in Palazzo Corsini in via della Lungara.

A lot of factors combined to create a "golden age of libraries" between 1600 and 1700: The quantity of books had gone up, as the cost had gone down, there was a renewal in the interest of classical literature and culture, nationalism was encouraging nations to build great libraries, universities were playing a more prominent role in education, and renaissance thinkers and writers were producing great works. Some of the more important libraries include the Bodleian Library at Oxford, the Library of the British Museum, the Mazarine Library in Paris, and the National Central Library in Italy, the Prussian State Library, the M.E. Saltykov-Shchedrin State Public Library of St. Petersburg, and many more.

Public Libraries

The earliest example in England of a library to be endowed for the benefit of users who were not members of an institution such as a cathedral or college was the Francis Trigge Chained Library in Grantham, Lincolnshire, established in 1598. The library still exists and can justifiably claim to be the forerunner of later public library systems.The beginning of the modern, free, open access libraries really got its start in the U.K. in 1847.

Parliament appointed a committee, led by William Ewart, on Public Libraries to consider the necessity of establishing libraries through the nation: In 1849 their report noted the poor condition of library service, it recommended the establishment of free public libraries all over the country, and it led to the Public Libraries Act in 1850, which allowed all cities with populations exceeding 10,000 to levy taxes for the support of public libraries. Another important act was the 1870 Public School Law, which increased literacy, thereby the demand for libraries, so by 1877, more than 75 cities had established free libraries, and by 1900 the number had reached 300. This finally marks the start of the public library as we know it. And these acts led to similar laws in other countries, most notably the U.S.

1876 is a well known year in the history of librarianship. The American Library Association was formed, as well as The American Library Journal, Melvil Dewey published his decimal based system of classification, and the United States Bureau of Education published its report, "Public libraries in the United States of America; their history, condition, and management." The American Library Association continues to play a major role in libraries to this day, and Dewey's classification system, although under heavy criticism of late, still remains as the prevailing method of classification used in the United States.

As the number of books in libraries increased, so did the need for compact storage and access with adequate lighting, giving birth to the *stack system*, which involved keeping a library's collection of books in a space separate from the reading room, an arrangement which arose in the 19th century. Book stacks quickly evolved into a fairly standard form in which the cast iron and steel frameworks supporting the bookshelves also supported the floors, which often were built of translucent blocks to permit the passage of light (but were not transparent, for reasons of modesty). With the introduction of electrical lighting, it had a huge impact on how the library operated. Also, the use of glass floors was largely discontinued, though floors were still often composed of metal grating to allow air to circulate in multi-story stacks. Ultimately, even more space was needed, and a method of moving shelves on tracks (compact shelving) was introduced to cut down on otherwise wasted aisle space.

Library 2.0, a term coined in 2005, is the library's response to the challenge of Google and an attempt to meet the changing needs and wants of the users by using web 2.0 technology. Some of the aspects of Library 2.0 include, commenting, tagging, bookmarking, discussions, using social software, plug-ins, and widgets. Inspired by web 2.0, it is an attempt to make the library a more user driven institution.

A Working Definition of Digital Library [1998]

For DLF partners effectively to "federate" digital libraries, they must share a comon understanding of what a digital library is. Here is their working definition.

"Digital libraries are organizations that provide the resources, including the specialized staff, to select, structure, offer intellectual access to, interpret, distribute, preserve the integrity of, and ensure the persistence over time of collections of digital works so that they are readily and economically available for use by a defined community or set of communities."

Of course, the concept of digital library has multiple senses that one might invoke in various contexts. For example, the concept may refer simply to the notion of collection without reference to organization, intellectual accessibility or service attributes. This extended sense seems to be in play, for example, when we hear the World Wide Web described as a digital library. The concept might also refer to the organization underlying the collection, or even more specifically to the computer-based system in which the collection resides. The latter sense seems to be most operative in the NSF digital library initiative programme. See, for example, C.L. Borgman, et al. *Social Aspects of Digital Libraries*. Digital *libraries* might also be distinguished from digital *archives* to emphasize the nature of the works collected or, as in *Preserving Digital Information: Report of the Task Force on the Archiving of Digital Information*, to stress the preservation function.

One could, of course, revise, refine, and otherwise improve this comprehensive definition. However, it is meant here mainly to suggest that there is a set of attributes that gives coherence to the concept of digital libraries. These attributes include functions of collection, organization, preservation, access and economy. A programme for the development of "federated" digital libraries needs to be defined and measured in terms of the development of these attributes. However, the proposed definition also emphasizes that "digital libraries" need to be defined and measured in relation to the communities they serve. Thus, the DLF programme aims to situate the development of digital libraries in a larger context of service. Given the complexity and costs of developing digital libraries, DLF efforts and investments need to be conscious of and strategically designed to address the larger institutional and social goals of its participants.

Art of Book Publishing and Copyright Act

Simpsons Solicitors

1. *General:* Graphic artists, illustrators, painters sculptors and particularly photographers, supply work to the publishing industry. The manner of their involvement varies from artist to artist and project to project.
   - (i) An illustrator may be: an employee on salary a contractor on annual retainer a contractor for a book (illustrations and/or cover) a contractor for a series of books
   - (ii) Painters and sculptors are commonly involved through the licensing of the right to reproduce their works either for critical or art historical review biography licensing reproductions of work for use on a cover
   - (iii) Photographers are regularly involved in all of these styles of relationship.
2. Given this disparity of purpose, function and relationship, it is clear that the terms of the legal relationships that each artist enjoys with his or her publisher will vary considerably.

Nor do publishers form a homogeneous group. Their internal corporate policies vary considerably as do their commercial needs. The publisher of a school text on physics will take a very different approach to the publisher of an illustrated children's book or the publisher of a biography. Generally, the principal uses that a publisher will have for artwork is:

- (i) covers
- (ii) diagrams charts, maps
- (iii) "internal" art

(iv) illustrations (e.g. childrens' books, cartoons)

(v) decorative borders

What I would like to do is look first at some aspects of copyright ownership and control that necessarily thread themselves between these divergent applications. Then I will examine the principal clauses that define the relationship between the individual artist and the individual publisher.

2. Dealing with copyright

(i) *Assignments or Licences?:* Increasingly publishers are realising that demanding an assignment of all rights can be both inappropriate and excessive. Until the last decade, it was standard practice for publishers to demand an assignment of copyright in respect of published artistic works. It was absolutely "take it or leave it".

Some publishers however still insist on a complete assignment of all rights. This may be perfectly reasonable in certain circumstances.

(a) *Commissioned Works:* If a non-fiction publisher wishes to produce a text on natural history or the operation of the combustion engine, it may commission an artist to do all the technical drawings for the text.

In such instances it is almost universal that the publisher will retain all rights-both in the artwork itself and the copyright therein.

These publishers consider the artist to be little, if anything, more than a technician. For the artist, this relationship works because he or she would not usually have any other use for the images; on the other hand, the publisher may well recycle the illustrations in reprints, new editions and even other of its publications.

If however the artist is commissioned to provide illustrations for, say, a book of humour, a licence would be quite common. That licence might be exclusive (for say volume rights) or non-exclusive. It all depends on the relative commercial needs and bargaining power of the parties.

(b) *Existing Works:* If the publisher wishes to incorporate an existing work in a book or on its cover, it is more likely to license the work rather than demand an assignment.

It is also useful to distinguish between the intended use of the artwork in order to determine whether assignment or licence is appropriate.

Generally, covers, "internal" art, illustrations are licensed while diagrams, charts, maps and decorative borders are assigned. Of course there are case by case exceptions.

(ii) *Nature of Rights Demanded and Required?:* A book publisher is going to certainly need to obtain rights for:

(a) reproduction in volume form, for

(b) the territory of the market of the book, and

(c) the duration of either the rights in the literary work or at least for the period that the book remains in print.

Whether it needs more, is going to be a matter of explanation and discussion.

As an example of the need to specify the rights that are appropriate, consider the following:

Rights to Characters

Who should own the rights to the author/artist's characters? Other than having the right to publish the work that it has contracted to publish, should the publisher have the right to either control or profit from subsequent uses of the character?

It is commonplace for contracts to be for more than one work or contain an option. Ignoring the desirability or otherwise of this, is it appropriate for a publisher to control the rights in the characters of the work? Should Penguin be able to prevent Leunig from drawing his whimsical little man or Mathew Martin from using his goggles-wearing duck, had the publisher insisted that the artists assign all rights in their works? Unlikely perhaps...but what about Tom Clancy and "The Hunt For Red October"?

(iii) *Exclusiveness or Non-exclusiveness?:* Rights need not be either exclusive or non-exclusive. Often a mix is more appropriate:

(a) The rights may need to be exclusive for a period of time. Then it may be appropriate for them to either revert completely or be enjoyed on a continuing but non-exclusive basis.

(b) The rights may need to be exclusive for a number of editions (or perhaps while the book remains continuously in print) and thereafter non-exclusive.

(c) They may be exclusive for certain uses but either non-exclusive or indeed non-existent for other purposes.

(d) The rights may be non-exclusive from the outset and remain so either for the length of copyright or until some predetermined event occurs;

(e) They may be exclusive from the outset .....

The combinations are numerous but the point is simple:

Licences are enormously flexible and allow one to take exactly what one needs in order to achieve one's commercial purpose whilst still allowing the copyright owner to keep some economic interest in his or her own work.

(iv) *Fair Dealing for the Purpose of Criticism and Review:* Many publishers have a very inflated idea of what "fair dealing" permits them to do without permission. In Sillitoe & Ors v. McGraw-Hill Book Co (UK) Ltd (1983) FSR 545 the judge spelled out that for the use to be protected by s.41 the reproduction had to be:

(a) a fair dealing,

(b) for the purpose of criticism or review, either of that work or another work, and

(c) a "sufficient acknowledgment" of the work had to be made.

Fair dealing isn't defined in the Copyright Act. The cases (such as Hubbard v. Vosper (1972) 2 QB 84) seem to emphasise that what is "fair" will be a matter of fact to be determined in each case. What is the extent of the use in comparison to the supporting text? Has the work been previously published?

The purpose of criticism or review is also often misunderstood. It does not, for example, give the publisher the right to use an artist's paintings when the article or book is about the painter's life generally. The criticism or review has to be of the works themselves. I believe that there is a good argument for stretching that to include the 'ideas behind the works' but eventually there must be a line drawn at the point that the focus of the reproduction is not the criticism or review of the work but of something else.

Sufficient acknowledgment: Many publishers forget that "sufficient acknowledgment" is actually defined in the Copyright Act. Section 10(1) says that in relation to a Work" it means "an acknowledgment identifying the work by its title or other description and, unless the work is anonymous or pseudonymous or the author has previously agreed or directed that an acknowledgment of his name is not to be made, also identifying the author".

Types of Libraries: Their Functions and Objectives

Libraries can be divided into categories by several methods: by the entity (institution, municipality, or corporate body) that supports or perpetuates them

- o academic libraries
- o corporate libraries
- o government libraries
- o historical society libraries
- o private libraries
- o public libraries
- o school libraries

by the type of documents or materials they hold:

- o data libraries
- o digital libraries
- o picture (photograph) libraries
- o slide libraries
- o tool libraries

by the subject matter of documents they hold

- o architecture libraries
- o fine arts libraries
- o law libraries
- o medical libraries
- o theological libraries (See: Theological Libraries and Librarianship)

by the users they serve

- o military communities
- o users who are blind or visually/physically handicapped (see National Library Service for the Blind and Physically Handicapped)

by traditional professional divisions

- *o Academic Libraries:* These libraries are located on the campuses of colleges and universities and serve primarily the students and faculty of that and other academic institutions. Some academic libraries, especially those at public institutions, are accessible to members of the general public in whole or in part.
- *o Public Libraries or Public Lending Libraries:* These libraries provide service to the general public and make at least some of their books available for borrowing, so that readers may use them at home over a period of days or weeks. Typically, libraries issue library cards to community members wishing to borrow books. Many public libraries also serve as community organizations that provide free services and events to the public, such as reading groups and toddler story time.
- *o Research Libraries:* These libraries are intended for supporting scholarly research, and therefore maintain permanent collections and attempt to provide access to all necessary material. Research libraries are most often academic libraries or national libraries, but many large special libraries have research libraries within their special field and a very few of the largest public libraries also serve as research libraries.

- o *School Libraries:* Most public and private primary and secondary schools have libraries designed to support the school's curriculum.
- o *Special Libraries:* All other libraries fall into this category. Many private businesses and public organizations, including hospitals, museums, research laboratories, law firms, and many government departments and agencies, maintain their own libraries for the use of their employees in doing specialized research related to their work. Special libraries may or may not be accessible to some identified part of the general public. Branches of a large academic or research libraries dealing with particular subjects are also usually called "special libraries": they are generally associated with one or more academic departments. Special libraries are distinguished from special collections, which are branches or parts of a library intended for rare books, manuscripts, and similar material.

The final method of dividing library types is also the simplest.

Many institutions make a distinction between circulating libraries (where materials are expected and intended to be loaned to patrons, institutions, or other libraries) and collecting libraries (where the materials are selected on a basis of their natures or subject matter). Many modern libraries are a mixture of both, as they contain a general collection for circulation, and a reference collection which is often more specialized, as well as restricted to the library premises.

Also, the governments of most major countries support national libraries. Three noteworthy examples are the U.S. Library of Congress, Canada's Library and Archives Canada, and the British Library. A typically broad sample of libraries in one state in the U.S. can be explored at Every Library In Illinois.

General Library Objectives

The general objective of the Skowhegan Free Public Library shall be:

1. To assemble, preserve and circulate, as budget and resources permit, books and other resources necessary to provide information, self education and recreation for the people of the greater Skowhegan area.
2. To serve the community as a center of reliable information.
3. To provide a place where inquiring minds may encounter valid information, multiple viewpoints, and original ideas so necessary in a democratic society that depends for its survival on a free and open exchange of information.
4. To support the educational, civic, and cultural activities of groups and organizations.
5. To provide information, programmes, and services that support literacy development to people of all ages.
6. To seek continually to identify community needs and to provide programmes and library services to meet those needs.
7. To provide free library services to Skowhegan residents and students.

Functions & Objectives

Being one of the most important facilities in any learning institution, a library is center for knowledge acquisition and development. Our library provides the following functions.

1. References, printing services and book loans on various subjects.
2. Provide all possible information needs for researchers, students, academic staff as well as neighboring communities.
3. Provide central classification of all documents, books, periodicals, journals and even E-sources.
4. Serve as a documentation center.
5. Establish and maintain both Card as well as an Online Public Access catalogues (OPAC) of Library materials.
6. Establish and maintain a Library webpages.

7. Offer ICT services to students, academic staff as well as neighboring communities.
8. Establish and promote cooperation with similar centers at national as well as international levels.
9. The library will also provide technical services such as book binding, printing, editorial and photographic services.

Laws of Library Science and Implications in Teacher Education Libraries

S. R. Ranganathan, known as the "the father of library science in India," and respected by librarians all over the world, proposed five laws of library science. Many librarians worldwide accept them as the foundations of their philosophy (e.g. Koehler et al, 2000)

These laws are:

1. Books are for use.
2. Every reader his [or her] book.
3. Every book its reader.
4. Save the time of the User.
5. The library is a growing organism.

The Five Laws of Library Science are some of the most influential concepts in that field. Since they were published in 1931, these five laws "have remained a centerpiece of professional values..." (Rubin 2004). These basic theories of Library Science continue to directly affect the development of this discipline and the service of all libraries.

S. R. Ranganathan's early education was cf a mathematic background. This systematic way of thinking, he later applied to his work in library science, most notably his work on library classification and administration. (Indian Statistical Institute Library, et al 2007) "From the middle of the nineteenth century, librarians in the west felt the need and started emphasizing the importance of enhanced services to library patrons. Formulation of the Five Laws of Library Science at long last, provided a solid and lasting foundation in this direction." (Kabir 2003).

An Explanation of the Five Laws

First Law: Books are for Use: The 1st law of library science is "Books are for use' Which implies that a book should be durable & the material of which it is made should have longevity.

The 1st law insists upon intensifying the use of books by every possible method and it urges the library profession to select such edition of the book which is readable & pleasing to the eye. A book is to select for easy understanding by the majority of the user of the library.A book that is written with flair for simple style, language & clarity of expression should be purchased...

Second Law: Every Reader His or Her Book: Any patron from the library community should have access to the books in the library. Any person has a right to use the collections housed in the library. There are not certain books or collections that some audiences within the population can not access. Collections should be developed that every part of the population will be interested in.

Third Law: Every Book its Reader: This law is about items in the library's collection, and who uses them. Each book in the library has a member of the community that will find the book useful or interesting. One of the major developments that Ranganathan contributed through this law is the idea that if a book is not being used often it needs exposure to groups of readers who will find it useful.

Fourth Law: Save the Time of the Reader: This law makes it clear that if readers find what they are looking for in a timely manner they will be more satisfied, and more likely to feel like their needs have been met. This not only makes library service more efficient, but also makes the reader feel like their search has been an effective one.

Fifth Law: The Library is a Growing Organism: This law says that the library is dependent on life and change. Without the human and organizational changes that occur, the library would neither function properly, nor meet its purpose.j

Variants

In 1998, librarian Michael Gorman (past president of the American Library Association, 2005-2006), recommended the following laws in addition to Ranganathan's five in his small book, "Our Singular Strengths":

1. Libraries serve humanity.
2. Respect all forms by which knowledge is communicated.
3. Use technology intelligently to enhance service.
4. Protect free access to knowledge.
5. Honour the past and create the future.

In 2004, librarian Alireza Noruzi recommended applying Ranganathan's laws to the web in his paper, "Application of Ranganathan's Laws to the Web":

1. Web resources are for use.
2. Every user has his or her web resource.
3. Every web resource its user.
4. Save the time of the user.
5. The Web is a growing organism.

The expanding role of privatization in education: implications for teacher education and development.

Introduction

The merits of a marketplace model for public education have been among the most prominent themes in education policy discussions over the last two decades. Advocates of market approaches to education reform contend that creating a market in educational services will foster competition among providers and thus spur delivery of better services at the same or lower cost than providing them through traditional public schools. Whether this is the case is debatable. It is clear, however, that the policy preferences of the past 25 years have increasingly leaned toward privatization. These preferences have been expressed in repeated efforts to promote educational vouchers and by the advocacy of "strong" state charter school laws. Most recently, the reauthorization of the Elementary and Secondary Education Act, popularly known as the "No Child Left Behind"

Act (NCLB), has accelerated the three decade-long trend toward private, for-profit activities in public education.

This chapter provides an overview of privatizing initiatives in K-12 public education and discusses current policies that encourage the expanded involvement of the private sector. Also, we discuss the implications of privatizing activities for aspiring and practicing teachers.

The Growth and Scope of Entrepreneurship in Education

Within K-12 education, privatizing activity falls into two broad categories: overall management or operation of schools, and provision of supplemental educational services. Each is discussed in turn. Among the for-profit firms engaged in the management or operation of K-12 schools, only a small number actually own private schools and charge tuition to students. The bulk of entrepreneurial activity in the management or operation of K-12 education falls under the umbrella of what Wall Street analysts have dubbed the Education Management Organization (EMO) industry. Although the analogy is far from perfect, Wall Street coined the term EMO as an analog to Health Maintenance Organizations (HMOs) (Toch, 1996). EMOs are for-profit firms such as Edison Schools and Mosaica, that are hired to manage public district schools or charter schools. Most often, for-profit firms manage charter schools as agents of not-for-profit charter holders.

Initially voucher programmes seemed to offer the most significant opportunity for-profit firms to compete for public tax dollars. However, with vouchers getting little political traction, EMO growth has largely been fueled by state charter school legislation. Although charter schools are public schools operated with public funds, they are generally established by organizations independent of school districts and are given considerable freedom in their day-to-day operations in return for meeting contractual performance goals. In theory, charter schools are held accountable by the market because parents are given the right to "vote with their feet" and choose to enroll or withdraw their children from the charter school of their choice. Since state funding formulas are based on student enrollment, charter schools with insufficient enrollment, proponents argue, would be forced to close their doors. In contrast to voucher proposals, charter schools have enjoyed strong, bipartisan support, further contributing to their growth.

At the federal level, the No Child Left Behind (NCLB) legislation favors the expansion of privatizing approaches to education through district to charter school conversions of schools labeled failing and by creating a market for supplemental education services. NCLB requires schools, in return for federal education aid, to conduct standardized testing annually in grades 3 through 8. Schools that fail to demonstrate Adequate Yearly Progress (AYP) face a series of "corrective actions" that escalate in severity if a school continues to under-perform according to NCLB standards. Sanctions for a school that has failed to achieve AYP after five consecutive years include privatizing options such as reopening as a charter school and contracting with an outside organization to manage the school.

The Growth of Education Management Organizations

For-profit companies typically manage two forms of public schools: district public schools, which EMOs may manage under a contract with a local school district, and charter schools. Charter holders may include academic institutions, nonprofit foundations, and groups of parents, teachers, or both. Charter holders frequently contract with for-profit EMOs to manage charter schools on their behalf. Less often, EMOs hold charters directly (Molnar et al, 2004).

The Profiles of For-Profit Education Management Organizations (Profiles), an annual report that compiles information on for-profit EMOs that manage traditional and/or charter schools, has tracked the growth of EMOs for the past seven years. In 1989-1999, the first year of the report, 13 for-profit companies operated 135 schools in 15 states. In the most recent report (2005-2006), 51 education management organizations managed 521 schools, with a total enrollment of 237,179 students across 29 states and the District of Columbia. Over the past eight years, the number of EMOs has nearly quadrupled. Simultaneously, the number of schools managed by EMOs has nearly quadrupled as well.

Charter schools account for a large and growing majority of EMO contracts: 84% of the privately managed schools covered in the 2005-2006 Profiles report are charter schools. Furthermore, EMOs enroll a large percentage of the total charter school population nationwide. In 2005-2006, the 51 EMOs in the Profiles report account for 25% of all students enrolled in charter schools. A closer look at EMO enrollment counts reveals that EMO-managed charter schools represent enroll an even larger share of primary charter school students, 36% of all charter primary school students are enrolled in the EMO-managed charter schools tracked in the Profiles report (Molnar et al, 2006). These data suggest that for-profit firms have concentrated their efforts on primary schools.

User Education in Academic Libraries

Developments in computers, microelectronics, and communication technologies have radically changed the library and information environment. Gone are the days of stand-alone libraries, in which a library was judged less by the quality of its resources and services than by the number of documents it had available. Traditional libraries were dominated by print publications and the access mechanisms were also by-and-large manual. The paradigm shift from stand-alone libraries to library and information networks, available via the Internet, can provide end-users with a seamless connection to Internet-based services. Moreover, we are surrounded by automated, digital, and virtual libraries as well as by networked data, specialized networks, and library networks. Multimedia and the Internet have further made the job of library and information professionals more challenging.

The development of new technology makes direct access to information easier for users, and, while information skills are required to collect and present that information, in the future there is likely to be less of a role for information workers as intermediaries between users and information sources.

In fact, there is a paradigm shift from a parent-child relationship between information provider and user to an "adult-adult" relationship. While new formats and mechanisms are being developed to cope with this rapidly changing environment, the existing gap between the generation and use of information is further widening in the present situation. A major aim of user education is therefore to widen the use of a range of library resources, which will enable academics to improve their teaching and research, and students to learn more and achieve better results in their work.

In the print-based environment we spoke of library instruction, bibliographic instruction, and user education programmes. Initiation of users, lectures to library users, library tours, pamphlets and brochures, audio-visual aids, and, in a few cases, user education programmes were the main tools and techniques for enabling patrons to make good use of the library. These tools and techniques must now be supplemented. End-user training should now be the focus of user education.

The Need for End-user Education

User education is essential. It helps publicize library services. It improves the image of the library. Above all, user education and training are the best ways to implement Ranganathan's five laws of library science. User education and training are often fee-based, because developing the infrastructure for the network environment is very costly.

The Challenge in Information Services

Information has become more complex and expensive. The traditional services, such as reference service, current awareness services, and selective dissemination of information need be supplemented by "Selective *Elimination* of Information," the evaluation of information to separate quality information from junk. In this context, the basic challenge is to convince and convert traditional users into users of Internet-based resources and services. Information literacy can contribute to developing information technology (IT) related competencies among end-users as it includes basic computer and network literacy. The aim of information literacy is to make information users capable of locating, retrieving, and using information.

Planning Strategies

Traditionally, librarians instructed the end-users in the use of print publications, but a balance between print and digital documents will be a basic norm in the near future. In this context, training and retraining the end-users in the use of IT-based resources and services, such as e-mail, ftp, telnet, www, browsers, search engines, opacs, databases, system software, application software, electronic journals, computer conferences, scholarly discussion lists, mailing lists, Usenet newsgroups, websites, CDs, and DVDs should become an integral part of a library's user education programme. This is where strategic planning comes in, in order to develop a comprehensive user-education and training programme at the national level.

The University Grants Commission (UGC), the National Information system for Science and Technology (NISSAT), National Social Science Documentation Centre (NASSDOC), Indian National Scientific Doumentation Centre (INSDOC), Defence Scientific Information & Documentation Centre (DESIDOC), university libraries, library associations, library and information science departments can play a pivotal role in this direction. Such national programmes can be customized at the local level to suit institutional needs.

The Changing Academic Library

During the recent economic recession, money for education and libraries in India became very tight, requiring cuts in serial subscriptions and book purchases for academic libraries. At the same time, subscription prices were soaring, as were the costs and number of databases and journals available. Library planning is now essential in order to maximize available resources and take advantage of emerging technologies. A Library Planning and Action Initiative (LPAI) should now be implemented by academic libraries in India.

To accomplish the goals of the LPAI, a planning team should be established in every academic library. An advisory task force must be formed to work closely with the planning team. The advisory task force members could be chancellors, vice-chancellors, other academic administrators, academic librarians, a representative from the Librarian's Association, information technologists, and other faculty including representation from faculty governance bodies.

The LPAI task force should use the following strategies to guide the academic library's transition to the digital future:

Seek Innovative and Cost-effective Means to Strengthen Resource Sharing: Resource sharing should extend throughout academic libraries (and other important libraries) as a strategy to maximize the resources available for print collections that meet the needs of students and faculty for information needed in teaching and research.

Create Digital Libraries: The Academic Digital Library (ADL) should provide new services and extend existing ones to guide libraries in the successful integration of traditional and digital formats. The programmes of the ADL should support information access and delivery via electronic communications; information preservation, storage, and retrieval; information management consultation and training; new forms of scholarly and scientific communication; and development of the knowledge network of the university.

Mutually Beneficial Collaboration of Academic Libraries with Libraries, Museums and Industry: Collaboration is a strategy to extend library access, share the costs of library collections and services, and develop an academically and economically sustainable model of scholarly communication.

Information Infrastructure that Supports the Dissemination of and Access to Scholarly and Scientific Information in a Networked Environment: A sophisticated and robust technological infrastructure is required to disseminate and access digital information. Academic libraries must invest in technology to support the delivery of digital collections and be tightly integrated into information management and technology planning at all levels.

Organize an Environment of Continuous Planning and Innovation: The environment for scholarly information is expected to be highly fluid for at least the next decade, as universities attempt to meet the challenges of scholarly and scientific communication in the 21st century. The academic library should develop a planning process that will support our libraries as they continue to engage in innovation and the development of organizational, technical, policy, and financial structures needed to make the transition to integrated print and digital collections. Planning structures should also encourage and support strategies to enhance the transmission of scholarly and scientific communication in a digital environment.

Conclusion

At the end of the 20th century, college and university libraries face enormous challenges and opportunities. As campuses move into the information age, the mission and role of the library is being redefined. While the amount of information libraries need to acquire continues to increase, the resources available to do so are insufficient. Moreover, administrators need to assess the relationship between the library and the computer center, as both fight for limited resources.

The growing universe of print-based publications and digital documents on the one hand, and the declining universe of library budgets on the other, can be handled confidently by adopting certain strategies, such as by developing critical thinking skills, as well as promoting information literacy at large In the near future, uses should expect timely access to quality information. This information must be accurate, relevant, comprehensive, and engaging. This can be done successfully by incorporating end-user education and training components, in the academic libraries developing continuing professional education and training programmes for the library and information professionals, as well as the end-users will have to develop learning attitude and network related competence to us by the information and communication technologies.

Role of Teacher as a Library Teacher

In recent years, there has been much discussion regarding the title of that member of teaching staff in the education system who is employed in the position of "Teacher Librarian". Whilst there is support in some academic areas that the label is precise, adequate and appropriate, there are others who argue that it is self-limiting, obsolete and inaccurate.

Although there can be no doubt as to the duel role of both teacher (in the sense of educator) and librarian (as the person in charge of the library), it would appear that the conflict arising from the allocation of the title is a reflection of the changing scope of this position, rather than simply one of nomenclature.

This paper outlines a number of issues that are a direct result of recent technological developments, societal changes and educational advances that have impacted upon the Teacher Librarian, and includes recommendations for changes to improve the educational outcomes for all members of the school community.

Introduction

As the information professional within a school, the Teacher Librarian is presented with a cacophony of tasks, often with inadequate resources, and generally insufficient support.

A Teacher Librarian has a unique role, requiring the integration of teaching skills and competency in librarianship. Angus (1993) notes that they are also qualified to take an active role in curriculum support, design and implementation.

Gorman (1998) states that a "librarian's job" is to preserve forms of recorded knowledge, foster public education and continue a historical mission that provides a foundation for democratic society. This is indeed a noble brief for librarians in general, but inadequate in the contemporary educational context.

Todd (in Todd, Henri and Rowen,1996) notes that Teacher Librarians may be involved in curriculum development, staff training and student learning and welfare and thus the position should be elevated to that equivalent to a Leading Teacher in a secondary setting, or an Executive Teacher in an infants/ primary school. To this end, Todd supports the proposal of the creation of the position of Director of Information Resources (DIS). In some sections of the teacher-librarianship community, this was interpreted as threatening the tenure and status of the profession.

Henri (1996) reaffirms the importance of retaining the word "teaching" in the title of Teacher Librarian, stating that Teacher Librarians have a whole-school curriculum perspective in addition to their managerial experience. The possibility of replacing Teacher Librarians with librarians and technicians is of major concern to Henri, who states that a DIS has a different role to that of a Teacher Librarian.

Adding to the above debate is Rowan (1996), who presents an emotive case with her contention that a library is "a place, not a service". She disparages of synonyms for libraries, stating that titles such as "multimedia resource centres, global information services and information services units" are merely elaborate pieces of whimsy, without justification.

However, Lemke (1993) notes that the fundamental assumptions of academic education are incompatible with the present, let alone future, needs of a postmodern society. With education diverging into multimedia applications, and curriculum developments demanding a higher degree of technologically advanced methodology, Lemke avows that new educational theory will deal with a multitude of new issues concerning student and teacher roles.

For Teacher Librarians to deny the inevitable changes is to render themselves liable to extinction. Should administrators fail to acknowledge the scope and importance of the school Teacher Librarian, regardless of position title, will not only render them politically vulnerable but also negligent in their responsibilities to education services.

Scope of Teacher Librarian's Role

Within the generally accepted responsibilities of a Teacher Librarian are the management of the "books", but it is widely acknowledged that information is no longer limited to containment in print form. Boyle (1998) notes that in the future, sources of information will become more fluid, dynamic and readily available.

Additionally, not only will the sources of information evolve with technology, but also the amount of data will`increase. Magire, Kazlaukas and Weir (1994) estimate that the volume of information has doubled every five years for the last 20 years, causing a fragmentation of knowledge and resulting in a multitude of specialised information professionals.

To fulfill the emerging role for librarians, Boaden (1991) emphasises the need to be:

- more innovative
- use technology in a better way
- undertake research and planning
- carry out special needs surveys
- take on a broader role than currently

Similarly, Teacher Librarians are advised to accept new roles and to be more interactive with other staff. In this way, they will become more valued for their information expertise and technological know-how (ALA, 1990).

Further to developing and expanding their role within the provision on information services, Teacher Librarians must also be cognisant of their legal responsibilities external to teaching. The International Federation of Library Associations and Institutions included in their Strategic Plan 1998-1999 the expectation of [Teacher Librarians] to comprehend and action legalities such as copyright, fair use and licencing models.

In addition to the issues that are external to the education system are those requirements generated by the system itself. The Finn Report identified Information Literacy as being a core competency (Burnheirm, 1992), with Skrzeczynski (1995) identifying the Teacher Librarians' involvement in literacy education as including areas of:

-resources-curriculum-professional development-environment-assessment-evaluation

Angus (1993) identified an extensive list of roles that are undertaken by a Teacher Librarian. Each one of the eighteen items on her checklist amounted to almost a full-time position. For example, one of the eighteen roles was that of "planning, teaching and evaluating cooperatively with teachers to ensure effective integration of information resources and technologies into student learning".

Similarly, the ALIA/ASLA Joint Statement on Teacher Librarians (1994) identified seventeen different facets of the role, with seven separate areas of responsibility.

Dillon & Henri (1998) concur that Teacher Librarians have to provide broader services and better access to information, despite less funding. Even within the traditional areas of library-only services, collections must be constantly reviewed, evaluated, compared, upgraded and publicised.

Walsh (1997) admonishes that libraries must respond to the needs of [their] local communities, and school libraries are no exception. With the introduction of Internet facilities to schools, the Teacher Librarian finds that as the access point for the Internet is generally located in the library, their role is extended once again, to include supervision of this facility. In schools that have been networked to provide multiple access points, the Teacher Librarian obviously cannot provide supervision in other parts of the school, and thus is required to provide teaching-staff training in this area.

Lacey (1998) despairs of the fact that the Department of Education and Training (DET) has not conducted an investigation of the role of Teacher Librarians nor the changing nature of school libraries. Whilst the DET has imposed mandatory accountability functions, practicing Teacher Librarians are required to perform their managerial duties often with time-constraints imposed by their educational commitments. The roles that Lacey identifies include:

- educator
- curriculum advisor
- information professional
- resource manager, advisor and selector

- trainer for students, teachers and school assistants
- team-teacher
- computer technology advisor and troubleshooter
- Internet trainer and supervisor
- network coordinator
- literacy consultant and advisor
- cataloguer
- librarian

Clearly, it is not possible to undertake all the above functions and perform each to an ultimate degree of success There is neither the time nor the resources for this to be accomplished.

Todd's summation that the quality of some Teacher Librarians is questionable must lead one to assume that he does not have an appreciation for the realities of life as a Teacher Librarian. Whilst there is no doubt that Teacher Librarians of lesser competency and commitment do exist, this is the norm in any profession, trade or indeed pursuit.

The recent deplorable practice in North America of replacing school librarians with library technicians does not offer an acceptable model for change. However, some of the American states are now investigating this issue (Chicago Tribune, 1998), with findings to date recognising the gross underestimation of the value of Teacher Librarians. Additionally, recommendations have been made that higher degrees in librarianship should be appropriately rewarded in salary scales.

Recommendations

Lacey's appeal to the Minister for Education and Training (1998) for an immediate investigation into the role of Teacher Librarians and the changing functions of the school library warrants merit as a starting point for underpinning the debate regarding the scope of the position. As the DET has not supplied a proscribed job description, the function of the Teacher Librarian is open to manipulation and professional abuse.

The NSW Teachers Federation (1998) notes with concern that when teaching staff were reduced by 2,000 positions statewide, Teacher Librarians had to undertake Relief from

Face to Face (RFF) duties. Little more than a childminding role, these duties are continuing despite the fact that the DET has now reinstated the previously lost teaching positions.

Much time is spent by Teacher Librarians in the performance of tasks of a clerical nature, despite the fact that most school libraries have access to an amount of clerical time. It is interesting to note that Angus (1993) recommends the appointment of two teacher librarians should the number of staff (teaching and ancillary) be above 50, and three Teacher Librarians where the staff number more than 86. Similarly, ancillary hours are recommended well above the current allocations prevalent in most schools. However, it is noted that the allocation of ancillary hours is at the discretion of the school's principal, whilst the appointment of a Teacher Librarian is at the behest of the DET. The formulation of mandatory guidelines by the DET would resolve this issue.

Further, should schools be permitted to have more than one Teacher Librarian, it is obvious that there needs to be an appropriate Head Teacher. Angus notes that the number of students enrolled in a school is insufficient in itself to dictate appropriate staffing for a school, and factors such as student profile and special needs must be considered.

The matter of appropriate assistance is also one of great importance. Whilst some clerical duties may be performed by ancillary staff on secondment from other duties (in line with the DET policy of "multiskilling"), the lack of suitably trained staff is an issue that must be addressed. A suitable analogy is that of the science faculty laboratory assistant, who requires specialist skills in many of the science disciplines in order to satisfactorily undertake required tasks. Should Teacher Librarians be supplied with assistants with library technical skills, many of the more routine tasks of library operation could be delegated, enabling the Teacher Librarian to engage in higher level pursuits.

ALIA delineates between the roles of Teacher Librarians and library technicians, with the Teacher Librarian being responsible for the design, management, direction and policy formulation of a library. The library technician's role is one concerning operational and technical aspects of library function, such as the maintenance of systems which support the acquisition, organization and management of the library.

Lee (1996) comments that Teacher Librarians are the personnel best placed within the teaching ranks to support a school's move into the information age. However, few received any technological training in regard to either OASIS Library nor SCIS Cataloguing, let alone any instruction regarding technology tools. Whilst the DET now provides minimalist assistance in this area with their Technology in Teaching and Learning (TILT) modules delivered via the District Offices in NSW, the depth of the instruction is generally less than that of students entering Year 7.

McKenzie (1998) recommends that for professional development to be effective:

15-60 hours annually per teacher must be committed

10%-25% of technology budget should be spent on staff learning

traditional staff training and development should be replaced by adult learning

the emotional dimension of the challenge of transfer must be addressed.

Similarly, ALA (1998) suggests that it is necessary to enroll in on-line workshops, attend conferences and become informed regarding developments in the sphere of library administration.

The Department of Training and Education Coordination (1997) issued documentation regarding the computer proficiency of personnel in education, and promotes the requirement to keep abreast of technology. The implications for both teaching and administration are outlined, with both spheres being applicable to Teacher Librarians by virtue of their duel roles.

Many school districts and (former) regional divisions have an affiliation of Teacher Librarians. This is an important support network serving both social and professional functions. However, it is of interest to note that the Hunter Region School Libraries

Association has used their collegial bonds to develop a strategic plan developed in collaboration with Teacher Librarians across what was then four Educational Recourse Centres (ERCs).

This initiative was supported by the then Director of Schools and also by the then Director, Teaching and Learning (Barry, 1995). The success of this medium is self-evident, and provides a suitable model for collaborative, supported planning for the future.

Conclusion

Taylor (1997) bemoans the fact that successful educational practices depend on the alignment of education with cultural and social policy, rather than economic priorities.

As the governing body of education in the state of New South Wales, the DET imposes staff formulae that determine the number of Teacher Librarians, library assistants, and budget allocations.

An intensive investigation into the role of Teacher Librarians must reveal that they are unable to adequately fulfill all the tasks that have been imposed on them unless sufficient funds are made available to employ more Teacher Librarians, allocate a greater number of ancillary hours, make provision for appropriate training and development, raise the status of Teacher Librarians by recognising their specialist skills by making their position an executive one, and ensure suitably qualified personnel are employed in this critical position within the education system.

In conclusion, in order that Teacher Librarians are able to maximise the educational opportunities for members of the school community, it is necessary to increase library budgets in order that:

- schools have adequate numbers of personnel to allow access to appropriate information
- library personnel are appropriately qualified
- the professional attributes of Teacher Librarians are acknowledged

- professional development is on-going, appropriate and substantial.

Further, the DET should investigate the role of Teacher Librarians, and provide an appropriate statement of duties for this position.

Without these changes, school libraries risk becoming what McKenzie (1996) refers to as "information ATMs" where knowledge is to be withdrawn in the same manner that money can be accessed from banks. Whilst in some circumstances this may be sufficient, school libraries are charged with the responsibility of not only providing access to information, but also with the didactic challenge of providing instruction on the use, evaluation, and methods of obtaining that information.

Library Committee

The purpose of the Library Committee is to act as a channel of communication and dialogue between the University Library and its users. The Committee's main objective is to aid in the establishment a bridge between the Library and the UOB neighboring community.

Many activities have been organized by the Committee, including the Annual Inter-Faculty Library Challenge. Other activities of importance are exhibitions, writing workshops with renowned journalists, and workshops to encourage reading in young learners.

If you have any suggestions, please contact the Committee through the Library or the members.

The Role of Students

Students must understand that the opportunity to learn with a host employer and their staff in the workplace is important and valued.

They will have a purpose and focus for their learning.

Students are to behave with courtesy and respect, follow all reasonable instructions and not do anything that would jeopardise the safety of themselves or others in the workplace.

Students are to inform their library supervisor and the contact from the school if they are not able to attend the workplace. Students also need to inform their library supervisior of any injury, accident or incident that may occur during their placement.

Students must respect workplace confidentiality at all times. They are not to convey any knowledge or information of this kind to any person outside the host employer's workplace.

Student preparation plays an important part in the online medium of e-learning, they are learning through action online. One of the defining traits of online learning is the increased independence of learners who are trying to set up Home Office for Online Learning. Only if they are motivated, disciplined and self directed can e-learning be successful. Online students can contribute to successful learning and preparation through the following:

Awareness

The student must be able to evaluate expectations, assess appropriate length of time needed to complete the work and understand value of the learning. He must also have the ability to assess personal, technical and study skills.

Orientation

As opposed to a traditional classroom, an e-learner goes through several stages of preparation before engaging the content. This includes the virtual classroom, software, instructor and then finally the content. Different students will enter a course at different levels of preparedness; in online courses, the instructor should be able to accommodate a student at any level.

Discipline and Motivation

The student should be disciplined and motivated to follow course schedule and complete assignments.

Organized

The student must be organized enough to schedule study time and online time to ensure all course obligations are met.

Self-directed

The learner must motivate himself and ask for help when needed.

Role of the Instructor

The instructor too plays a crucial role in this online medium of e-learning. The instructor should be involved in and be aware of student experiences and suggest ways to address it. He can offer simple assessments on computer skills needed, introductions at the start of a course, offer links to student resources, provide clear schedules, provide for discussions, chat times, instant messaging etc.

Some other roles that an instructor needs to carry out are:

In the absence of face-to-face learning, it is imperative for the instructor to establish rapport with students, make them feel comfortable with the online experience and encourage them to participate .

The channels of communication between the instructor and the student must be open and constant. It should be driven by regular emails, active involvement in discussion forums and chats.

The essence of e-learning is flexibility and convenience. Often online learners are adults who have varying time constraints; one has to adapt to such scenarios.

The instructor creates and maintains the online environment-levels of respect, concern for learning, etc. are all set by the instructor. An attitude that accepts failure as critical to learning is needed.

Teachers and Librarians: Collaborative Relationships

Since the early 1980s, library literature has examined progress toward establishing successful collaborative relationships between classroom teachers and library media specialists. In 1989, Berkowitz and Eisenberg acknowledged the gap between the library media specialist's potential as a curriculum consultant in theory and in practice, noting that library media specialists' interest in being involved in curriculum dates back to the 1950s. Assignments developed in partnership between teachers and library media specialists are known to be more "authentic"-exhibiting a higher degree of meaning and significance (Gross & Kientz, 1999). When not guided in the use of a process, students tend to approach research as though there is only one right answer, and fail to learn how to use information to construct their own meaning (Kuhlthau, 1995). This ability to construct meaning is at the heart of information literacy, which collectively describes the skills students will need to cope in a complex world with access to an ever increasing wealth of information.

The results of a study by the Library Service Center of the Colorado State Library offer the most recent support for library media specialists and teachers working collaboratively. The study concludes that test scores increase as school librarians spend more time collaborating with and providing training to teachers, providing input into curricula, and managing information technology for the school (Manzo, 2000). A significant number of prior studies also indicate a positive relationship between the library media programme and academic achievement. Didier (1984) examines 38 of these studies, including Gaver's (1963) study of the impact of elementary library service on test scores; Greve's (1974) research on the effect of library service on the academic achievement of high school seniors; and Snider's (1965) investigation of the relationship between college success and knowledge of information skills.

Collaboration Defined

Collaboration is based on shared goals, a shared vision, and a climate of trust and respect (Muronago & Harada, 1999). Each partner fulfills a carefully defined role; comprehensive planning is required; leadership, resources, risk, and control are shared; and the working relationship extends over a relatively long period of time (Callison, 1999). The teacher brings to the partnership knowledge of the strengths, weaknesses, attitudes and interests of the students, and of the content to be taught. The media specialist adds a thorough understanding of information skills and methods to integrate them, helping the teacher to develop resource-based units that broaden the use of resources and promote information literacy (Doiron & Davies, 1998). Additional benefits include more effective use of both resources and teaching time, integration of educational technologies, and a reduced teacher/student ratio (Doiron & Davies, 1998).

Teachers with experience in collaborative planning and teaching view the role of the library media specialist more positively and welcome continued collaboration. Participants believe that the results of the collaboration are more powerful and significant than the results of their individual efforts (Friend & Cook, 1996).

Conditions Favorable to Collaborative Partnerships
Administrative Factors

Studies of successful collaborative partnerships have helped us to learn more about the factors conducive to this type of relationship. A recognized barrier to successful collaboration is lack of time (Bishop & Larimer, 1999). Library media specialists with flexible schedules are able to devote more time to planning and working with teachers (Callison, 1999). While media specialists on a fixed schedule spend up to five minutes planning with a teacher, a media specialist on a flexible schedule spends more than 30 minutes (Haycock, 1998).

Media specialists with flexible schedules also develop four and one-half times as many integrated units of study than do those on fixed schedules, as well as teaching more information skills lessons integrated with classroom instruction (Tallman & van Deusen, 1994). Scheduling common planning time for teachers and media specialists also promotes collaboration. The greatest amount of collaboration occurs when the media specialist has a flexible schedule and team planning is encouraged by the principal (Tallman & van Deusen, 1994).

Several Canadian studies have shown that principals have a better understanding of the school library programme and view it more positively than do classroom teachers (Oberg, 1995). Their critical role in promoting collaborative relationships goes beyond scheduling. Principal support includes working directly with teachers to develop their understanding of the role of the library. This is accomplished through staff inservices, featuring library activities in staff meetings, stating expectations of teachers regarding library use both during the hiring process and afterwards, and serving as a role model by effectively using the library and its information literacy programme (Oberg, 1995). Administrators who ask how teachers are using the resources of the media center and the expertise of the library media specialist create an atmosphere where collaboration is more likely to occur (Bishop & Larimer, 1999).

Interpersonal Factors

Successful collaboration involves changing both the attitudes toward and expectations of the role of the library media specialist (Wolcott, 1996). Research shows that most students, teachers, and administrators don't perceive library media specialists and media centers as integral to their own success (Hartzell, 1997). Library media specialists are often viewed as storytellers and providers of resources rather than co-teachers who share common goals (Bishop & Larimer, 1999). It is up to the library media specialist to take steps to change this by serving on curriculum committees, attending planning meetings, and sharing ideas for integrating the media center into the curriculum (Bishop & Larimer, 1999).

Likewise, teachers need help to make the transition from independent teaching to collaboration. The library media specialist can help facilitate this change by acting as the change agent, innovator, opinion leader and/or monitor (Haycock, 1999). The qualities of a library media specialist most often mentioned in discussions of collaboration are initiative, confidence, communication skills, leadership qualities, and, above all, the willingness to take risks. Library media specialists must assume partnership and look for opportunities to plan with teachers, rather than waiting to be asked (Callison, 1999). Effective social skills are necessary to realizing the vision of collaboration set forth in Information Power: Building Partnerships for Learning (1998). Indeed, cognitive styles have been examined, and library media specialists defined as "field-dependent" were found to engage more frequently in collaborative efforts with classroom teachers regardless of time and resource limitations (Montgomery, 1991). Field-dependent library media specialists were characterized by their interest in people, use of others as a source of reinforcement, focus on socially-oriented subject matter, and preference for working with others. Less outgoing library media specialists should note that in the collaborative relationship, both leadership, and risk are shared.

Continued Commitment to the Goal

Haycock (1999) notes that collaborative programme planning and team teaching are complex evolutionary changes which require time-perhaps two to five years-to reach effective levels. In the case of library media specialist/teacher collaboration, the transition has been slow. Although library literature reflects more than two decades of interest in collaborative planning, and library media specialists are well-trained to perform in this capacity, there are still fewer examples of instructional partnerships than might be expected (Haycock, 1999). However, commitment to the goal remains strong.

The term "collaboration" is one of the most frequently used terms in Information Power: Building Partnerships for Learning (Callison, 1999). "Instructional consultant" has been upgraded to instructional and curriculum "partner," reflecting a collaborative relationship where the teacher and library media specialist are viewed as equal contributors (Muronago & Harada, 1999). The future of the library media programme will be shaped by the vision for a student-centered library media programme described in this revised document. This vision for the future is based on three central ideas which suggest a framework to support the authentic student learning that is the goal of the successful, student-centered library media programme. These central ideas are collaboration, leadership, and technology.

Teachers and Parents for Effective Use of Library

A well-equipped and adequately staffed school library can help improve instruction and can be the center of learning by providing extensive enrichment materials. The school library is a necessary part of every school. Education department recommends standards based on school size, and the respective agencies sponsors school library development projects. These developments indicate the growing interest in nationwide school library projects. However, there is a great need for properly trained personnel, for more space, and more allocations. The school library programme should be coordinated with the entire school curriculum in order to structure teaching units, to meet special student needs, and to promote professional relations. The school library's work should be related to community needs through the parent teachers association.

UNIT-II

Information Sources

Information

Information as a concept has a diversity of meanings, from everyday usage to technical settings. Generally speaking, the concept of information is closely related to notions of constraint, communication, control, data, form, instruction, knowledge, meaning, mental stimulus, pattern, perception, and representation.

Many people speak about the Information Age as the advent of the Knowledge Ageor knowledge society, the information society, the Information revolution, and information technologies, and even though informatics, information science and computer science are often in the spotlight, the word "information" is often used without careful consideration of the various meanings it has acquired.

Etymology

According to the Oxford English Dictionary, the first known historical meaning of the word *information* in English was the act of *informing*, or giving form or shape to the mind, as in education, instruction, or training. A quote from 1387: "Five books come down from heaven for information of mankind." It was also used for an *item* of training, *e.g.* a particular instruction. "Melibee had heard the great skills and reasons of Dame Prudence, and her wise information and techniques." (1386)

The English word was apparently derived by adding the common "noun of action" ending "*-ation*" (descended through

French from Latin "*-tio*") to the earlier verb *to inform*, in the sense of to give form to the mind, to discipline, instruct, teach: "Men so wise should go and inform their kings." (1330) *Inform* itself comes (via French) from the Latin verb *informare*, to give form to, to form an idea of. Furthermore, Latin itself already even contained the word *informatio* meaning concept or idea, but the extent to which this may have influenced the development of the word *information* in English is unclear.

As a final note, the ancient Greek word for *form* was "ìïñöÞ" (morf-> morphe, Morph) and also *åßäïò* eidos (kind, idea, shape, set), the later word was famously used in a technical philosophical sense by Plato (and later Aristotle) to denote the ideal identity or essence of something (see Theory of forms). "Eidos" can also be associated with thought, proposition or even concept.

As a Message

Information is a term with many meanings depending on context, but is as a rule closely related to such concepts as meaning, knowledge, instruction, communication, representation, and mental stimulus. Simply stated, information is a message received and understood. In terms of data, it can be defined as a collection of facts from which conclusions may be drawn. There are many other aspects of information since it is the knowledge acquired through study or experience or instruction. But overall, information is the result of processing, manipulating and organizing data in a way that adds to the knowledge of the person receiving it.

Information is the state of a system of interest. Message is the information materialized.

Information is a quality of a message from a sender to one or more receivers. Information is always *about* something (size of a parameter, occurrence of an event, value, ethics, etc). Viewed in this manner, information does not have to be accurate; it may be a truth or a lie, or just the sound of a falling tree. Even a disruptive noise used to inhibit the flow of communication and create misunderstanding would in this view be a form of information. However, generally speaking, if the *amount* of information in the received message increases, the message is more accurate.

This model assumes there is a definite sender and at least one receiver. Many refinements of the model assume the existence of a common language understood by the sender and at least one of the receivers. An important variation identifies information as that which would be communicated by a message if it were sent from a sender to a receiver capable of understanding the message. In another variation, it is not required that the sender be capable of understanding the message, or even cognizant that there is a message, making information something that can be extracted from an environment, e.g., through observation, reading or measurement.

Communication theory provides a numerical measure of the uncertainty of an outcome. For example, we can say that "the signal contained thousands of bits of information". Communication theory tends to use the concept of information entropy, generally attributed to Claude Shannon, see below.

Another form of information is Fisher information, a concept of R.A. Fisher. This is used in application of statistics to estimation theory and to science in general. Fisher information is thought of as the amount of information that a message carries about an unobservable parameter. It can be computed from knowledge of the likelihood function defining the system. For example, with a normal likelihood function, the Fisher information is the reciprocal of the variance of the law. In the absence of knowledge of the likelihood law, the Fisher information may be computed from normally distributed score data as the reciprocal of their second moment.

Even though information and data are often used interchangeably, they are actually very different. Data is a set of unrelated information, and as such is of no use until it is properly evaluated. Upon evaluation, once there is some significant relation between data, and they show some relevance, then they are converted into information. Now this same data can be used for different purposes. Thus, till the data convey some information, they are not useful and therefore not information.

Measuring Information Entropy

The view of information as a message came into prominence with the publication in 1948 of an influential paper by Claude Shannon, "A Mathematical Theory of Communication." This paper provides the foundations of information theory and endows the word *information* not only with a technical meaning but also a measure. If the sending device is equally likely to send any one of a set of *N* messages, then the preferred measure of "the information produced when one message is chosen from the set" is the base two logarithm of *N* (This measure is called *self-information*). In this paper, Shannon continues:

> *The choice of a logarithmic base corresponds to the choice of a unit for measuring information. If the base 2 is used the resulting units may be called binary digits, or more briefly bits, a word suggested by J. W. Tukey. A device with two stable positions, such as a relay or a flip-flop circuit, can store one bit of information. N such devices can store N bits...*

A complementary way of measuring information is provided by algorithmic information theory. In brief, this measures the information content of a list of symbols based on how predictable they are, or more specifically how easy it is to compute the list through a programme: the information content of a sequence is the number of bits of the shortest programme that computes it. The sequence below would have a very low algorithmic information measurement since it is a very predictable pattern, and as the pattern continues the measurement would not change. Shannon information would give the same information measurement for each symbol, since they are statistically random, and each new symbol would increase the measurement.

It is important to recognize the limitations of traditional information theory and algorithmic information theory from the perspective of human meaning. For example, when referring to the meaning content of a message Shannon noted "Frequently the messages have *meaning*... these semantic aspects of communication are irrelevant to the engineering problem. The significant aspect is that the actual message is one selected *from a set of possible messages*" (emphasis in original).

In information theory signals are part of a process, not a substance; they do something, they do not contain any specific meaning. Combining algorithmic information theory and information theory we can conclude that the most random signal contains the most information as it can be interpreted in any way and cannot be compressed. Michael Reddy noted that "'signals' of the mathematical theory are 'patterns that can be exchanged'. There is no message contained in the signal, the signals convey the ability to select from a set of possible messages." In information theory "the system must be designed to operate for each possible selection, not just the one which will actually be chosen since this is unknown at the time of design".

As a Pattern

Information is any represented pattern. This view assumes neither accuracy nor directly communicating parties, but instead assumes a separation between an object and its representation. Consider the following example: economic statistics represent an economy, however inaccurately. What are commonly referred to as data in computing, statistics, and other fields, are forms of information in this sense. The electro-magnetic patterns in a computer network and connected devices are related to something other than the pattern itself, such as text characters to be displayed and keyboard input. Signals, signs, and symbols are also in this category.

On the other hand, according to semiotics, data is symbols with certain syntax and information is data with a certain semantic. Painting and drawing contain information to the extent that they represent something such as an assortment of objects on a table, a profile, or a landscape. In other words, when a pattern of something is transposed to a pattern of something else, the latter is information. This would be the case whether or not there was anyone to perceive it.

But if information can be defined merely as a pattern, does that mean that neither utility nor meaning are necessary components of information? Arguably a distinction must be made between raw unprocessed data and information which possesses utility, value or some quantum of meaning. On this view, information may indeed be characterized as a pattern; but this is a necessary condition, not a sufficient one.

An individual entry in a telephone book, which follows a specific pattern formed by name, address and telephone number, does not become "informative" in some sense unless and until it possesses some degree of utility, value or meaning. For example, someone might look up a girlfriend's number, might order a take away etc. The vast majority of numbers will never be construed as "information" in any meaningful sense. The gap between data and information is only closed by a behavioral bridge whereby some value, utility or meaning is added to transform mere data or pattern into information.

When one constructs a representation of an object, one can selectively extract from the object (sampling) or use a system of signs to replace (encoding), or both. The sampling and encoding result in representation. An example of the former is a "sample" of a product; an example of the latter is "verbal description" of a product. Both contain information of the product, however inaccurate.

When one interprets representation, one can predict a broader pattern from a limited number of observations (inference) or understand the relation between patterns of two different things (decoding). One example of the former is to sip a soup to know if it is spoiled; an example of the latter is examining footprints to determine the animal and its condition. In both cases, information sources are not constructed or presented by some "sender" of information. Regardless, information is dependent upon, but usually unrelated to and separate from, the medium or media used to express it.

In other words, the position of a theoretical series of bits, or even the output once interpreted by a computer or similar device, is unimportant, except when someone or something is present to interpret the information. Therefore, a quantity of information is totally distinct from its medium.

Definitions of Information

One of the most common ways to define information is to describe it as one or more statements or facts that are received by a human and that have some form of worth to the recipient. For example, the Sesame Street character "Cookie Monster" describes information as "news or facts about something," or, as the first definition in the *Random House College Dictionary* suggests for information, "knowledge communicated or received concerning a particular fact or circumstance; news." Cookie Monster's definition is consistent with the common notions that information must:

1. be something, although the exact nature (substance, energy, or abstract concept) isn't clear;
2. provide "new" information: a repetition of previously received messages isn't informative;
3. be "true:" a lie or false or counterfactual information is *mis-information*, not information itself;
4. be "about" something.

This approach to information, like most human-centered approaches to information, leads one to emphasize the meaning and use of message, "what the message is about?" and "what is known already?" over the information carrying messenger and the message itself. When the message is essentially random, or the message is of no value to the recipient, such as a repeated message previously received and understood, it is colloquially said that no information was received and no information was transmitted.

Some individuals equate information with meaning [Mil87]. Hearing a statement isn't enough to make an event an informative act; its meaning must be perceived to make the statement informative. Arguing against this approach, Bar Hillel points out that "it is psychologically almost impossible not to make the shift from the one sense of information, ... i.e. information = signal sequence, to the other sense, information = what is expressed by the signal sequences" [BH55]. As Stonier reminds us, "we must not confuse the detection and/or interpretation of information with information itself" [Sto90]

For many who have worked with quantitative models of information in the engineering disciplines, this concern with meaning lies outside the scope of the traditional mathematical theory of information; communication engineers seldom concern themselves professionally with the meaning of messages.

In an approach similar to defining information as meaning, information is often understood in terms of knowledge that is transmitted to a sentient being. For example, Peters defines information as " knowledge with the human body taken out of it" [Pet88]. Similarly, information may be understood as "that which occurs within the mind upon the absorption of a message" [Pra82].

Information and its cousin entropy have long been studied as fundamental characteristics of physical systems and structures. Systems of molecules are often studied by considering an imaginary being, Maxwell's demon, a hypothetical gatekeeper between two sections of a closed system of molecules [LR90]. Assume that molecules move in a frictionless way. If the demon opens and closes the door at just the right times, can it essentially allow particles with higher levels of energy through to one side of the doorway and particles with lower levels of energy through to the other? Is this a perpetual motion machine, with the demon expending no energy, pumping energy to wherever it is wanted? This would violate the second law of thermodynamics. If the demon can't perform as described, why is it limited in its capabilities?

Attempts to solve this paradox have centered on the relationship between information and structure of the systems and the information needed and used by the demon in decision making, as well as the energy involved in making an observation and remembering the state of the system. The description of the positions of the molecules, the structure of the system, can be described using concepts and formulae consistent with some communication models, such as Shannon's model of communications.

The form or structure of systems is viewed by some as being equivalent to information. Thus, "information is what remains after one abstracts from the material aspects of physical reality" [Res89]. The information in a structure is an immaterial ghost that co-exists with the physical object about which it informs. The word "form" comes from the same etymological roots as "information." Form or state of nature may be reflected in the set of characteristics' values in the output of a producing process.

The randomness associated with an information producing process about a system's form and structure may be understood as the inverse of information. Consider a pile of coins on a counter; whether they are "heads" or "tails" is information, while if we have no such information, their heads or tails orientation is random to us. Receiving information about the orientation of a coin may result in the removal of uncertainty, decreasing the ignorance or lack of information about the structure.

Information has long been understood as a concept appropriate for discussion in the humanities and social sciences [Rit91]. Electrical engineers began using the term to describe data transmission during the first half of the twentieth century. Instead of providing a definition of information, these engineers focused on measuring information, as they attempted to maximize information transmitted or received, or minimize noise, or both. The social science literature of the 1950s and 1960s used ideas about information measurement developed by Shannon and Weaver in the late 1940s crossing back from engineering to the liberal arts. Outside of electrical engineering, Shannon's formal ideas about information are used most profitably today in the computing and cognitive sciences.

All of these ideas about information serve to facilitate discourse for those describing discipline specific concepts, each used in solving a particular set of problems. Electrical engineers wish to study the capacity of pieces of hardware and the physical connections between them. Linguists wish to understand how information is transmitted by languages and the nature of what lies at the core of communication. Mathematicians and computer scientists wish to study the processes by which software transforms input into output and the fundamental characteristics of transforming processes.

Researchers in these disciplines want tools that manipulate the phenomena of their domains. These needs have produced ideas about information having varying degrees of overlap, as well as areas where they fail to intersect. Given the number of definitions or metaphors that have been proposed for information, how does one compare them? We propose a commonality within these definitions; this underlying commonality can be defined, studied, and measured.

We suggest here a general definition of information: *information is produced by all processes and it is the values of characteristics in the processes' output that are information.* This captures most concepts of information in individual disciplines. The number of possible values in the output and their relative frequencies of occurrence may be used in measuring the amount of information present.

Sources of Information

Information can come from virtually anywhere—personal experiences, books, articles, expert opinions, encyclopedias, the Web—and the type of information you need will change depending on the question you are trying to answer. Look at the following sources of information. Notice the similarities between them.

Primary and Secondary Sources of Information

Primary sources of information allow the learner to access original and unedited information. A primary source requires the learner to interact with the source and extract information. Secondary sources are edited primary sources, second-hand versions. They represent someone else's thinking.

Advertisements

Primary Sources:

- Person
- Interview
- E-Mail contact
- Event
- Discussion

- Debate
- Community Meeting
- Survey
- Artifact
- Observation of object (animate and inanimate)

Secondary Sources:

- Reference Material
- Book
- CD Rom
- Encyclopedia
- Magazine
- Newspaper
- Video Tape
- Audio Tape
- TV

Primary or Secondary

- Internet Web Site
- Graph, chart, diagram, table

Privacy Policy: This privacy policy is reviewed and revised from time to time. You may wish to revisit it regularly.

This site does not collect or store data from you with the purpose of selling or renting the data or sending marketing emails. We collect no more data about each visitor than most other websites.

When posting a comment, a name and email address are required. You do not have to select your real name. Your email address will not published.

Comments, trackbacks, pingbacks and forms submitted here will be identified by your IP address. It's sometimes possible to use these numbers to trace/identify someone or the ISP or employer/ educational institution the IP address is registered to. Your IP address could potentially be used in conjunction with other data to identify you. If this is a concern please use an anonymous browsing service.

Some of the facilities on this site are usable only if you have cookies enabled. Some advertising networks like Google also store cookies. You may wish to clear these cookies and the browser cache if you wish to refrain from revealing any identifying information, especially if you are using a public or shared computer.

Any time you visit a page on the internet, you send quite a bit of information to the server. The web servers that host this site maintain access logs with the information that you send. These servers are owned by third parties and this information is used to provide site statistics and to get an idea of popular pages and what sites link here. We do not intend to use these logs to identify legitimate users. The data logged may be used by us to solve technical problems with the site and, in cases of abuse of this site, to investigate the abuse.

Again, if you are concerned about attempts to match your IP address to your identity, you may wish to use an anonymous browsing service or attempt some means to obfuscate your real IP address.

In general, it is not our practice to disclose personal information to third parties. We may share personal information we collect in the following circumstances:

- As required by law, such as in response to a valid request from law enforcement.
- To designated third parties to resolve or investigate abuse complaints or to enhance, add or maintain functionality of this site
- When the information is related to spiders or bots, usually when investigating technical issues.
- For abusive users, we may release information to assist in attempting to block the abusive user or to complain to that user's Internet Service Provider.
- If necessary to defend legal claims against us by third parties.
- When we deem it necessary to protect the property or rights of the user community, or this website.

You are required to give your email address when you post a comment. We will not sell information collected via this site, such as your email address, to third parties. If you are concerned, you may wish to get a free email account or attempt to use a remail service.

We implement reasonable security measures to protect against unauthorized access to or interception of personal information that we store or control. However, no site can fully eliminate security risks and we make no guarantee that the information that you provide us cannot be unlawfully intercepted/ accessed. Please notify us if any such security breach occurs.

Primary Source

Primary source is a term used in a number of disciplines. In historiography, a primary source (also called original source) is a document, recording or other source of information, such as a paper or a picture for instance, that was created at the time being studied, by an authoritative source, usually one with direct personal knowledge of the events being described.

It serves as an original source of information about the topic. Primary sources are distinguished from secondary sources, which often cite, comment on, or build upon primary sources.

Similar (but not identical) definitions are used in library science, and other areas of scholarship. A primary source could be a first-hand source from the past, such as a diary or artifact. Primary sources have been described as those sources closest to the origin of the information or idea under study. Primary sources have been said to provide researchers with "direct, unmediated information about the object of study."

They may contain original research or new information not previously published elsewhere. They serve as an original source of information or new ideas about the topic. *Primary* and *secondary*, however, are relative terms, and often a given source may be classified as either primary or secondary, depending on how it is used.

The Significance of Source Classification in Various Disciplines

History and Historiography: The delineation of sources as primary and secondary first arose in the field of historiography, as historians attempted to identify and classify the sources of historical writing. In scholarly writing, an important objective of classifying sources is to determine the independence and reliability of sources. In contexts such as historical writing, it is almost always advisable to use primary sources if possible, and that "if none are available, it is only with great caution that [the author] may proceed to make use of secondary sources." Many historians believe that primary sources have the most objective connection to the past, and that they "speak for themselves" in ways that cannot be captured through the filter of secondary sources.

Many scholars have commented on the difficulty in producing secondary source narratives from the "raw data" which makes up the past. Historian/philosopher Hayden White has written extensively on the ways in which the rhetorical strategies by which historians construct narratives about the past, and what sorts of assumptions about time, history, and events are embedded in the very structure of the historical narrative. In any case, the question of the exact relation between "historical facts" and the content of "written history" has been a topic of discussion among historians since at least the nineteenth century, when much of the modern profession of history came into being.

As a general rule, modern historians prefer to go back to primary sources, if available, as well as seeking new ones, because primary sources, whether accurate or not, offer new input into historical questions, and most modern history revolves around heavy use of archives for the purpose of finding useful primary sources. On the other hand, most undergraduate research projects are limited to secondary source material.

Other Fields

In scholarly writing, the objective of classifying sources is to determine the independence and reliability of sources. Though the terms *primary source* and *secondary source* originated in historiography as a way to trace the history of historical ideas, it has been applied to many other fields. For example, this idea may be used to trace the history of scientific theories, literary elements, and other information that is passes from one author to another. In scientific literature, a primary source is the original publication of a scientist's new data, results, and theories. In political history, primary sources reflect documents such as official reports, speeches, pamphlets, posters, or letters by participants, official election returns, and eyewitness accounts. In the history of ideas or intellectual history, the main primary sources are books, essays and letters written by intellectuals. A study of cultural history could include fictional sources such as novels or plays. In a broader sense primary sources also include physical objects like photographs, newsreels, coins, paintings or buildings created at the time. Historians may also take archaeological artifacts and oral reports and interviews into consideration. Written sources may be divided into three main types.

- Narrative sources or literary sources tell a story or message. They are not limited to fictional sources (which can be sources of infcrmation for contemporary attitudes), but include diaries, films, biographies, leading philosophical works, scientific works, and so on.
- Diplomatic sources include charters and other legal documents which usually follow a set format.
- Social documents are records created by organizations, such as registers of births, tax records, and so on.

In the study of historiography, when the study of history is itself subject to historical scrutiny, a secondary source becomes a primary source. For a biography of a historian, that historian's publications would be primary sources. Documentary films can be considered a secondary source or primary source, depending on how much the filmmaker modifies the original sources.

The Lafayette College Library, for example, provides the following synopsis of primary sources in several basic areas of study:

"The definition of a primary source varies depending upon the academic discipline and the context in which it is used.

- In the humanities, a primary source could be defined as something that was created either during the time period being studied or afterward by individuals reflecting on their involvement in the events of that time.
- In the social sciences, the definition of a primary source would be expanded to include numerical data that has been gathered to analyze relationships between people, events, and their environment.
- In the natural sciences, a primary source could be defined as a report of original findings or ideas. These sources often appear in the form of research articles with sections on methods and results."

Finding Primary Sources

Although many documents that are primary sources remain in private hands, the usual location for them is an archive. These can be public or private. Documents relating to one area are usually spread over a large number of different archives. These can be distant from the original source of the document. For example, the Huntington Library in California houses a large number of documents from the United Kingdom.

In the US, digital primary sources can be retrieved from a number of places. The Library of Congress maintains several online Digital Collections where they can be retrieved. Examples of these are American Memory and the Prints and Photographs Online Catalog (PPOC). The National Archives and Records Administration also has such a tool, called Access to Archival Databases (AAD).

In the UK, the National Archives provides a consolidated search of its own catalogue and a wide variety of other archives listed on the Access to Archives index. Digital copies of various classes of documents at the National Archives (including wills) are available from DocumentsOnline. Most of the available documents relate to England and Wales. Some digital copies of primary sources are available from the National Archives of

Scotland. Many County Record Offices collections are included in Access to Archives, while others have their own on-line catalogues. Many County Record Offices will supply digital copies of documents.

In the Republic of Ireland, available digital documents include the censuses of 1901 and 1911 which are available from the National Archives of Ireland.

In Australia, the National Archives of Australia has digitised a number of classes of records and will produce digitised copies of suitable documents on demand.

Using Primary Sources

History as an academic discipline is based on primary sources, as evaluated by the community of scholars, who report their findings in books, articles and papers. Arthur Marwick says "Primary sources are absolutely fundamental to history." Ideally, a historian will use all available primary sources created by the people involved, at the time being studied. In practice some sources have been destroyed, while others are not available for research.

Perhaps the only eyewitness reports of an event may be memoirs, autobiographies, or oral interviews taken years later. Sometimes the only documents relating to an event or person in the distant past were written decades or centuries later. This is a common problem in classical studies, where sometimes only a summary of a book has survived. Potential difficulties with primary sources have the result that history is usually taught in schools using secondary sources.

Historians studying the modern period with the intention of publishing an academic article prefer to go back to available primary sources and to seek new (in other words, forgotten or lost) ones. Primary sources, whether accurate or not, offer new input into historical questions and most modern history revolves around heavy use of archives and special collections for the purpose of finding useful primary sources. A work on history is not likely to be taken seriously as scholarship if it only cites secondary sources, as it does not indicate that original research has been done.

However, primary sources-particularly those from before the 20th century-may have hidden challenges. "Primary sources, in fact, are usually fragmentary, ambiguous and very difficult to analyse and interpret." Obsolete meanings of familiar words and social context are among the traps that await the newcomer to historical studies. For this reason, The interpretation of primary texts is typically taught as part of an advanced college or postgraduate history course, however advanced self-study or informal training is also possible.

The following questions are asked about primary sources:

- What is the tone?
- Who is the intended audience?
- What is the purpose of the publication?
- What assumptions does the author make?
- What are the bases of the author's conclusions?
- Does the author agree or disagree with other authors of the subject?
- Does the content agree with what you know or have learned about the issue?
- Where was the source made? (questions of systemic bias)

In journalism, education, and other fields, these are sometimes known as the five Ws-who, what, when, where and why.

Secondary Source

In library and information science, historiography and other areas of scholarship, a secondary source is a document or recording that relates or discusses information originally presented elsewhere. A secondary source contrasts with a primary source, which is an original source of the information being discussed. Secondary sources involve generalization, analysis, synthesis, interpretation, or evaluation of the original information. *Primary* and *secondary* are relative terms, and some sources may be classified as primary or secondary, depending on how it is used. An even higher level, the tertiary source, resembles a secondary source in that it contains analysis, but attempts to provide a broad overview of a topic that is accessible to newcomers.

Source Classification

Many sources can be considered either primary and secondary, depending on the context in which they are used. Moreover, the distinction between *primary* and *secondary* sources is subjective and contextual, so that precise definitions are difficult to make. For example, if a historical text discusses old documents to derive a new historical conclusion, it is considered to be a primary source for the new conclusion, but a secondary source of information found in the old documents. Other examples in which a source can be both primary and secondary include an obituary or a survey of several volumes of a journal counting the frequency of articles on a certain topic.

Whether a source is regarded as primary or secondary in a given context may change, depending upon the present state of knowledge within the field. For example, if a document refers to the contents of a previous but undiscovered letter, that document may be considered "primary", since it is the closest known thing to an original source, but if the letter is later found, it may then be considered "secondary".

Attempts to map or model scientific and scholarly communication need the concepts of primary, secondary and further "levels". One such model is the UNISIST model of information dissemination. Within such a model these concepts are defined in relation to each other, and the acceptance of this way of defining the concepts are connected to the acceptance of the model.

Other languages, like German, call the secondary sources *Sekundärliteratur*, leaving *Sekundärquelle* to historiography. A *Sekundärquelle* is a source that can tell about a (lost) *Primärquelle*, e.g. a letter is quoting from minutes that no longer exist and can not be consulted by the historian.

Typical Secondary Sources in Various Fields

Historiography and Historical Scholarship: The delineation of sources as primary and secondary first arose in the field of historiography, as historians attempted to identify and classify the sources of historical writing. In scholarly writing, an important objective of classifying sources is to determine the independence and reliability of sources. In contexts such as historical writing, it is almost always advisable to use primary sources if possible, and that "if none are available, it is only with great caution that [the author] may proceed to make use of secondary sources." Many scholars have commented on the difficulty in producing secondary source narratives from the "raw data" which makes up the past. Historian/philosopher Hayden White has written extensively on the ways in which the rhetorical strategies by which historians construct narratives about the past, and what sorts of assumptions about time, history, and events are embedded in the very structure of the historical narrative. In any case, the question of the exact relation between "historical facts" and the content of "written history" has been a topic of discussion among historians since at least the nineteenth century, when much of the modern profession of history came into being.

As a general rule, modern historians prefer to go back to primary sources, if available, as well as seeking new ones, because primary sources, whether accurate or not, offer new input into historical questions, and most modern history revolves around heavy use of archives for the purpose of finding useful primary sources. On the other hand, most undergraduate research projects are limited to secondary source material.

Library and Information Science

In library and information sciences, secondary sources are generally regarded as those sources that summarize or add commentary to primary sources in the context of the particular information or idea under study.

Secondary Sources in Family History

"A secondary source is a record or statement of an event or circumstance made by a non-eyewitness or by someone not closely connected with the event or circumstances, recorded or stated verbally either at or sometime after the event, or by an eye-witness at a time after the event when the fallibility of memory is an important factor." Consequently, an autobiography written after the event is a secondary source, even though it may be the first published description of an event. For example, many first hand accounts of events in the 1st world war that were written in the post war years were influenced by the then prevailing perception of the war which was significantly different from contemporary opinion.

Secondary Legal Sources

In the legal field, source classification is important because the persuasiveness of a source usually depends upon its history. Primary sources may include cases, constitutions, statutes, administrative regulations, and other sources of binding legal authority, while secondary legal sources may include books, articles, and encyclopedias. Legal writers usually prefer to cite primary sources because only primary sources are authoritative and precedential, while secondary sources are only persuasive at best.

Secondary Sources of Scientific and Mathematical Ideas and Data

Source classification is a useful tool for tracing the history of scientific and mathematical ideas, including who is credited as the primary source of the idea and how it has been propagated. A review article is an example of such a secondary source, and some scientific journals only publish review articles.

One important use of secondary sources in the field of mathematics has been to make difficult mathematical ideas and proofs from primary sources more accessible to the public.

Tertiary Source

The term tertiary source is a relative term. What is considered tertiary depends on what is considered primary and secondary. A tertiary source may thus be understood as a selection, distillation, summary or compilation of primary sources, secondary sources, or both. The distinction between primary source and secondary source is standard in historiography, while the distinction between these sources and tertiary sources is more peripheral, and is more relevant to the scholarly research work than to the published content itself. In some contexts typical instances of tertiary sources are bibliographies, library catalogs, directories, reading lists and survey articles. Encyclopedias and textbooks are examples of written materials that typically embrace both secondary and tertiary sources, presenting on the one hand commentary and analysis, while on the other attempting to provide a synoptic overview of the material available on the topic.

A different definition is used by the UNISIST model in which secondary sources are understood as bibliographies, while tertiary sources are understood as synthesis of primary literature.

Using Reference Sources

As you go through school, you will need to use reference sources to find information about topics, locate facts, and answer questions. Here are five types of reference sources you should use. Each type is available in print forms, on CD-ROMs, and on the Internet.

1. *Dictionary:* A dictionary provides information about the meaning, pronunciation, and spelling of words. Unabridged dictionaries attempt to be complete by including all words currently in use in a language. They provide extensive information about the words included. Abridged dictionaries omit words that do not regularly appear in books, magazines, and newspapers. Specialized dictionaries provide detailed information about the words that apply to a particular subject such as space, math, biology, psychology, and many more. They include technical words that are rarely used outside of the subject.
2. *Thesaurus:* A thesaurus contains synonyms for commonly used words. A synonym is a word that has the same meaning or nearly the same meaning as another word. For example, "simple" is a synonym for "easy." A thesaurus contains many more synonyms for a word than does a dictionary. A thesaurus can help you precisely express your ideas when writing.

3. *Encyclopedia:* An encyclopedia contains articles on a variety of subjects. The articles are written by experts on each of the subjects. In addition to articles, encyclopedias may include illustrations and diagrams, definitions of some words, and references to additional information. A general encyclopedia includes overview articles on a wide range of topics.
4. *Almanac:* An almanac is an annual single-volume reference source that contains useful facts about a wide range of topics. You can learn about countries of the world, government, historical events, and many other topics. Because almanacs are revised each year, the information is current.
5. *Atlas:* An atlas is a collection of maps. The most common atlas contains maps that show the political and physical features of countries throughout the world. A political map shows government boundaries. A physical map shows the features of the earth's surface such as mountains, deserts, and bodies of water. You may also use a road map to learn how to get from place to place. There are also specialized atlases for such things as weather across the world, oceans of the world, and even the anatomy of the human body.

Wherever you study, be sure you have access to each of these important reference sources.

Types of Reference Sources

Different types of reference sources answer different types of questions. Listed below are common types of reference sources and the kind of information contained in each:

- Almanac-Compilations of facts and statistics, usually one volume.
- Atlas-Maps and geographical information.
- Biographical sources-Biographical information about individuals.
- Dictionary-Definitions of terms, either general or in relation to a specific subject or discipline.

- Encyclopedia-Comprehensive summaries of factual information, providing more detail than a dictionary.
- Handbook-Concise explanatory information on a topic.

References Sources in the Undergraduate Library

The reference books listed below are all included in the Undergraduate Library's Reference Collection. These are suggested as good starting points for getting started in the various subject areas listed below. This is by no means a comprehensive list of sources. If you do not see a reference book that will help you find information on your topic, ask for assistance at the Research Desk.

Advertising/Marketing:

- The Advertising age encyclopedia of advertising Q. 659.103 Ad964
- Encyclopedia of major marketing campaign Q. 659.1073 En19

Crime and Law (including Violence and Guns):

- Encyclopedia of Crime and Punishment Q 364.03 En193
- Encyclopedia of gun control and gun rights 363.33097303 Ut8e
- The encyclopedia of violence: origins, attitudes, consequences 303.603 D547e
- Gun control: a reference handbook 363.330973 K945G
- Guns in American society: an encyclopedia of history, politics, culture, and the law 363.33097303 G957
- Violence in America: an encyclopedia Q. 303.6097303 V812
- Statistical handbook on violence in America Q. 303.60973021 St29
- Violence and the media: a reference handbook 303.6 N482v

Drugs-Their Use and Abuse:

- Berkshire Encyclopedia of World Sports (good section on performance enhancing drugs) 796.03 B455

- Drugs and drug policy in America: a documentary history 362.290973 B411d
- Encyclopedia of drugs and alcohol >Q. 362.2903 En19
- Encyclopedia of Smoking and Tobacco362.2960973 H616e

Education:

- Encyclopedia of American Education 370.973 Un 32e 2001
- Encyclopedia of Education and Human Development Q.370.3 En 194
- Encyclopedia of Educational Research 370.3 En192 1992
- Encyclopedia of Special Education Q.371.903 En 19 2000
- Learning Disabilities Sourcebook 371.926 L479
- Greenwood Dictionary of Education 370.3 G856
- Encyclopedia of Education (8 vol.) Q370.3 En194 2003
- Philosophy of Education: an encyclopedia 370.1 P5491

Environment:

- The encyclopedia of the environment 363.7003 En19
- Encyclopedia of Environmental Issues 363.7003 En192
- Environmental Encyclopedia Q.363.7003 En89 2003
- The McGraw-Hill Recycling Handbook 363.7282 M459 2001

Ethics:

- Bioethics: sex, genetics & human reproduction Q. 176 En191
- Encyclopedia of bioethics Q. 174.2 EN191995
- Encyclopedia of ethics 170.3 En192001

Fine Arts (Film, Music, Theater, Photography):

- 1/2/3/4 For the Play 016.8088241 H338o
- Encyclopedia of Popular Music781.6403 En191998
- Film Review Annual 791.437 F4873
- Greenwood Encyclopedia of Rock History 781.6609 G856
- History of the American Cinema 791.430973 H629
- The New York Times Film Reviews 791.43 N48

- The New York Times Theater Reviews Q.792 N485
- Play Index 016.80882 P69
- Virgin Encyclopedia of Popular Music 782.42164 V8192002

Health/Medicine:

- Encyclopedia of Diet Fads 613.2503 B489e
- Encyclopedia of Human Nutrition Q 612.303 En19
- Encyclopedia of Obesity and EatingDisorders 616.8526003 C272e2000
- The Gale encyclopedia of alternative medicine Q. 615.503 G132005
- The Gale encyclopedia of medicine Q. 616.003 G1312006
- Nutrition and Well-Being A to Z Q 613.203 N959
- Encyclopedia of sex 306.703 En192
- The Continuum complete international encyclopedia of sexuality Q. 306.703 In82004
- Human sexuality: an encyclopedia 306.703 H88

Literature:

- Masterplots 809 M393
- Literary Critics and Criticism Q.801.95 C8697
- Oxford Encyclopedia of American Literature Q.810.3 Ox25
- Greenwood Encyclopedia of Science Fiction and Fantasy 823.08 G856
- Short Story Index 016.80883 SH8

Media and Communication:

- Encyclopedia of Communication and Information Q. 302.203 En19
- Encyclopedia of Propaganda 303.37503 En19
- Media and politics in America: a reference handbook 302.230973 St41m
- Public opinion and polling around the world: a Historical Encyclopedia 303.38 P964
- Encyclopedia of television subjects, themes and settings 791.4575 T275e

- Encyclopedia of television Q. 791.4503 En192004

Political Science:

- Atlas of American Politics 1960-2000 Q320.97309045 At65
- Elections A to Z 324.6097303 M784e
- Encyclopedia of the Democratic Party Q324.273403 En19 v.3-4
- Encyclopedia of Presidential Campaigns, Slogans, Issues, and Platforms 324.973003 R543e
- Encyclopedia of the Republican Party Q324.273403 En19 v.1-2
- The Encyclopedia of Third Parties in AmericaQ324.273 K945e 2000
- Voting in America324.60973 D561v

Popular Culture:

- Bowling, beatniks, and bell-bottoms: pop culture of 20th-century America 306.09730904 B682
- American Decades Q. 973.91 Am353
- Encyclopedia of American Social History Q 301.0973 En19
- Encyclopedia of Contemporary American Culture 973.9203 En194
- The Greenwood guide to American popular culture 306.40973 G857
- The guide to United States popular culture Q. 306.097303 G941
- St. James encyclopedia of popular culture Q 973.9 St1

Psychology:

- Diagnostic and Statistical Manual of Mental Disorders 4th Edition (DSM-IV) 132 Am35d 1994
- Encyclopedia of Psychology 150.3 En19
- Magill's Encyclopedia of Social Science: Psychology 150.3M272
- Encyclopedia of human emotions Q. 152.403 En19

Race, Class, Culture, Sexual Orientation, Gender:

- American Immigrant Cultures Q 305.800973 Am354
- Countries and their cultures Q.306.03 C832
- Encyclopedia of the world's minorities Q.305.8003 En197
- Gale Encyclopedia of Multicultural AmericaQ 305.800973 G131 1999 Gay and lesbian issues: a reference handbook 305.9 St492g
- Gay and lesbian rights in the United States: a documentary history 305.90664 G256
- Gay rights on trial: a reference handbook 342.73085 W179g
- Lgbt, encyclopedia of lesbian, gay, bisexual, and transgender history in AmericaQ. 306.7660973 L599
- Racial and Ethnic Relations in America 305.800973 R1156
- Religion and American Cultures Q200.97303 R279
- Worldmark Encyclopedia of Cultures and Daily Life Q305.8003 W893

Religion:

- Cults in America 291 C899
- Encyclopedia of Religion Q.200.321 En19
- The encyclopedia of religion and nature 201.7703 En192
- The Encyclopedia of Unbelief 210.321 En19
- Gods, Goddesses and Mythology Q.201.303 G549
- Religions of the World Q.291 R2791

Social Problems (National & Domestic):

- Current issues: Macmillan social science library Q. 306.0973 C936
- Editorials on File Q.070 Ed46
- Encyclopedia of sociology Q. 301.03 En199 2000
- Facts on File 051 FACT
- Issues and Controversies on File 973.05 IS
- Social issues (Encyclopedia of Sociology) Q. 301.03 So13
- Social Issues in AmericaQ.361.97303 So1323

- Social issues in science and technology: an encyclopedia 303.48303 N482s

Sports/Recreation:

- Berkshire Encyclopedia of World Sports 796.03 B455
- Chronicle of the Olympics Q. 796.48 C468
- International Encyclopedia of Women and Sports Q.796.082 In82
- Native Americans in Sports 796.08997 N213

Terrorism:

- Encyclopedia of American Foreign Policy Q327.73003 H279e
- Encyclopedia of Espionage, Intelligence, and Security Q327.1203 En192
- Encyclopedia of Terrorism Q. 303.62503 C733e
- Spy Book: the Encyclopedia of Espionage 327.1203 P766s
- United States Intelligence: an encyclopedia 327.1273 Un3
- Waging War on Trial 327.73009 D627w

Women and Gender:

- Encyclopedia of women and gender: sex similarities and differences and the impact of society on gender Q. 305.403 En192
- Routledge international encyclopedia of women: global women's issues and knowledge Q. 305.403 R765Women in the
- Third World: an encyclopedia of contemporary issues Q. 305.42091724 W84221

Documenting Sources

The Internet and other digital sources of information are widely used tools for research, but since they are still relatively new tools, various disciplines are still deciding what the correct way to document electronic sources is, and disciplines are constantly changing their minds as to what the most appropriate ways are. To ensure accuracy, it's always best to consult the style manual and/or accompanying website for your discipline first before consulting other sources. We have a complete list of style manuals on our resources for documenting sources in the disciplines page, which also provides links to general information about documenting print sources (and in some cases, electronic sources). Other ways to determine the style you should use are to ask your instructor for guidelines or resources, or to locate the official website for publications in your discipline and see if they have any guidelines or style manuals available.

This resource contains links to sources that will help students, teachers, and anybody doing research on the Internet to cite electronic sources using different styles. We also have links to some of our OWL handouts on citing sources.

Electronic

Electronic learning (or e-Learning or eLearning) is a type of Technology supported education/learning (TSL) where the medium of instruction is through computer technology, particularly involving digital technologies. E-learning has been defined as "pedagogy empowered by digital technology". In some instances, no face-to-face interaction takes place. E-learning is used interchangeably in a wide variety of contexts. In companies, it refers to the strategies that use the company network to deliver training courses to employees. In the United States, it is defined as a planned teaching/learning experience that uses a wide spectrum of technologies, mainly Internet or computer-based, to reach learners. Lately in most Universities, e-learning is used to define a specific mode to attend a course or programmes of study where the students rarely, if ever, attend face-to-face for on-campus access to educational facilities, because they study online.

Market

The worldwide e-learning industry is estimated to be worth over thirty-eight (38) billion euros according to conservative estimates, although in the European Union only about 20% of e-learning products are produced within the common market. Developments in internet and multimedia technologies are the basic enabler of e-learning, with content, technologies and services being identified as the three key sectors of the e-learning industry. eLearning is a catch-all term that covers a wide range of instructional material that can be delivered on a CD-ROM or DVD, over a local area network (LAN), or on the Internet.

Growth of E-learning

By 2006, nearly 3.5 million students were participating in on-line learning at institutions of higher education in the United States. Many higher education, for-profit institutions, now offer on-line classes. By contrast, only about half of private, non-profit schools offer them. The Sloan report, based on a poll of academic leaders, says that students generally appear to be at least as satisfied with their on-line classes as they are with traditional ones. Private institutions may become more involved with on-line presentations as the cost of instituting such a system decreases. Properly trained staff must also be hired to work with students on-line. These staff members need to understand the content area, and also be highly trained in the use of the computer and Internet. Online education is rapidly increasing, and online doctoral programmes have even developed at leading research universities..

Technology

As early as 1993, Graziadei, W. D. described an online computer-delivered lecture, tutorial and assessment project using electronic Mail, two VAX Notes conferences and Gopher/ Lynx together with several software programmes that allowed students and instructor to create a Virtual Instructional Classroom Environment in Science (VICES) in Research, Education, Service & Teaching (REST). In 1997 Graziadei, W.D., et al., published an article entitled "Building Asynchronous and Synchronous Teaching-Learning Environments: Exploring a Course/Classroom Management System Solution". They described a process at the State University of New York (SUNY) of evaluating products and developing an overall strategy for technology-based course development and management in teaching-learning. The product(s) had to be easy to use and maintain, portable, replicable, scalable, and immediately affordable, and they had to have a high probability of success with long-term cost-effectiveness. Today many technologies can be, and are, used in e-Learning, from blogs to collaborative software, ePortfolios, and virtual classrooms. Most eLearning situations use combinations of these techniques.

Along with the terms learning technology, instructional technology, and Educational Technology, the term is generally used to refer to the use of technology in learning in a much broader sense than the computer-based training or Computer Aided Instruction of the 1980s. It is also broader than the terms Online Learning or Online Education which generally refer to purely web-based learning. In cases where mobile technologies are used, the term M-learning has become more common. E-learning, however, also has implications beyond just the technology and refers to the actual learning that takes place using these systems.

E-learning is naturally suited to distance learning and flexible learning, but can also be used in conjunction with face-to-face teaching, in which case the term Blended learning is commonly used. E-Learning pioneer Bernard Luskin argues that the "E" must be understood to have broad meaning if e-Learning is to be effective. Luskin says that the "e" should be interpreted to mean exciting, energetic, enthusiastic, emotional, extended, excellent, and educational in addition to "electronic" that is a traditional national interpretation. This broader interpretation allows for 21st century applications and brings learning and media psychology into the equation.[citation needed]

In higher education especially, the increasing tendency is to create a Virtual Learning Environment (VLE) (which is sometimes combined with a Management Information System (MIS) to create a Managed Learning Environment) in which all aspects of a course are handled through a consistent user interface standard throughout the institution. A growing number of physical universities, as well as newer online-only colleges, have begun to offer a select set of academic degree and certificate programmes via the Internet at a wide range of levels and in a wide range of disciplines. While some programmes require students to attend some campus classes or orientations, many are delivered completely online. In addition, several universities offer online student support services, such as online advising and registration, e-counseling, online textbook purchase, student governments and student newspapers.

e-Learning can also refer to educational web sites such as those offering learning scenarios, worksheets and interactive exercises for children. The term is also used extensively in the business sector where it generally refers to cost-effective online training.

The recent trend in the e-Learning sector is screencasting. There are many screencasting tools available but the latest buzz is all about the web based screencasting tools which allow the users to create screencasts directly from their browser and make the video available online so that the viewers can stream the video directly. The advantage of such tools is that it gives the presenter the ability to show his ideas and flow of thoughts rather than simply explain them, which may be more confusing when delivered via simple text instructions. With the combination of video and audio, the expert can mimic the one on one experience of the classroom and deliver clear, complete instructions. From the learners point of view this provides the ability to pause and rewind and gives the learner the advantage to move at their own pace, something a classroom cannot always offer. One such example of e-Learning platform based on screencasts is YoHelpOnline.

Services

E-learning services have evolved since computers were first used in education. There is a trend to move toward blended learning services, where computer-based activities are integrated with practical or classroom-based situations.

Goals of E-learning

E-Learning lessons are generally designed to guide students through information or to help students perform in specific tasks. Information based e-Learning content communicates information to the student. Examples include content that distributes the history or facts related to a service, company, or product. In information-based content, there is no specific skill to be learned. In performance-based content, the lessons build off of a procedural skill in which the student is expected to increase proficiency.

Computer-based Learning

Computer Based Learning, sometimes abbreviated to CBL, refers to the use of computers as a key component of the educational environment. While this can refer to the use of computers in a classroom, the term more broadly refers to a structured environment in which computers are used for teaching purposes. The concept is generally seen as being distinct from the use of computers in ways where learning is at least a peripheral element of the experience (e.g. computer games and web browsing).

Computer-based Training

Please help improve this article by adding reliable references. Unsourced material may be challenged and removed. (September 2007)

Computer-based training (CBT) services are where a student learns by executing special training programmes on a computer relating to their occupation. CBT is especially effective for training people to use computer applications because the CBT programme can be integrated with the applications so that students can practice using the application as they learn. Historically, CBTs growth has been hampered by the enormous resources required: human resources to create a CBT programme, and hardware resources needed to run it. However, the increase in PC computing power, and especially the growing prevalence of computers equipped with CD-ROMs, is making CBT a more viable option for corporations and individuals alike. Many PC applications now come with some modest form of CBT, often called a tutorial. Web-based training (WBT) is a type of training that is similar to CBT; however, it is delivered over the Internet using a web browser. Web-based training frequently includes interactive methods, such as bulletin boards, chat rooms, instant messaging, videoconferencing, and discussion threads. Web based training is usually a self-paced learning medium though some systems allow for online testing and evaluation at specific times. Recent years have seen an explosion in online training for educators by content providers such as Knowledge Delivery Systems, Atomic Learning, PBS Teacherline, and more.

Computer Supported Collaborative Learning (CSCL)

"Computer-supported collaborative learning (CSCL) is one of the most promising innovations to improve teaching and learning with the help of modern information and communication technology. Collaborative or group learning refers to instructional methods whereby students are encouraged or required to work together on learning tasks. It is widely agreed to distinguish collaborative learning from the traditional 'direct transfer' model in which the instructor is assumed to be the distributor of knowledge and skills." Lehtinen et al.

Pedagogical Elements

Pedagogical elements are an attempt to define structures or units of educational material. For example, this could be a lesson, an assignment, a multiple choice question, a quiz, a discussion group or a case study. These units should be format independent, so although it may be implemented in any of the following methods, pedagogical structures would not include a textbook, a web page, a video conference or Podcast.

When beginning to create e-Learning content, the pedagogical approaches need to be evaluated. Simple pedagogical approaches make it easy to create content, but lack flexibility, richness and downstream functionality. On the other hand, complex pedagogical approaches can be difficult to set up and slow to develop, though they have the potential to provide more engaging learning experiences for students. Somewhere between these extremes is an ideal pedagogy that allows a particular educator to effectively create educational materials while simultaneously providing the most engaging educational experiences for students.

Web Learning Sources

What is the Internet?

The Internet is an international computer network made up of smaller networks. Originally designed as a way for government and academic researchers to share information, the net now connects universities, schools, corporations, non-profit organizations, and individuals. Unlike most networks, the Internet remains usable even if one or more of its network connections should fail. Therefore the Internet is a very robust tool both for sharing information and, more recently, for conducting electronic commerce.

What is the World Wide Web?

The term "World Wide Web" refers to the Internet's ability to display and link files containing text, images, and a variety of other information. For example, a person creates a web site containing a series of pages that describes a science project. These files can also contain links to other files located anywhere in the world. The links are typically based on content related to the page containing the reference. The result is an ability to continually branch from a single starting point to any number of pages of related content located at sites all over the world.

What is the Difference between a Web Site and a Web Page?

A web site is made up of a web page(s).

A web site is similar to a file folder. A folder contains and organizes information and documents. These documents are similar to web pages.

For example-www.teachersfirst.com is the main page of the TeachersFirst web site. The links from this page are separate web pages. All of these pages together make up the web site.

Many personal web sites consist of a single page. On the other hand, the site created by IBM for the 1998 Winter Olympics contained over 30,000 pages.

For consistency, we will refer to information placed on the Web as web sites since these encompass web pages as well.

What can I Find on the Web?

Content on the Web is as diverse as the people and cultures of the world. Web content covers an array of subjects that makes it more extensive than even the largest bookstore. The originality of the Web has no comparison and thousands of new web sites and information is added to the Internet every day.

Web sites are created by individuals and companies and contain the variety of information one would expect from such organizations. While the Web was originally conceived as a way to share academic information, today it contains far more. There remains a wealth of academic content for all levels, as well as a huge amount of corporate information that range from sites seeking to sell or advertise everything from computers to real estate. There are also promotional and informational sites operated by non-profit, political, and a variety of other organizations. In many respects, the Web is an international library, almanac, yellow pages, and flea market all rolled into one. Unfortunately, the Web contains a fair amount of material which is unsuitable for children and young adults. So while it is a powerful teaching tool, it is a tool which should be used with deliberate caution.

An important thing to remember is that the Internet is huge; it is unstructured, and it is growing rapidly. Therefore, if you can not find the information you want today, it may be available next week. Keep looking!

Why Use the Web?

The World Wide Web is an invaluable tool in today's teaching environment. You can find a seemingly endless amount of information on the Web: teaching materials, pictures, videos, sound clips, exercises, games and so much more to enhance your instructional materials. Keeping students motivated and interested in learning is the goal of all teachers. TeachersFirst links can help you do that.

What is Wrong with All Caps?

You should not use ALL CAPS when using Internet applications. This is important! If you use all caps you are

YELLING at someone, not emphasizing a point. Unless you really are upset and wish to yell at someone, use normal sentence case. Internet users can be very touchy about this. They will know you are a newbie and if they are in a bad mood they may send you a nasty reply (flame) or get others to spam you.

What is a Browser?

A browser is a software programme/application which allows users to view and navigate the content of the World Wide Web. The two most popular browser programmes are Netscape's Navigator and Communicator, and Microsoft's Internet Explorer. Basic versions of these programmes can be downloaded free from their publishers web site, or you can click on the icons in the TeachersFirst Toolbox to download either programme. TeachersFirst has a complete browser tutorial, but the following paragraphs should give enough information to get you started.

Browsers do not have precisely the same features, but their basic capabilities are very similar. If you are a typical user, you'll probably find that 80% of your time on the Web is spent using 20% of your browser's capabilities. These capabilities are:

1. *Viewing and Navigating the Web*: A browser displays web sites. As you move from one site to another you have the option to go back to the previous page as well as going forward to a page you just viewed if you have used the back key. These keys are very useful when viewing a web site that has not placed links to different pages on their site.
2. *Marking Favorite Pages:* Browsers can store a list of sites to which you want to return. Netscape calls these "bookmarks," and Explorer calls them "favorite places." Remember that these are links to web sites and are not stored copies of the files themselves. This means that when you click on a bookmark/favorite place, your browser will load the most recent version of that website.
3. *Saving Pages:* Your browser has the ability to save the contents of a page to your computer. It is important to

remember that a single web page may contain numerous pictures and graphic files. Each of these files must be saved separately. You must also have software applications that are capable of viewing those images or you are saving them for nothing.

What is a URL?

The acronym URL stands for "uniform resource locator," a fancy term for the unique location of a particular web file on the Internet. A typical URL looks like this:

http: / / www.TeachersFirst.com / history / ushistory.htm

Why is this important? If you know what a URL means, you can tell a lot about the source of the pages you are viewing. THIS IS IMPORTANT. Let's begin by breaking the URL into its component parts.

http:// is the protocol (a set of operating rules) by which computers on the Internet send files back and forth. The protocol for the Web "http" is called " hypertext transfer protocol."

www.TeachersFirst.com is the domain name. The domain name is the unique name for the network which contains the web site you are viewing.

/history/ is the pathname. A pathname is the location within the web site where a specific web page is located. This is similar to a subfolder or a folder within a folder. Also, this is not always part of a URL. Pathnames can be called anything that the web sites creator came up with. In most cases, the use of a tilde "~" in a pathname indicates a web site reserved for a given individual's personal use.

Ushistory.htm is the file name. It is the name of a single hypertext file, web page, located on the Internet.

All Internet addresses contain these components in varying combinations.

Go to URL Anatomy Tutorial

What is html?

HTML stands for Hyptertext Markup Language. This is the code that creates the page format (layout, font, size, colour, pictures, etc.) of a web page. HTML was developed in order to have a standard to ease communication across the Internet. Since all browser applications read HTML, it eliminates the necessity to convert files or data so that all users can read them. The HTML standard is responsible for the ease in access and ultimately, the growth of the Internet.

How do I begin?

There are only three requirements to begin using the World Wide Web.

1. a computer
2. Internet access
3. browser software

Since you are viewing this page you have these items or are borrowing them from someone.

The World Wide Web's greatest frustration is locating the information you need. That's why we created TeachersFirst – to provide content which concentrates entirely on the needs of K-12 teachers. This site is designed to save you time and facilitate finding useful information for your teaching and your students.

If this is your first experience with the World Wide Web, we suggest the following:

1. Work through the browser tutorial to learn how to use your browser software. Navigating the Web is a lot easier once you master a few simple commands and how to use them.
2. Take a look at the "URL Anatomy" tutorial. It will help you understand those long web addresses to which we constantly refer.
3. Browse through the TeachersFirst contents, especially the "Classroom Materials" section.

E-book

An e-book (short for electronic book, also written eBook or ebook) is an e-text that forms the digital media equivalent of a conventional printed book, often protected with a digital rights management system. E-books are usually read on personal computers or smart phones, or on dedicated hardware devices known as e-book readers or e-book devices. Many mobile phones can also be used to read e-books.

History

Early e-books were generally written for specialty areas and a limited audience, meant to be read only by small and devoted interest groups. The scope of the subject matter of these e-books included technical manuals for hardware, manufacturing techniques, and other subjects.

Numerous e-book formats emerged and proliferated, some supported by major software companies such as Adobe's PDF format, and others supported by independent and open-source programmers. Multiple readers naturally followed multiple formats, most of them specializing in only one format, and thereby fragmenting the e-book market even more. Due to exclusiveness and limited readerships of e-books, the fractured market of independents and specialty authors lacked consensus regarding a standard for packaging and selling e-books.

E-books continued to gain in their own underground markets. Many e-book publishers began distributing books that were in the public domain. At the same time, authors with books that were not accepted by publishers offered their works online so they could be seen by others. Unofficial (and occasionally unauthorized) catalogs of books became available over the web, and sites devoted to e-books began disseminating information about e-books to the public.

As of 2008, new marketing models for e-books were being developed and dedicated reading hardware was produced. E-books (as opposed to ebook readers) have yet to achieve global distribution. Only two e-book readers dominate the market, Amazon's Kindle model or Sony's PRS-500. However, not all authors have endorsed the concept of electronic publishing. J.K Rowling, author of the Harry Potter series, has stated that there will be no e-versions of the books.

- 1971: Michael S. Hart launch the *Gutenberg Project*.

- 1993: Zahur develops the first software to read digital books. Digital Book v.1 and the first ebook is published *On Murder Considered as one of the Fine Arts* (Thomas de Quincey).
- 1993: Digital Book offers the first 50 ebooks in Floppy disk with Digital Book Format (DBF).
- 1993: Hugo Award for Best Novel nominee texts published on CD-ROM by Brad Templeton.
- 1993: Bibliobytes, a project of free digital books online in Internet.
- 1995: Amazon starts to sell physical books in Internet.
- 1996: The Project Gutemberg reachs the 1.000 titles. The target is 1.000.000
- 1998: Launched the first ebook Readers: Rocket ebook and Softbook.
- 1998-1999: Websites selling ebooks in English, like *eReader.com* and *eReads.com*.
- 2000: Stephen King offers his book "Riding Bullet" in digital file, it only can be read in computer.
- 2001: Open 'Todoebook.com' the first website selling ebooks in Spanish.
- 2002: Random House and HarperCollins start to sell digital versions of their titles in English.
- 2005: Amazon bought Mobipocket like a strategic positioning.
- 2006: Sony presents the *Sony Reader* with e-ink.
- 2006: LibreDigital Launched BookBrowse as an online reader for publisher content.
- 2007: Amazon launched Kindle in US.
- 2008: Adobe and Sony agreeded to share their technologies (Reader and DRM).
- 2008: Sony sells the *PRS-505* in UK and France
- 2008: Amazon launched Kindle2 in US.

Formats

Comparison of e-books with printed books:

Advantages

- Text can be searched automatically and cross-referenced using hyperlinks.
- A single e-book reader containing several books is easier to carry around (less weight and volume) than the same books (or sometimes even a single book) in printed form. Even hundreds or thousands of books may be stored on the same device. Using removable media even more can be carried around easily.
- Also at a fixed place such as at home it can be an advantage that an e-book collection requires very little space.
- Mobile availability of e-books may be provided for users with a mobile data connection, so that these e-books need not be carried around.
- E-books can allow non-permanent highlighting and annotation.
- Font size and font face can be adjusted.
- E-books may allow animated images or multimedia clips to be embedded.
- E-books allow for greater fidelity in colour reproduction compared to CMYK colour printing (although some e-book readers have only monochrome displays).
- Depending on the device an e-book may be readable in low light or even total darkness.
- An e-book can automatically open at the last read page.
- While an e-book reader costs much more than one book, the electronic texts are generally cheaper. Moreover, a great share of books are available for free, without any charge at all. For example, all fiction from before the year 1900 is in the public domain.
- Text-to-speech software can be used to convert e-books to audio books automatically.
- An e-book can be offered indefinitely, without ever going "out of print".

- Depending on possible digital rights management, it may be easy and cheap to produce a back-up for the case that the e-book is lost or damaged, and/or it may be possible to get a free new copy if that happens.
- It is easier for authors to self-publish e-books.
- A free e-book can stimulate the sales of the printed version.
- The production of e-books does not consume paper, ink, etc.

Disadvantages

- Reading e-books requires an electronic device and software. Even in the case of reading it on a personal computer one already has, it may require additional software.
- A small book is easier to carry around than a typical e-book reader.
- E-book readers require electrical power; in the case of mobile use, the battery can get exhausted.
- E-book readers are more fragile than paper books and more susceptible to physical damage.
- E-book readers can malfunction and e-books can be damaged due to faults in hardware or software.
- E-book readers are more likely to be stolen than paper books.
- Depending on the device an e-book may be difficult to read in bright sunlight.
- Most publishers don't produce the e-book equivalent of their printed books. In other cases the product quality is lower or it is released later.
- E-books can be easily hacked through the use of hardware or software modifications and widely disseminated on the Internet and/or other e-book readers, without approval from the author or publisher (piracy). This is a disadvantage for publishers, but at the same time an advantage for readers, since they don't have to pay for reading a book.

- If an e-book device is stolen, lost, or broken beyond repair, all e-books stored on the device may be lost. This can be avoided by backup either on another device or by the e-book provider.
- There is a loss of tactility and aesthetics of book-bindings. Also lost is the ability to very quickly riffle through the pages to search for a particular section or to get a sense of the book merely by sight.
- Screen resolution of reading devices may be lower than actual paper.
- Due to the digital rights management reselling or lending out an e-book may have complications.
- Some books available as e-book cannot be read on some e-book readers because they are not supplied in a format those readers allow.
- While printed books remain readable for ages, changing technologies and less durable electronic storage media require e-books to be copied to a new carrier after some years.
- E-book readers require various substances to produce, and are an environmental hazard as they're non-biodegradable.
- Piracy is also a serious issue. It's difficult to make an illegal copy of a printed book where as e-books can easily be copied. Most proprietary software come with anti-piracy codes etc... but soon pirated copies were widely available. The same could be said of the e-book as well.

Digital Rights Management

Anti-circumvention techniques may be used to restrict what the user may do with an e-book. For instance, it may not be possible to transfer ownership of an e-book to another person, though such a transaction is common with physical books. Some devices can phone home to track readers and reading habits, restrict printing, or arbitrarily modify reading material. This includes restricting the copying and distribution of works in the public domain through the use of "click-wrap" licensing, effectively limiting the rights of the public to distribute, sell or use texts in the public domain freely.

Most e-book publishers do not warn their customers about the possible implications of the digital rights management tied to their products. Generally they claim that digital rights management is meant to prevent copying of the e-book. However in many cases it is also possible that digital rights management will result in the complete denial of access by the purchaser to the e-book. With some formats of DRM, the e-book is tied to a specific computer or device. In these cases the DRM will usually let the purchaser move the book a limited number of times after which he cannot use it on any additional devices. If the purchaser upgrades or replaces their devices eventually they may lose access to their purchase. Some forms of digital rights management depend on the existence of online services to authenticate the purchasers. When the company that provides the service goes out of business or decides to stop providing the service, the purchaser will no longer be able to access the e-book.

As with digital rights management in other media, e-books are more like rental or leasing than purchase. The restricted book comes with a number of restrictions, and eventually access to the purchase can be removed by a number of different parties involved. These include the publisher of the book, the provider of the DRM scheme, and the publisher of the reader software. These are all things that are significantly different from the realm of experiences anyone has had with a physical copy of the book.

E-Journal

This module is a powerful production publishing system. It allows you to create and control your own electronic (and possibly printed) journals in Drupal-you can set up as many journals as you want, add authors and editors. Module gives you issue management, basic user and access control, vocabularies and archives. This module was inspired by Open Journal System which is an open-source online submission and manuscript tracking system. The Drupal platform is more flexible though, it gives you many ways to extend your publishing system.

Currently, the module is made of the following packages (needless to say, you can combine them with other modules):

ejournal-the core functionality of an publications / issue management

ejournalaccess-for setting access to different group of users

ejournalauthors-use Drupal taxonomy as user profiles links

ejournalcitation-construct citation reference beneath published articles

ejournalshortly-for publication of short messages along side with the main content

E-learning

Electronic learning (or e-Learning or eLearning) is a type of Technology supported education/learning (TSL) where the medium of instruction is through computer technology, particularly involving digital technologies. E-learning has been defined as "pedagogy empowered by digital technology". In some instances, no face-to-face interaction takes place. E-learning is used interchangeably in a wide variety of contexts. In companies, it refers to the strategies that use the company network to deliver training courses to employees. In the United States, it is defined as a planned teaching/learning experience that uses a wide spectrum of technologies, mainly Internet or computer-based, to reach learners. Lately in most Universities, e-learning is used to define a specific mode to attend a course or programmes of study where the students rarely, if ever, attend face-to-face for on-campus access to educational facilities, because they study online.

Market

The worldwide e-learning industry is estimated to be worth over thirty-eight (38) billion euros according to conservative estimates, although in the European Union only about 20% of e-learning products are produced within the common market.

Developments in internet and multimedia technologies are the basic enabler of e-learning, with content, technologies and services being identified as the three key sectors of the e-learning industry. eLearning is a catch-all term that covers a wide range of instructional material that can be delivered on a CD-ROM or DVD, over a local area network (LAN), or on the Internet.

Growth of E-learning

By 2006, nearly 3.5 million students were participating in on-line learning at institutions of higher education in the United States. Many higher education, for-profit institutions, now offer on-line classes. By contrast, only about half of private, non-profit schools offer them. The Sloan report, based on a poll of academic leaders, says that students generally appear to be at least as satisfied with their on-line classes as they are with traditional ones. Private institutions may become more involved with on-line presentations as the cost of instituting such a system decreases. Properly trained staff must also be hired to work with students on-line. These staff members need to understand the content area, and also be highly trained in the use of the computer and Internet. Online education is rapidly increasing, and online doctoral programmes have even developed at leading research universities..

Technology

As early as 1993, Graziadei, W. D. described an online computer-delivered lecture, tutorial and assessment project using electronic Mail, two VAX Notes conferences and Gopher/Lynx together with several software programmes that allowed students and instructor to create a Virtual Instructional Classroom Environment in Science (VICES) in Research, Education, Service & Teaching (REST). In 1997 Graziadei, W.D., et al., published an article entitled "Building Asynchronous and Synchronous Teaching-Learning Environments: Exploring a Course/Classroom Management System Solution". They described a process at the State University of New York (SUNY) of evaluating products and developing an overall strategy for technology-based course development and management in teaching-learning. The product(s) had to be easy to use and maintain, portable, replicable, scalable, and immediately affordable, and they had to have a high probability of success with long-term cost-effectiveness. Today many technologies can be, and are, used in e-Learning, from blogs to collaborative software, ePortfolios, and virtual classrooms. Most eLearning situations use combinations of these techniques.

Along with the terms *learning technology*, *instructional technology*, and Educational Technology, the term is generally used to refer to the use of technology in learning in a much broader sense than the computer-based training or *Computer Aided Instruction* of the 1980s. It is also broader than the terms *Online Learning* or *Online Education* which generally refer to purely web-based learning. In cases where mobile technologies are used, the term M-learning has become more common. E-learning, however, also has implications beyond just the technology and refers to the actual learning that takes place using these systems.

E-learning is naturally suited to distance learning and flexible learning, but can also be used in conjunction with face-to-face teaching, in which case the term Blended learning is commonly used. E-Learning pioneer Bernard Luskin argues that the "E" must be understood to have broad meaning if e-Learning is to be effective. Luskin says that the "e" should be interpreted to mean exciting, energetic, enthusiastic, emotional, extended, excellent, and educational in addition to "electronic" that is a traditional national interpretation. This broader interpretation allows for 21st century applications and brings learning and media psychology into the equation.

In higher education especially, the increasing tendency is to create a Virtual Learning Environment (VLE) (which is sometimes combined with a Management Information System (MIS) to create a Managed Learning Environment) in which all aspects of a course are handled through a consistent user interface standard throughout the institution. A growing number of physical universities, as well as newer online-only colleges, have begun to offer a select set of academic degree and certificate programmes via the Internet at a wide range of levels and in a wide range of disciplines. While some programmes require students to attend some campus classes or orientations, many are delivered completely online. In addition, several universities offer online student support services, such as online advising and registration, e-counseling, online textbook purchase, student governments and student newspapers.

E-Learning can also refer to educational web sites such as those offering learning scenarios, worksheets and interactive exercises for children. The term is also used extensively in the business sector where it generally refers to cost-effective online training.

The recent trend in the e-Learning sector is screencasting. There are many screencasting tools available but the latest buzz is all about the web based screencasting tools which allow the users to create screencasts directly from their browser and make the video available online so that the viewers can stream the video directly. The advantage of such tools is that it gives the presenter the ability to show his ideas and flow of thoughts rather than simply explain them, which may be more confusing when delivered via simple text instructions. With the combination of video and audio, the expert can mimic the one on one experience of the classroom and deliver clear, complete instructions. From the learners point of view this provides the ability to pause and rewind and gives the learner the advantage to move at their own pace, something a classroom cannot always offer. One such example of e-Learning platform based on screencasts is YoHelpOnline.

Services

E-learning services have evolved since computers were first used in education. There is a trend to move toward blended learning services, where computer-based activities are integrated with practical or classroom-based situations.

Goals of E-learning

E-Learning lessons are generally designed to guide students through information or to help students perform in specific tasks. Information based e-Learning content communicates information to the student. Examples include content that distributes the history or facts related to a service, company, or product. In information-based content, there is no specific skill to be learned. In performance-based content, the lessons build off of a procedural skill in which the student is expected to increase proficiency.

Computer-based Learning

Computer Based Learning, sometimes abbreviated to CBL, refers to the use of computers as a key component of the educational environment. While this can refer to the use of computers in a classroom, the term more broadly refers to a structured environment in which computers are used for teaching purposes. The concept is generally seen as being distinct from the use of computers in ways where learning is at least a peripheral element of the experience (e.g. computer games and web browsing).

Computer-based Training

Computer-based training (CBT) services are where a student learns by executing special training programmes on a computer relating to their occupation. CBT is especially effective for training people to use computer applications because the CBT programme can be integrated with the applications so that students can practice using the application as they learn. Historically, CBTs growth has been hampered by the enormous resources required: human resources to create a CBT programme, and hardware resources needed to run it.

However, the increase in PC computing power, and especially the growing prevalence of computers equipped with CD-ROMs, is making CBT a more viable option for corporations and individuals alike. Many PC applications now come with some modest form of CBT, often called **a tutorial. Web**-based training (WBT) is a type of training that is similar to CBT; however, it is delivered over the Internet using a web browser.

Web-based training frequently includes interactive methods, such as bulletin boards, chat rooms, instant messaging, videoconferencing, and discussion threads. Web based training is usually a self-paced learning medium though some systems allow for online testing and evaluation at specific times. Recent years have seen an explosion in online training for educators by content providers such as Knowledge Delivery Systems, Atomic Learning, PBS Teacherline, and more.

Computer-Supported Collaborative Learning (CSCL)

"Computer-supported collaborative learning (CSCL) is one of the most promising innovations to improve teaching and learning with the help of modern information and communication technology.

Collaborative or group learning refers to instructional methods whereby students are encouraged or required to work together on learning tasks. It is widely agreed to distinguish collaborative learning from the traditional 'direct transfer' model in which the instructor is assumed to be the distributor of knowledge and skills. " Lehtinen et al.

Pedagogical Elements

Pedagogical elements are an attempt to define structures or units of educational material. For example, this could be a lesson, an assignment, a multiple choice question, a quiz, a discussion group or a case study. These units should be format independent, so although it may be implemented in any of the following methods, pedagogical structures would not include a textbook, a web page, a video conference or Podcast.

When beginning to create e-Learning content, the pedagogical approaches need to be evaluated. Simple pedagogical approaches make it easy to create content, but lack flexibility, richness and downstream functionality.

On the other hand, complex pedagogical approaches can be difficult to set up and slow to develop, though they have the potential to provide more engaging learning experiences for students. Somewhere between these extremes is an ideal pedagogy that allows a particular educator to effectively create educational materials while simultaneously providing the most engaging educational experiences for students.

Subject Gateways

What is a Subject Gateway?

"Subject gateways are online services and sites that provide searchable and browseable catalogues of Internet based resources. Subject gateways will typically focus on a related set of academic subject areas."

Many of the activities and research projects within DESIRE are focused on developing the ideas behind this definition of a subject gateway, as well as developing methodology and tools that provide the functionality needed for a subject gateway to function. DESIRE is also concerned with promoting the implementation of subject gateways.

Reference Services

Reference Desk

General reference services are provided from the Library's Reference Desks at the Murdoch, Rockingham and Peel campuses. The librarians can help you make effective use of the Library's resources by advising you on the use of the catalogue and website and suggesting appropriate databases for your subject area.

Ask a Librarian

Ask a Librarian is an email reference service provided for Murdoch University students and staff. Send us your question and we will respond by the next working day.

Online Librarian

Online Librarian lets you get answers to your basic reference questions in real-time using chat.

Specialised Reference Services

The subject and liaison librarians provide specialised reference services and research skills training programmes from their offices. They also provide a subject request service for eligible external students. Forms for this service are available online.

On-line searching of databases on behalf of clients is also available. Contact the relevant subject librarian for further information and costs.

Learning Resource Centre

Since 2004, with the help of Learning for Life (LFL), SIDH has been able to construct a new campus-our Learning Resource Center, or LRC, on two acres of land near the existing Bodhigram campus. It will house various short and long courses, workshops, and seminars on education for young children, adolescents, and adults – both from urban and rural areas. Our future plans include two year-long residential courses – a gap year college and a teacher's training course. Apart from the fees from these courses, we hope to generate further income for SIDH by hiring out the premises to NGOs, institutes, and individuals/research scholars. The LRC is being constructed in phases. The first phase was the construction of dormitories that have been utilized since June 2005. The second phase will be completion of the kitchen and administrative block. The third phase will be individual rooms and studio apartments for resource persons (if we succeed in generating the required funds).

Dormitories in six different clusters, in a modular manner, have been constructed to ensure privacy and enable more than one group to stay at the same time. At present 44 people can stay very comfortably but with extra beds, this number can be increased to accommodate 88 people. A complex with staff quarters, kitchen and dining area is nearing completion. The entire complex with above facilities will cost nearly 85 lakhs out of which nearly 62 lakhs have been provided by Vitol Corporation through our partner – Learning for Life (LFL). The balance amount has come from donations raised by SIDH over the years from individual well-wishers and miscellaneous internal earnings. We intend to construct 6 individual rooms with toilets and bath for resource persons and 6 studio apartments for long-term stay of scholars and researchers. We will also have to construct two more lecture halls, equip the building with proper furniture and fixtures, and install a solar water heating system for the entire campus.

UNIT-III

Organization of Information

Collection Development Policy of Information Resources for Teacher Education Institution Libraries

In her recently published book, *Fundamentals of Collection Development and Management*, Peggy Johnson provided a definition of a 'collection development policy' that would probably be broadly acceptable to most in the library and information profession:

> *A formal written statement of the principles guiding a library's selection of books and other materials, including the criteria used in selection, de-selection, and acceptance of gifts. It may also address intellectual freedom, future goals, and special areas of attention (2004: 311).*

But if there are few who would be unwilling to accept this definition, there would probably also be few who were excited by it or felt that it related to a particularly dynamic branch of information provision. Collection development policies have been with us for a long time: Johnson (2004: 73) herself suggests that they were becoming prominent in United States libraries by the 1950s and 1960s. While their 'golden age' was probably later than this, at least in Australia where they attracted most attention in the late 1980s and early 1990s, there can be no doubt that in the early years of the twenty-first century they are not a burning issue.

One possible reason for this may suggest itself from looking at the wording of Johnson's definition. It will be noticed that it mentions 'books' but does not explicitly mention digital materials. This is not of course because Johnson is unaware of such material: she in fact devotes a section of her book to a discussion of what might appear in a policy document devoted to 'e-resources' (2004: 80, 83). There has been considerable discussion in the literature of what should appear in collection development policies devoted to digital resources, and of whether it is more appropriate to have a separate policy for such resources or a policy document that combines consideration of both print and digital resources.

The website *Electronic Collections Development* (2002) provides numerous examples of collection development policies largely or entirely devoted to digital resources. Notwithstanding this, however, Peter Clayton and Gary Gorman were able to observe in a book published as recently as 2001 that 'Most existing collection development policies are strong on their approach to traditional print materials but weak on electronic materials-if, indeed, they are covered at all'.

If this is true, and collection development policies are closely linked to print materials in the minds of librarians, it is hardly surprising that collection development policies are not a major focus of attention in the library and information profession at the beginning of the twenty-first century. For many professionals and paraprofessionals today, in particular those working in major academic and research libraries, it is digital resources that are of primary importance, and it is digital resources that their clients seem most to want and need.

These digital resources may come in many different forms, including computer-mediated materials like CD-ROMs brought into the library and owned by it, and others not owned by the library but accessed remotely when needed from terminals either within the library or linked to the library from the homes and offices of the library's clients. Familiar examples include websites on the World Wide Web and digital versions of serials. Increasingly there are available digital counterparts of all the familiar kinds of print and audiovisual materials-some straightforward machine-readable counterparts of items that may have been created decades or centuries before the advent of computerisation, and others digital editions of such materials which exploit the possibilities of hypertext-as well as items which exist only in digital form and indeed would be inconceivable employing technology such as print.

Libraries today often see themselves as 'hybrid' institutions, making available both print and digital resources, and many observers see this as a transitional stage on the way to the digital library, defined by Oppenheim and Smithson as 'an information service in which all the information resources are available in computer-processable form, and the functions of acquisition, storage, preservation, retrieval, access and display are carried out through the use of digital technologies' (1999: 97). A visit to a large university library today is not likely to convince anyone that this prediction is fanciful: typically the bays of print materials are areas of largely undisturbed tranquillity, while crowds, queues, and frantic keyboard activity identify where the computer terminals linked to electronic resources are to be found.

Even in this environment there may be few ready to commit themselves in print to the view that written collection development policies are 'Wasted words' (Snow 1996), or willing to join Hazen in stating that:

> *Collection development policies as traditionally conceived are static, reactive, and of little practical utility. They have outlived their purpose (1995: 29).*

The recent collection management texts of Evans and Zarnosky (2000), Clayton and Gorman (2001), and Johnson (2004) all devote considerable space to such policy documents. But clearly many practitioners have 'voted with their feet' (or at least the allocation of their time). Despite exceptions such as the State Library of New South Wales, which published on the internet the first part of a new two-part collection development policy, completed in 2002, part two of which is yet to appear (State Library of New South Wales 2004), creating new collection development policies, or revising those now several years old, is not a major activity in the profession now focusing ever more intently on digital resources.

Of course, the reason for this neglect of such policies among practitioners is not merely that they are associated with print materials and other resources that the library purchases in a tangible form for in-house processing and eventual location on its shelves. It is not merely that they have come to seem old-fashioned. The very concept of collecting has been called into question as a primary activity of libraries. When increasingly the resources that the library makes available are ones which are not physically collected and brought within its walls but to which it provides access if and when they are needed, it would hardly be surprising if some came to regard a document that seeks to guide its collecting activities as of diminishing relevance.

Furthermore, now that it is an easy task to explore online the records of the holdings of almost all major libraries and many lesser ones in the developed world, the question might arise as to whether the traditional role of collection development policies in communicating to interested parties the collecting strengths and collecting intentions of libraries is as important as it was when discovering 'who held what' meant consulting cumbersome print or microform catalogues, or even long journeys by land, sea, and air.

Collecting in a Digital Environment

The idea that in a digital environment libraries no longer collect does not really stand up to closer scrutiny, however. They may increasingly not collect physical objects that can be admired in serried rows on the shelves, and they may only to a limited extent collect files that occupy server storage in computers under the direct control of the library. But they do assemble virtual collections of materials to which they have access.

However strong a library's commitment to relying on digital resources accessed remotely when needed, it is most unlikely not to identify the resources that it considers to be of particular interest to its clients, and to conclude agreements with the vendors of these items to make them available. Often this will in fact be the only way to ensure prompt access to the resources in question: electronic publishers and vendors frequently insist on a contract or licence before making their products such as digital versions of scholarly journals available if and when needed. In some circumstances such 'anticipatory' arrangements may not be strictly necessary-access to an item on a fee per individual use may be possible. But such 'pay-as-you-go' access is likely to be clumsy to operate in a busy library and significantly less economic than prior purchase of access if the resource in question is one likely to be used frequently by library clients.

Though recent years have seen some resources, such as digital versions of newspapers, move from being available free of charge on the internet to being available only for a fee, it remains true that many useful resources (as well as immense dross) are available free of charge to the user on the internet. Few information professionals, however, would take the view that if they provide computer terminals and access to Google their duty to the clients of their library in respect to such material has been fully discharged. Most professionals see as part of the library's role the identification of what is worthwhile and of particular relevance to their clients amidst the bewildering overabundance of the anarchic internet, and the bringing of this material to the attention of clients by establishing links to it from the library's web pages or its OPAC.

What this means is that in a very real sense libraries continue to collect in a digital environment. They select from the universe of digital publications those that to some extent they bring under their control, by paying fees to ensure access to them or by establishing well-defined pathways to them. The control may be more intangible and impermanent than that which exists over printed items sitting on the library shelves; it may even vanish overnight when a subscription is not renewed or an internet site disappears. The content of the collection may be more fluid than it ever was in any print collection subject to the ravages of theft and physical deterioration. But the fact of collecting seems beyond dispute.

Traditional Collection Development Policy Functions in a New Context

If collecting occurs there is a need for management of the process. In any organisation accountable for the funding it receives, collecting obviously needs to be systematic. Decisions need to be made as to what should be collected to serve the purposes for which the library exists within the limitations set by the funding available to it. For digital resources, as for traditional print ones, the available funding will provide access to only a fraction of what has been 'published' (and probably of what clients would like to have available to them), so there need to be principles to guide the act of selection in individual cases, with a view to ensuring that funds are optimally spent to serve the needs of the clientele. More is involved than just payments to publishers and vendors: the library needs to ensure that the time of its staff is used wisely, rather than on mater ial not likely to be of value to the users of the library. Consideration also needs to be given to the fact that what finds its way into the digital collection does not necessarily have a justification for remaining there indefinitely: the digital library may not have to worry about its shelves being cluttered by material that is outmoded, no longer relevant, dirty, or torn, but it does need to concern itself about paying for access to what is no longer of value, and about the cluttering of catalogues and web pages with links that lead to outmoded material if indeed they lead anywhere at all.

The collection development policy for digital resources is an essential planning device in a way broadly similar to the policy for print resources. It should also fulfil a broadly similar communication function for, unlike a good collection development policy, digital access to the catalogues of a library indicates the individual items it holds or makes available, not the principles and policies which inform the work of those building and maintaining its collection. As in the case of print resources a collection development policy can provide some protection for library staff in the legitimate performance of their selection duties by laying down the principles governing selection that have the sanction of the library's parent body. This protection is at least as important in a digital environment as in a print one, since, for example, potentially offensive sites displayed by clients of the library on the screens of its computer terminals in public areas are more likely to cause outrage than material less obtrusively retained with the covers of a printed volume.

New and Enhanced Functions

Such considerations suggest that a collection development policy for digital resources is as important as one for print resources. The reality, however, is that the policy is more important in the case of digital resources than it ever was in the case of print.

Partly this is because of the nature of digital resources. In the 'pre-digital' era libraries did acquire materials such as audio disks and microforms that required equipment to access the data they contained, and there was of course the 'time bomb' of the slow physical deterioration of most twentieth century paper-based materials. But most collections were predominantly print and most libraries most of the time were able to operate without giving much consideration to these problems. In general, materials once acquired and placed on the shelves, could be expected to be readily available several decades later. Digital materials, in contrast to paper-based ones, require computer hardware and if they are to be used, the library must ensure that the appropriate kinds of hardware and software are available in sufficient quantities. In the case of material not owned but accessed remotely the problem may usually be minor, as vendors will normally ensure their material operates on standard software; but digital resources that the library purchases outright and maintains on its own electronic systems pose a potentially far greater problem. Finding that changes in information technology, including rapid obsolescence may make it difficult or impossible to access a resource created several years earlier is quite a common experience. This means that the selection decision becomes more complicated, because it involves what are in effect new and possibly unpredictable factors to be considered. In the words of Ellis Weinberger, 'The institution will need to determine the possibility and cost of preserving the object before obtaining it' (2000: 68). Collection development policies must include consideration of both the equipment to use and the preservation implications of the digital materials to which they refer.

The complexities of collecting digital resources also stem partly from the ways in which such resources are made available to libraries. Publishers of digital materials, a cynic might say, have avoided many of the mistakes made by print publishers, who allowed a situation to develop in which libraries purchasing examples of their products were free to make them available to whomsoever they choose, including casual visitors to the library and even individuals in other libraries who sought access to the items through an interlibrary loan service. In the case of digital resources publishers' interests are typically protected by licensing conditions that they impose, or attempt to impose, on libraries seeking to purchase access to their products.

The library may find itself confronted with extremely restrictive conditions attempting to govern to whom and under what conditions it may make the digital resource in question available, and further, imposing on it legal liability for any breaches of these conditions by people who access the resource through the library. Consideration of licensing conditions needs to form part of the selection or acquisition procedures for digital resources. Negotiation may well be necessary, for in extreme cases the licensing conditions proposed, if taken literally, would make library use of the resources impossible. The library may have its own conditions which it wishes to insist on writing into the licence agreement, such as a requirement that digital resources provide a satisfactory level of use statistics (Johnson 2004: 83). The services of legal advisers may even be needed. A digital resources collection development policy should probably not be a detailed negotiator's manual, but if it is to be an effective planning device it will need to outline the procedures to be followed in dealing with the complexities of licensing.

In many cases the library will not be acting alone. Some digital resources are very expensive, and libraries band together in purchasing consortia to obtain access to them. Such consortia inevitably restrict to some extent the library's collecting autonomy, and modern collection development policies need to make provision for the possibility of the library's entering into consortia agreements that convey both advantages and obligations on it. It is not merely in relation to other members of a consortium that a library may find its autonomy somewhat circumscribed in a digital environment. In concerning itself with digital resources the library is entering territory to which the parent organisation's computer centre might lay claim, since the centre might well argue that matters relating to computer hardware, computer software, and even data files are its area of expertise. The matter may be dealt with, if not always resolved, by amalgamating the library and the computer centre, but whether or not this happens, an important role of the collection development policy may be staking out the claim of the library to be the collecting agency for files collected for their information content rather than as tools required in the conduct of the organisation's operations.

A different kind of demarcation is involved when, as is usually still the case, the library actively collects print materials despite its emphasis on digital resources. When does the library purchase only the digital version, when only the print version, and when both? Increasingly academic and research libraries appear to be resolving this issue by declaring that digital versions are preferred, and print versions will be acquired only when digital ones are not available. But this may not always be a desirable option, particularly for public libraries, and a collection development policy may need to address the issue. (This, of course, is an important argument for not having completely separate print and digital policy documents: if a library does collect in both formats, efficient use of its budget requires the coordination of development of the two.)

The hybrid or the digital library does need a collection development policy, and it needs a policy prepared with as much care and consultation as was devoted to the creation of print policies when creating them was a 'fashionable' library activity. In fact, the further the library ventures into the rich variety and complexity of different kinds of digital resources, with the challenges of licensing and consortia negotiations, the greater the need for a collection development policy is likely to be. Clearly too, the rapid and constant transformation of the world of digital resources and information technology make revision of the policy at regular and reasonably frequent intervals more important than the often-neglected revision of the print policy ever was. The content of the policy will indeed need to be somewhat different from that of policies of earlier decades to take account of new problems and new complexities such as those outlined above.

There may even be a case for abandoning the word 'collection' as being too redolent of a bygone age when libraries boasted of the number of volumes that sat ready for use on their shelves. But arguably the case for retaining it and emphasising that today collecting activity includes acquiring access to resources in digital format, is even stronger, since it is essential to keep in mind that even in an entirely digital environment, libraries are still in a vital sense collecting institutions.

Library Collection Development Policy

Purpose of Policy Statement: This collection development policy for the Brooks Library is intended for the use and guidance of librarians and faculty responsible for the building of collections that strongly support the learning and instructional needs and programmes of Central Washington University. The collections also seek to support the general cultural and intellectual formation of students and the work of staff engaged in university business. A library collection should have both the resource depth and breadth to serve institutional goals and objectives for learning, teaching, and other mission activities. Funding, staffing, and services to support materials acquisition, processing, and maintenance must be provided in suitable and adequate measure.

In order to meet the immediate needs and future goals of the university, the acquisition and maintenance of library resources and materials require constant attention. These activities are guided by a policy that sets priorities and distributes decision-making among the Collection Management Librarian, Library Liaisons, and Library Representatives. The policy also stands as a means of communicating the library's collection policy to the university community and other users. The Collection Development Policy of Brooks Library outlines the broad perimeters of collection development activities within the library. It is accompanied by the document titled "Collection

Development Procedures and Information For Department Representatives and Library Liaisons" and the Materials Withdrawal Guidelines to provide a complete account of collection management efforts related to the Circulating, Reference and Serials Collections. Government Documents and Special Collections have individual policies not contained in this document.

Brooks Library Mission Statement: According to the Brooks Library Mission, the library "provide[s] resources and services to stimulate intellectual curiosity and to facilitate learning and research within the academic community." To that end, this policy will clearly define the types of resources collected. It considers the presence of electronic formats, university centers, and the cooperative efforts of the Orbis-Cascade Alliance and their effects on materials acquisition.

The primary mission of the Brooks Library is to support the mission and goals of Central Washington University, particularly in its commitment to teaching as the means to facilitate learning. The library supports a relationship between teacher and student that makes both partners in learning, scholarship, research, creative expression, and the application of knowledge to solve human and societal problems.

The library presents information services and collections of materials that directly support quality education to students and foster the physical, intellectual, social, and ethical development of each student. Assistance in the preparation of students for meaningful and productive careers and the development of independent, life-long learning are central goals. Our information resources and services show students how to locate, use and evaluate information and help students become conscious of their role as members of a pluralistic society through emphasis on the collection and presentation of multicultural resources.

With firm commitment to responsibilities as a resource to the local community and region as well as the university community, the library shares its resources with other institutions and with the citizens of Washington.

A guiding vision of the Brooks Library is the development of a completely integrated information resources center in which all users will find the best available materials regardless of the format or media in which it occurs. The library must continue to act as a regional presence for preserving locally produced knowledge. The library is committed to providing access and delivery of services utilizing the best available technologies as well as anticipating changes within the information technology marketplace.

Collection Development Objectives:

- Advance the missions of the university and library through the implementation of relevant activities and programmes
- Build a collection that meets the instruction, research and information needs of students, faculty and the university community
- Coordinate collection development activities with Library Liaisons and Department Representatives, with special emphasis in promoting involvement of teaching faculty
- Recommend and implement collection development policy
- Modify collection development policy and programmes in response to changes in the curriculum
- Spend the materials budget allocation to achieve the greatest benefit possible
- Manage the collection so as to accommodate budget changes, space needs and new trends in curriculum and research
- Maintain the fiscal accounting and bibliographic systems used to administer collection development activities
- Conduct periodic evaluations of the various collections and correct deficiencies, including weeding the collection, purchasing materials to fill gaps, and replacing missing materials as needed
- Pursue cooperative and coordinated collection development with the Orbis-Cascade Alliance libraries

General Policies

Selection Priorities: Acquisitions are financed chiefly by appropriations from the university budget. Library funds from the university appropriation are allocated to academic departments and certain Library units for the purchase of materials.

Contingent on library funding, the following priorities shall be observed in the allocation of collection development funds for library materials and electronic resources:

- Support for student learning in, and faculty preparation for, existing prerequisites, major/minor courses, and graduate majors are given the highest level of priority
- Support for student learning in, and faculty preparation for, general education courses and electives.
- Support for non-curriculum related but mandated government programmes, such as maintaining our government document depository and regional public services of the documents library and cooperative library projects adopted by the Orbis-Cascade Alliance.
- Support for new majors and new graduate programmes consistent with clearly formulated and approved departmental, college, and university strategic plans, to the extent of the availability of additional funds provided for these new programmes by the state legislature and the university.
- Non-course related intellectual development of students and the general information needs of students, faculty, and other university personnel.
- Library materials and electronic resources for faculty research and development consistent with clearly formulated and approved departmental, college, and university strategic plans. These activities shall be supported by the library to the extent of the availability of funds provided for these programmes by the state legislature, the university, or from grant monies intended by granting agencies for the support of university infrastructure.

- Library materials and electronic resources for supporting the public services functions of Central Washington University in the local community and in Central Washington when funds are made available by the state and the university.

Resource Sharing

The Central Washington University interlibrary loan programme provides access to material from many other educational institutions in Washington, the Northwest states and throughout the nation. Access is also provided to our materials to other institutions of higher education for borrowing purposes. Some shared collection development activity has been coordinated through the Collection Development and Management Committee of the Orbis-Cascade Alliance.

Intellectual Freedom

The Brooks Library is committed to providing a balanced collection that represents a diversity of perspectives on issues and ideas. Material is primarily selected to meet the teaching, research, and service needs of the University community. The library adheres to the principles of intellectual freedom as outlined in the Library Bill of Rights of the American Library Association. Article 1 of the Library Bill of Rights states "Books and other library resources should be provided for the interest, information, and enlightenment of all people of the community the library serves." Materials should not be excluded because of the origin, background, or views of those contributing to their creation." Article 2 says "Libraries should provide materials and information presenting all points of view on current and historical issues. Materials should not be proscribed or removed because of partisan or doctrinal disapproval." Academic Freedom is also protected by the Central Washington University Faculty Code. Any individual or group questioning the appropriateness of material within the collection will be referred to the Library's Challenged Materials Policy.

Current versus Retrospective Selection

Primary emphasis is on the selection and acquisition of current (recently published, in-print) materials. The library will attempt to obtain retrospective materials as determined by systematic collection analysis when funds permit. Librarians and faculty are encouraged to use any and all information sources available to identify materials for selection and acquisition within their subject areas. Contact with the faculty of the academic units is vital, especially through Departmental Library Representatives. The use of Choice cards and the approval slips from book vendors aid both librarians and faculty in this process.

Collection Evaluation and Deselection

Librarians will conduct periodic evaluations of the collection to ensure that it reflects the changing and growing needs of the university community. The "Materials Withdrawal Guidelines" address these activities.

Collection Scope

The primary consideration of the Brooks Library collections is to provide books contributive to and supportive of the undergraduate curriculum of Central Washington University. As the university's curriculum grows, adapts, and otherwise changes in relation to the world and human knowledge, so the monograph collection must evolve. Collections related to the undergraduate curriculum should be as broad and deep as the monographic budget allows. Of secondary importance are the graduate curriculum, faculty research areas, and the larger body of published knowledge that has no direct connection to the university's instructional programmes. Purchases in these areas will be highly selective.

Format of materials is chosen based on the consideration of permanence, utility, accessibility, and appropriateness to content. Formats collected include:

- monographs
- serials
- videotapes
- digital video discs
- scores
- compact discs

- electronic databases
- electronic journals
- electronic books

Monograph Collection Development

The Library primarily selects single editions of cloth or paperbound books/monographs.

Textbooks, workbooks, study guides, etc., are generally not collected. Possible exceptions would be textbooks that are considered important in their field or if they are the best source of information on a certain topic.

The Summit catalog and the collections it represents provide an immensely valuable body of literature to consider alongside local collections. Availability of materials in Summit does impact acquisition behavior in Brooks Library, though with limited effect. Materials represented in Summit may nevertheless be purchased for the local collection if deemed necessary, or their accessibility through Summit may be considered adequate.

Library Liaisons are encouraged to write specific collection development policies for the subject areas for which they are responsible.

Recognition of Teacher Education Institutions

Recognition of institutions offering course or training in teacher education.

(1) Every institution offering or intending to offer a course or training in teacher education on or after the appointed day, may, for grant of recognition under this Act, make an application to the Regional Committee concerned in such form and in such manner as may be determined by regulations:

Provided that an institution offering a course or training in teacher education immediately before the appointed day, shall be entitled to continue such course or training for a period of six months, if it has made an application for recognition within the said period and until the disposal of the application by the Regional Committee.

(2) The fee to be paid along with the application under subsection (1) shall be such as may be prescribed.

(3) On receipt of an application by the Regional Committee from any institution under sub-section (1), and after obtaining from the institution concerned such other particulars as it may consider necessary, it shall,-

(a) if it is satisfied that such institution has adequate financial resources, accommodation, library, qualified staff, laboratory and that it fulfils such other conditions required for proper functioning of the institution for a course or training in teacher education, as may be determined by regulations, pass an order granting recognition to such institution, subject to such conditions as may be determined by re-gulations;or

(b) if it is of the opinion that such institution does not fulfil the requirements laid down in sub-clause (a), pass an order refusing recognition to such institution for reasons to, be recorded in writing:

Provided that before passing an order under sub-clause (b), the Regional Committee shall provide a reasonable opportunity to the concerned institution for making a written representation.

(4) Every order granting or refusing recognition to an Institution for a course or training in teacher education under sub-section (3) shall be published in the Official Gazette and communicated In writing for appropriate action to such institution and to the concerned examining body, the local authority or the State Government and the Central Government.

(5) Every institution, in respect of which recognition has been refused shall discontinue the course or training in teacher education from the end of the academic session next following the date of receipt of the order refusing recognition passed under clause (b) of sub-section (3).

The Gazette of India Extraordinary

(6) Every examining body shall, on receipt of the order under subsection (4),-

(a) grant affiliation to the institution, where recognition has been granted; or

(b) cancel the affiliation of the institution, where recognition has been refused.

Permission for a New Course on Training by Recognised Institution

(1) Where any recognised institution intends to start any new course or training in teacher education, it may make an application to seek permission therefor to the Regional Committee concerned in such, form and in such manner as may be determined by regulations.

(2) The fees to be paid along with the application under sub-section (1) shall be such as may be prescribed.

(3) On receipt of an application from an institution under sub-section (1), and after obtaining from the recognised institution such other particulars as may be considered necessary, the Regional Committee shall,-

(a) if it is satisfied that such recognised institution has adequate financial resources, accommodation, library, qualified staff, laboratory, and that it fulfils such other conditions required for proper conduct of the new course or training in teacher education, as may be determined by regulations, pass an order granting permission, subject to such conditions as may be determined by regulation; or

(b) if it is of the opinion that such institution does not fulfil the requirements laid down in sub-clause (a), pass an order refusing permission to such institution, for reasons to be recorded in writing: Provided that before passing an order refusing permission under sub-clause (b), the Regional Committee shall provide a reasonable opportunity to the institution concerned for making a written re-presentation.

(4) Every order granting or refusing permission to a recognised institution for a new course or training in teacher education under sub-section (3), shall be published in the Official Gazette and communicated in writing for appropriate action to such recognised institution and to the concerned examining body, the local authority, the State Government and the Central Government.

Affiliating Body to Grant Affiliation after Recognition or Permission by the Council

Notwithstanding anything contained in any other law for the time being in force, no examining body shall, on or after the appointed day,-

(a) grant affiliation, whether provisional or otherwise, to any institution; or

(b) hold examination, whether provisional or otherwise, for a course or training conducted by a recognised institution, unless the institution concerned has obtained recognition from the Regional Committee concerned, under section 14 or permission for a course or training under section 15.

The Gazette of India Extraordinary [Part II]

Contravention of provisions of the Act and consequences thereof.

(1) Where the Regional Committee is, on its own motion or on any representation received from any person, satisfied that a recognised institution has contravened any of the provisions of this Act, or the rules, regulations, orders made or issued thereunder, or any condition subject to which recognition under sub-section (3) of section 14 or permission under sub-section (3) of section 15 was granted, it may withdraw recognition of such recognised institution, for reasons to be recorded in writing:

Provided that no such order against the recognised institution shall be passed unless a reasonable opportunity of making representation against the proposed order has been given to such recognised institution:

Provided further that the order, withdrawing or refusing recognition passed by the Regional Committee shall come into force only with effect from the end of the academic session next following the date of communication of such order.

(2) A copy of every order passed by the Regional Committee under sub-section (1),-.

(a) shall be communicated to the recognised institution concerned and a copy thereof shall also be forwarded simultaneously to the University or the examining body to which such institution was affiliated for cancelling affiliation; and

(b) shall be published in the Official Gazette for general information.

(3) Once the recognition of a recognised institution is withdrawn under subsection (1), such institution shall discontinue the course or training in teacher education, and the concerned University or the examining body shall cancel affiliation of the institution in accordance with the order passed under sub-section (1), with effect from the end of the academic session next following the date of communication of the said order.

(4) If an institution offers any course or training in teacher education after the coming into force of the order withdrawing recognition under sub-section (1), or where an institution offering a course or training in teacher education immediately before the appointed day fails or neglects to obtain recognition or permission under this Act, the qualification in teacher education obtained pursuant to such course or training or after undertaking a course or training in such institution, shall not be treated as a valid qualification for purposes of employment under the Central Government, any State Government or University, or in any school, college or

other educational body aided by the Central Government or any State Government.

Document Selection

Library always tries to select and purchase the most valuable document in the fields of interest to fulfill the requirements of its members.

Frequently Book selection Bulletin is sent through email to the members to receive their recommendations for Books.

Apart from this, members are always welcome to suggest titles of documents to be purchased by filling up the Purchase Request Form. The final decision will be taken by the Library Committee.

A member who suggests a document would be informed, if the document is acquired and the document will be automatically reserved for him/her, after display for a week.

No document shall be issued before it is processed and put on display.

A Finer Measure of Benefit in Document Selection?

If it makes sense to use a finer unit of measurement from the next lower level in our hierarchy for library selection, why not do the same in document selection? Might it not also, by the same argument, be excessively simple to judge documents as simply relevant or not relevant? Again, how ``relevant" does it have to be---or how much of it has to be relevant---for the whole document to be deemed relevant? By the reasoning we applied in our discussion of libraries, it would seem better to move down a level and compare documents in terms of how much of each one is of marginal benefit.

One might say that probabilistic retrieval systems avoid the crudeness of binary relevance judgments because they generate a ranking of documents with respect to relevance, but this is not the case. What is generated are probability estimates that a document is or is not relevant, which is not the same as a measure of the relevant content of a document. Binary relevance judgments are still being used.

But comparing documents in a metric of the next lower level in our hierarchy (data) has problems. Library collections can be divided rather easily into their constituent elements, documents, but documents themselves are not so easy to subdivide with respect to relevance.

There are physical divisions (pages and lines) and there are rhetorical divisions (chapters, paragraphs, and sentences). Back of book indexing usually refers to pages, but the physical divisions are largely irrelevant to the subject matter and the rhetorical divisions are only weakly and inconsistently related to intellectual content. Some exceptions can be found: Bibliographies and encyclopedias are documents composed of recognizable, discrete elements. Other documents commonly follow standardized rhetorical forms but in a much less clearly and usefully defined way.

The advantages of dividing documents into separate conceptual units, into hypertextual nodes, was recognized in the seventeenth century and received detailed attention from Hartlib and Drury and from Leibniz. This interest was renewed when there was interest in applying modern technology to information management. Already by 1911 the German chemist Wilhelm Ostwald and his colleagues in an organization called Die Bruecke (The Bridge) were discussing the ``monographic principle," their name for the hypertextual division of documents into smaller units which could then be organized independently. They saw such a development as similar in nature and in significance to Gutenberg's introduction of movable printing type. Commenting on the ease with which bibliographies lend themselves to being subdivided and even rearranged, Paul Otlet wrote in 1918 f the need:

> *"...to detach what the book amalgamates, to reduce all that is complex to its elements... This is the `monographic principle' pushed to its ultimate conclusion. ... What is a book, in fact, if not a continuous line which has initially been cut to the length of a page and then cut again to the length of a justified line? Now this cutting up, this division, is purely mechanical; it does not correspond to any division of ideas."*

Otlet foresaw ``selection machines" searching among these smaller units of recorded knowledge and workstations for manipulating and processing them, but how to divide documents into conceptual pieces remains an unsolved problem. There is research in this direction and some of it explores how parts of documents might be used in various information retrieval tasks. Examples include automatic discovery of the topic structure of text, use of rhetorical boundaries (e.g. chapters, paragraphs, and sentences) to improve retrieval performance, and the automatic creation of hypertext links within documents. However, their effective use outside the laboratory may still be some way off.

Accessing the Document

To access the Manage Document Libraries page, the user should meet one of the following criteria:

- Member of Content Administrators group, which is set to wpsContentAdministrators user group by default
  OR
- Manager authority on the Manage Document Libraries portlet plus user authority on the portal content page and at least one document library

Configuring Library Management

Before you Begin: To configure the settings for the Manage Document Libraries portlet, the user should meet one of the following criteria:

- Member of the Content Administrators group, which is set to wpsContentAdministrators user group by default
  OR
- Manager authority on the Manage Document Libraries portlet plus user authority on the portal content page and at least one document library

The Manage Document Libraries portlet requires some additional configuration by the administrator. The configuration settings you select determine the options that administrators see when managing their document libraries. When you configure the settings for Manage Document Libraries, your changes affect that portlet instance, which means that other administrators use the options that you specified for the portlet. For example, if the administrator disables the browser plug-in, other users of the Manage Document Libraries portlet will not be able to import documents from their local machines using the import feature—the Import documents icon will be disabled. Also, if the plug-in is disabled, other users will not see the plug-in section in edit mode, so they will not be able to enable or disable the browser plug-in. Follow the steps below in the Configuring the Manage Document Libraries portlet section of this topic.

Your company might have other administrators that only manage Document Manager, instead of the administering the entire Portal. These Document Manager administrators can customize their own view of the Manage Document Libraries portlet. The settings that you configure for the Manage Document Libraries portlet affect what the Document Manager administrators see. For example, if the browser plug-in is disabled on the Manage Document Libraries portlet configure page, Document Manager administrators will not see the option to enable the plug-in on the edit page. Follow the steps below in the Customizing your own view of the Manage Document Libraries portlet section of this topic.

Refer to the Document libraries topic for an overview of what you can do with the Manage Document Libraries portlet.

Configuring the Manage Document Libraries Portlet

Follow these steps to configure the Manage Document Libraries portlet. These settings affect the view that other administrators see when they use the Manage Document Libraries portlet.

1. Log in as an administrator.
2. Navigate to the Manage Document Libraries page.
3. Click the wrench icon in the portlet title bar.
4. Specify the following Manage Document Libraries portlet settings:

  - o Number of document libraries displayed per page
  - o Enable and disable the browser plug-in
5. Save your settings.

For step-by-step information about configuring the Manage Document Libraries portlet, see the online help that is available from the portlet title bar.

Customizing Your Own View of the Manage Document Libraries Portlet

Follow these steps to modify your own view of the Manage Document Libraries portlet. These settings do not affect the view that other administrators see when they use the Manage Document Libraries portlet.

1. Log in as an administrator.
2. Navigate to the Manage Document Libraries page.
3. Click the pencil icon in the portlet title bar.
4. Specify the following Manage Document Libraries portlet settings:
   - o Number of document libraries displayed per page
   - o Enable and disable the browser plug-in
5. Save your settings.

For step-by-step information about modifying the Manage Document Libraries portlet, see the online help that is available from the portlet title bar.

Navigating to Manage Document Libraries Page

Follow these steps to access the Manage Document Libraries page:

1. Log in as an administrator.
2. Click Administration to go to the Portal Administration page.
3. Click Portal Content.
4. Click Manage Document Libraries.

Next Steps

You have completed this step. Continue to the next step by choosing one of the topics below.

Assigning User Access

Before you Begin: To assign access and roles from the Manage Document Libraries or Document Manager page, the user should meet one of the following criteria:

- Member of the Content Administrators group, which is set to wpsContentAdministrators user group by default

  OR
- The user needs to possess the following authority or higher:
  - o User authority on the Portal Content administrative page
  - o User authority on the Manage Document Libraries portlet
  - o Administrator authority on the ICM_CONTENT_REPOSITORY virtual resource
  - o User authority on the Resource Permission page and the Resource Permission portlet
  - o Delegator authority on the User and User Groups resources. For information on setting the Delegator authority, see Setting the Delegator authority.

Setting the Delegator authority:

1. Under Portal Administration, click Access.
2. Click User and Group Permissions > Users
3. Select the user you want to give Delegator authority to and click the pencil icon.
4. Click Virtual Resources, then click the key for Users.
5. Click the box for the Delagator role.

Follow the same process for user groups, except after clicking Virtual Resources, click on User groups and choose the Delegator role.

This section gives the administrator the information necessary to assign users access to a document library by using the Manage Document Libraries portlet. Administrators should use the Manage Document Libraries portlet to restrict who can view, edit, copy, and delete document libraries. Setting such restrictions can help keep the document repository organized and can help prevent unwanted changes to document libraries. The Manage Document Libraries portlet uses the Resource Permissions portlet to assign user access.

Setting up Access for Document Manager

As part of setting up and maintaining your document management work environment, you will need to set access authority and assign roles for your users. Some Document Manager administrators may want to restrict who can view, edit, move or delete folders or files.

Setting such restrictions can help keep the document repository organized, and can help prevent unwanted changes to documents or folders. For example, an administrator may want only project managers to have authority to delete files, and only give writers the authority to open and edit files. Administrators determine user authorization for these tasks by setting access controls.

In order to create an administrator role, the user needs to have access to the Resource Permissions portlet. Adding the user to the Content Administrators user group automatically provides the user with authority on the Manage Document Libraries portlet.

The Document Manager administrator should use the Manage Document Libraries portlet to assign access. Clicking the Access icon opens the Resource Permissions Portlet. From there, administrators can grant users and groups access rights to document libraries.

After access control for groups is set for a document library, the administrator (and certain enabled users) can set access for documents and folders. Refer to the Document Manager online help for detailed instructions on setting access control.

Steps for Assigning Access to a Document Manager Resource

Follow these steps to set access to specific Document Manager resources, such as folders and documents:

1. Navigate to the Document Manager portlet instance.

2. Select the document or folder that you want to set access to.
   a. To set access to a document, click the name of the document to open the document view page, then click More Actions-> Set Access.
   b. To set access to a folder, select the check box next to the folder, then click Folder Actions-> Set Access to This Folder.

The following table displays the roles that are relevant to Document Manager:

WebSphere Portal role	Document Manager access rights
User	Read-only access to Document Manager resources. Users can see the resource, but cannot modify or contribute content of their own.
Editor	The ability to view and add new documents, folders, and views to the current resource. Editors can also modify the properties and content of existing documents and files. **Note:** The editor role **cannot** move files.
Manager	All the privileges of Editors, plus the ability to: • convert documents to another format • delete folders or documents underneath the current resource • move files
Administrator	The Administrator role can perform any operation.

The Privileged User, Delegator, or Security Administrator roles have no special meaning for Document Manager resources.

Access control gives special privileges to the owner of a resource. For instance, if a user with the Editor authority adds a document or folder, she has view, edit, delete, grant access and delegate permissions on that file or folder, even though she is only an editor.

Note: To set access on a folder or document, the user must have User authority on the Resource Permission page and the Resource Permission portlet. If the user does not have the correct level of authority, then the set access option will not be available in Document Manager.

For step-by-step instructions, see the online help that is available from the portlet title bar.

Assigning User Access and Roles for a Document Library, Documents, or Folders

Administrators set appropriate authority to users and groups to work with Document Manager. After a new document library is created, the administrator must assign permissions for that document library. After access control is set for the document library, the administrator and certain enabled users can set access for documents and folders. Refer to the Manage Document Libraries online help for detailed instructions on setting access control.

Steps for This Task: Follow these steps to assign user access to a document library.

1. Navigate to the Manage Document Libraries page.
2. Select the document library to which you want to assign access.
3. Click the **Access** icon to open the Resource Permissions page.
4. Assign the appropriate resource permissions.
5. Save your settings.

Setting up Document Management

Before you Begin: Ensure that you have created the document library that you plan to use for document management. The default working library is Document Manager, and your ability to modify its settings is limited. If you want to use a different working document library, you must create one. You have many configuration options available for the document libraries that you create. Refer to the Creating, editing, and deleting document libraries topic for more information about working with document libraries.

Important: Configure document management for importing large files by increasing the inbound buffer size. By default, 10 MB is the largest single file that can be imported. If your document repository contains any file larger than 10 MB, you need to increase the buffer size.

To increase the buffer size, do the following:

1. In the administrative console of WebSphere Application Server, click Servers > Application Servers > *portal_server* > Custom Properties > New.
2. Add the protocol_http_large_data_inbound_buffer property, and specify a value in bytes that can accommodate your largest single file.
3. Save your settings.
4. Restart your portal.

Administrators can configure and modify the settings for the Document Manager portlet instance. This section is designed to give the administrator the information necessary to set up the document management environment and modify settings for a Document Manager portlet. Refer to the Document management topic for more information about what users can do with Document Manager.

Steps for This Task: The Document Manager portlet requires some additional configuration by the administrator. The settings you modify affect only that particular instance of Document Manager. For example, you might have multiple instances of Document Manager installed on one page, and each instance can be configured differently. Document Manager A might be set up to use a different document library than that of Document Manager B.

1. Navigate to the Document Manager portlet that you want to modify and click the wrench icon to configure the settings for the Document Manager portlet instance.
2. Specify the following settings:
   a. *Set the Working Document Library:* Specifies the document library in which users will work for the Document Manager instance.
   b. *Turn on New Document Indicator:* Indicates documents that are new or have been recently modified by the word New! next to them. With the indicator turned on for the Document Manager instance, the user can set the number of days for

the indicator to display in the edit mode for his or her portlet instance.

c. *Include the Document Library in the Search Center:* Makes the document library searchable by the Search Center. Only the working document library for the portlet instance will be queried by the Search Center. With the appropriate permissions, users can access Document Manager documents that are returned by the Search Center.

d. *Enable Conversions:* Allows users to use the Productivity Components to work with documents that were originally cre ated in other file formats. See the Viewing documents in HTML topic for a list of file types that can be viewed in HTML.

e. *Enable Editors:* Allows users to work with the Productivity Components. Refer to the Productivity Components topic for more information.

f. *Disable the Browser Plug-in:* Disables the browser plug-in that allows users to edit documents using applications installed on their computer. With the plug-in disabled, users will only be able to create and edit documents using the Portal editors. Users will still be able to import other document types with the browser plug-in disabled. See the Setting up the browser plug-in topic for more information about enabling and disabling the browser plug-in.

g. *Enable the Folder Tree:* Turns on the folder tree option. With the folder tree enabled, users will have the option to display the document library folder hierarchy vertically, starting at the document library root folder. With the folder tree disabled, users will only be able to display the table view, which lists the contents of the current document library without the tree view on the left. Users click Show folders to display the tree view along with the table view, and users click Hide folders to display only the table view. Also, if you configure the folder tree to be enabled, the option to turn on the folder tree is also displayed in edit mode.

h. *Enable Active Content Filtering:* Removes potentially harmful active content (such as JavaScript, Java, and ActiveX) from HTML prior to displaying it in a browser.

i. *Specify the SMTP Mail Server:* Provides users the ability to send email links to documents and folders to other users. In order to use the Send a link feature of Document Manager, you must specify the appropriate SMTP mail server.

j. *Configure the Default Root Path for Your Portlet:* Allows the administrator to specify an existing subfolder within the current document library as the root folder for each portlet instance. Upon login, users will begin their session from this configured root folder. If you select a default root folder that has been deleted, renamed, or inaccessible to the current user, the default root path will revert to the current document library root. Users will still have the ability to navigate to any accessible folder in the document library.

Modified configuration settings take effect immediately. Be careful when modifying configuration settings while the Document Manager portlet is in use.

For step-by-step information about configuring an instance of the Document Manager portlet, see the online help that is available from the portlet title bar.

Set Preview Size

You can also adjust the size of the document preview. Documents that exceed the set size will not be displayed. To modify the document preview size, follow these steps:

1. Log in as administrator and click on Administration > Portlet Management > Portlets > Document Manager > Configure portlet.
2. Add the property previewSizeThreshold to the list and set the preview size.

- o The preview size must be a valid number of bytes such as 1024 (1KB) or 1048576 (1MB).
- o The default preview size for documents is 10485760 bytes, which is 10MB.
- o If you do not want a preview of the selected document to appear at all, you can set the previewSizeThreshold parameter to 0 (zero).

3. Click **Save** to save the changes.

4. Log out and then log back in to Document Manager for the setting to take effect.

Setting up the Browser Plug-in

Before you Begin: Ensure that you meet the following criteria:

- The browser plug-in must be enabled for users to use desktop applications. Refer to Setting up document libraries for more information.
- The browser must be configured for ActiveX and scripting in order to use desktop applications.
- *Important Note for Linux Users:* On Linux, a Java Applet is used to communicate with the client file system. This applet gives you the ability to edit files using your native editors, as well as to import multiple files and directories from the client file system. In order to run the applet, you will need to have a supported Java Runtime Environment installed on your browser. For installation instructions on Mozilla, visit http://plugindoc.mozdev.org/linux.html#Java and follow the instructions to install the Java Runtime Environment. Once the Java Runtime Environment is recognized in the browser, you should be prompted to accept an IBM certificate when you first visit the edit or administrative import pages. You should choose to always accept this certificate for the applet to be able to read and copy files from your local machine. After you accept the certificate, you might need to refresh the page. The plug-in attempts to read and write the files you are editing to the temporary directory defined in the java.io.tmpdir system property. Users need to have authority to create

directories and files in that path (usually /tmp). Lastly, the plug-in requires that KDE be installed and that the kfmclient be in the path. Visit http://www.kde.org for information about installing KDE. The kfmclient exec command is used to open files with the editors registered in KDE.

The Manage Document Libraries portlet provides a browser plug-in that allows users to import their local files into a document library. Also, the Document Manager portlet provides a browser plug-in that allows users to work with documents in editing applications that are installed on their computers. Enabling the browser plug-in gives users the options to either use their preferred editing applications or the Productivity Components that are provided with the product. This section contains the information necessary to enable and disable the browser plug-in, as well as instructions for configuring a browser to automatically open a file in a certain editing application.

Note: Plug-in upgrades are not automatic if you are using a Mozilla or Firefox browser. See Upgrading the Mozilla or Firefox browser plug-in for information on upgrading.

Upgrading the Mozilla or Firefox browser Plug-in

Browser upgrades are often installed automatically; however, if you require a new Mozilla or Firefox plug-in, you must manually install it.

Upgrading Plug-ins on Mozilla 1.4

In order to get new plug-ins on Mozilla 1.4, perform the following steps:

1. Be sure that you have only one version of Mozilla installed. Multiple instances of Mozilla could interfere with the plug-in installation.
2. Delete the Mozilla cache. The cache is located in c:/ Documents and Settings/*your_user*/Application Data/ Mozilla.
3. Delete the registry keys that bind the plug-in mime type to Document Manager by searching the registry for application/pdm-plugin under HKEY_USERS.

4. Uninstall and then reinstall Mozilla.
5. Start the Mozilla browser and navigate to the Document Manager portlet.
   - o If a plug-in install window opens, follow the provided install steps.
   - o If you do not see a plug-in install window, visit http://<hostname>:9081/wps/pdm/plugin/nsinstpdm.jsp?application/pdm-plugin where <hostname> is the name of your portal server.

Upgrading Plug-ins on Mozilla 1.7 and Higher

For current versions of Mozilla 1.7 and higher, perform the following steps to update the plug-in:

1. Delete the registry keys that bind the plug-in mime type to Document Manager by searching the registry for application/pdm-plugin under HKEY_USERS.
2. Delete the existing plug-in files from *Mozilla_install_dir*/plugins/*PDM*.dll and *Mozilla_install_dir*/components/nsIPDMPlugin.xpt.
3. Start the Mozilla browser and navigate to the Document Manager portlet.
   - o If a plug-in install window opens, follow the provided install steps.
   - o If you do not see a plug-in install window, visit http://<hostname>:9081/wps/pdm/plugin/nsinstpdm.jsp?application/pdm-plugin where <hostname> is the name of your portal server.

Upgrading Plug-ins on Firefox 1.0 and Higher

For current versions of FireFox 1.0 and higher, perform the following steps to update the plug-in:

1. Delete the existing plug-in files from *Firefox_install_dir*/plugins/*PDM*.dll and *Firefox_install_dir*/components/nsIPDMplugin.xpt.
2. Start the Firefox browser and navigate to the Document Manager portlet.
   - o If a plug-in install window opens, follow the provided install steps.

- o If you do not see a plug-in install window, visit http://<hostname>:9081/wps/pdm/plugin/nsinstpdm.jsp?application/pdm-plugin where <hostname> is the name of your portal server.

Setting up the Browser Plug-in

Enabling the browser plug-in allows users to create and edit documents using familiar applications that are installed on their desktop.

The browser plug-in is enabled by default, and it can be disabled for the Manage Document Libraries portlet, as well as for the Document Manager portlet. If you disable the plug-in in the Manage Document Libraries portlet, the setting for disabling the plug-in will not appear in edit mode. Also, by disabling the browser plug-in in the Manage Document Libraries portlet, the setting for disabling the plug-in will not appear in the portlet edit mode, and administrators will not be able to import documents from their local machines using the import feature.

Similarly, if you disable the plug-in in the Document Manager portlet, the setting for disabling the plug-in will not appear in edit mode, and users will not have the options to enable or disable the plug-in for that Document Manager portlet instance.

1. Follow these steps to disable the browser plug-in for the Manage Document Libraries portlet:
   a. Log in as an administrator.
   b. Click **Administration**, then click **Portal Content**.
   c. Click **Manage Document Libraries**.
   d. Click the wrench icon in the portlet title bar to see the configuration options.
   e. Select **Disable browser plug-in** to prevent users from using the plug-in.
   f. Click **OK** to save your changes.
2. Follow these steps to disable the browser plug-in for the Document Manager portlet:
   a. Log in as an administrator.

b. Navigate to the Document Manager portlet you want to configure.

c. Click the wrench icon in the portlet title bar to see the configuration options.

d. Select **Disable browser plug-in** to prevent users from using the plug-in.

e. Click **OK** to save your changes.

Setting up Draft Approvals

Before you Begin:

- Ensure that you have assigned the appropriate permissions for your users:
  - o Users must have access to the document library.
  - o Users must have access to the Portal Content page and the Manage Document Libraries portlet.
  - o Users with review responsibility must be in the Document Reviewer user group.
  - o In order to override document locks, users must have at least User-level access in a user group to which the lock owner belongs. The lock owner might belong to multiple groups. As long as the user has User access in any of those groups, then the user can override the document lock.
  - o In order for a reviewer to edit a document submitted for approval by an author, the reviewer must have at least User-level access in a user group to which the author belongs. The author might belong to multiple groups. As long as the reviewer has User access in any of those groups, then the reviewer can edit the document.
- Confirm that WebSphere Application Server security is enabled. The draft approvals option is only available if security is enabled on your system. See the topic Enabling WebSphere Application Server security for WebSphere Portal for more information.

This section gives the administrator the information necessary to set up the draft approvals process for a document library.

Steps for This Task: Workflow roles are first administered through the WebSphere Portal User group administrative portlet. When the administrator configures the document library, he or she can select a user group to be the Document Reviewer group for the library's approval process. This subset is specified when the administrator elects to turn on the Document Manager approvals workflow option.

1. From the Manage Document Libraries page, select the working document library for the draft approvals process.
2. Open the Edit the document library settings page.
3. Under Approvals workflow, select Enable workflow.
4. Select the appropriate approver group.
5. Save your settings. The draft approvals process is now enabled for the document library.

For step-by-step information about working with drafts, see the online help that is available from the portlet title bar.

Once a document draft is submitted for review, the document appears in the Submitted Drafts view of the assigned reviewers. Although multiple users can have review responsibility, only one reviewer can accept or reject the document change.

Once a document change is accepted by a reviewer, it becomes visible in the Document Manager folder hierarchy. If a reviewer rejects the draft, the document returns to the Private Drafts view of the originator of the change for further modification, then a subsequent submit reactivates the approval step. Refer to the Working with drafts topic for more information.

Setting up File Type Definitions

This section describes how to set up file type definitions and enable Document Conversion Services for the Document Manager portlet, which provides users the ability to open various file types in HTML format. Documents produced by many standard applications (such as word processors or spreadsheets) can be viewed as HTML pages using the Document Conversion Services. For example, documents received as attachments to an e-mail can be viewed in a browser, even if the application that created the document is not installed. Document Conversion Services also allows documents to be searched by content. Refer to the Viewing documents in HTML topic for a list of file types that can be viewed in HTML.

Note: The document conversion process will delete previous versions of the document.

Steps for This Task: Setting up file type definitions is part of configuring Productivity Components. For details, see Configure Productivity Components. Ensure that you followed the instructions that the WebSphere Portal Customization Dialog generated for that task. One step in these instructions involves updating the content-types.properties file with the following content.

These extensions are case-sensitive.

- **Microsoft Office:**
  application/msword: \
  description=Microsoft Word;\
  file_extensions=.doc
- application/vnd.ms-excel: \
  description=Microsoft Excel;\
  file_extensions=.xls
- application/vnd.ms-powerpoint: \
  description=Microsoft PowerPoint;\
  file_extensions=.ppt
- **Lotus SmartSuite:**
  application/vnd.lotus-freelance: \
  description=Lotus Freelance;\
  file_extensions=.prz
- application/vnd.lotus-1-2-3: \
  description=Lotus 1-2-3;\
  file_extensions=.123
- application/vnd.lotus-wordpro: \

description=Lotus WordPro;\
file_extensions=.lwp

- **OpenOffice:**
  application/vnd.sun.xml.writer: \
  description=Open Office;\
  file_extensions=.sxw
- application/vnd.sun.xml.writer.template: \
  description=Open Office;\
  file_extensions=.stw
- application/vnd.sun.xml.writer.global: \
  description=Open Office;\
  file_extensions=.sxg
- application/vnd.sun.xml.calc: \
  description=Open Office;\
  file_extensions=.sxc
- application/vnd.sun.xml.calc.template: \
  description=Open Office;\
  file_extensions=.stc
- application/vnd.sun.xml.impress: \
  description=Open Office;\
  file_extensions=.sxi
- application/vnd.sun.xml.impress.template: \
  description=Open Office;\
  file_extensions=.sti
- application/vnd.sun.xml.draw: \
  description=Open Office;\
  file_extensions=.sxd
- application/vnd.sun.xml.draw.template: \
  description=Open Office;\
  file_extensions=.std
- application/vnd.sun.xml.math: \
  description=Open Office;\
  file_extensions=.sxm

Maintaining Your Search Index

Successful searching within Document Manager requires an up-to-date, valid search index. These important tips and procedures will help you maintain your search index.

Backing up and Recovering the Search Index

To ensure that your Document Manager search continues to work correctly, consider performing the following steps as part of your database back up and recovery procedures.

- Each time that you back up your database(s), you should also back up the Juru search indexes that have been built and coincide with the current state of your database(s).

  To back up Juru indexes:

  You need to back up the directory tree containing the Juru indexes. After you unzip the juruIndexes.zip file, these indexes are maintained under *wp_root*/jcr/search in the Indexes directory. Use any standard zip tool or operating system command that recursively collects the contents within a directory and its subdirectories.
- To restore the Juru indexes, simply unzip the backup copy to an empty directory (this is the default).

  For z/OS, the default directory is *wp_root*/jcr/search.

Changing the Search Indexing Interval

The time between rebuilding the search indexes is set to 30 minutes by default. To change the search indexing interval, you must change a setting in the icm.properties file. To change the interval:

1. Edit the icm.properties file.
2. Edit the line
   - jcr.textsearch.indexmaintenance.interval = 30
3. Set the interval number to the desired value in minutes. For example, if the interval is set to 90 minutes, the line looks like this:
   - jcr.textsearch.indexmaintenance.interval = 90

4. Save the properties file.
5. Restart the WebSphere Portal server.

Technical Processing

Major activities of this Section are:

- Writing process slip for assigning call no. for the book received from the Acquisition section.
- Checking the process slip with the Catalogue and SL cards.
- Assigning call no. for the book with the help of UDC Scheme and the Authority file.
- Arranging the process slip for the preparation of NAL monthly bulletin
- Pasting the Spine and Date labels in the book and noting the Call no.& Cop. No on the spine label and Accession no on the date label along with the Call no. and Cop.no.
- Arranging the processed project book for informing the concerned Project Co-ordinator
- Arranging the library book along with other processed books to be displayed on each month.
- Merging the SL card in the cabinet alphabetically after noting the Call no on it.
- Preparing the list of the processed books during a month with bibliographical details, Accession no and location using Microsoft Word.
- Announcing this list on the Library Web Site at the beginning of the month.
- Sending the processed books for display on each month after entering the required details of the book in the OPAC.
- Removing the already displayed books to the stack after keeping the reserved books on the reservation desk .
- Reminding the Project Co-ordinator or Faculty member to collect the processed books which are not collected

and to be issued on Permanent Loan or Department Loan.

Physical Verification of Collection

Physical verification is a process whereby an IC layout design is checked via EDA software tools to see if it meets certain criteria. Verification involves DRC (Design rule check), LVS (Layout versus schematic), ERC (Electrical Rule Check), XOR (Exclusive OR), and Antenna Checks.

XOR Check

This step involves comparing two layout databases/GDS by XOR operation of the layout geometries. This check results a database which has all the mismatching geometries in both the layouts. This check is typically run after a metal spin, where in the re-spin database/GDS is compared with the previously taped out database/GDS.

Antenna Check

Antenna checks are used to limit the damage of the thin gate oxide during the manufacturing process due to charge accumulation on the interconnect layers (metal, polysilicon) during certain fabrication steps like Plasma etching, which creates highly ionized matter to etch. The antenna basically is a metal interconnect, i.e., a conductor like polysilicon or metal, that is not electrically connected to silicon or grounded, during the processing steps of the wafer. If the connection to silicon does not exist, charges may build up on the interconnect to the point at which rapid discharge does take place and permanent physical damage results to thin transistor gate oxide. This rapid and destructive phenomenon is known as the antenna effect. The Antenna ratio is defined as the ratio between the physical area of the conductors making up the antenna to the total gate oxide area to which the antenna is electrically connected.

ERC (Electrical Rule Check)

ERC (Electrical rule check) involves checking a design for all well and substrate areas for proper contacts and spacings thereby ensuring correct power and ground connections. ERC steps can also involve checks for unconnected inputs or shorted outputs. They can also check for structures suceptible to ESD damage

Shared Responsibility for Electronic Materials Management

The CIC-EJC has provided the opportunity for the CIC libraries to define their role in electronic scholarship both independent of and in relation to publishers and computer specialists. The CIC Center for Library Initiatives has provided coordination and leadership for the CIC-EJC as it has for other CIC-wide library projects. CICNet has provided technical support, guidance, and implementation. It has conducted all development and maintenance of the technical aspects of the system, including acquisition and archiving of electronic journals, publisher relationships and permissions, organization and display of bibliographic data, development of indexing and search utilities, and hardware and software support. The CIC member librarians share responsibility for evaluation of available information resources including selection, deselection, cataloging, and quality control.

Other projects within the CIC provide an opportunity for collaboration in the development of related electronic information resources and access. The CIC libraries, with shared licenses negotiated by the CIC Center for Library Initiatives, have purchased commercial databases and are sharing them across the CIC institutions' regional network. This activity has served as a model of how to work together and reach mutually beneficial collective decisions. These efforts have put CIC in the forefront in collective licensing negotiations with publishers.

The Virtual Electronic Library (VEL), funded through a U.S. Department of Education grant, will develop the technical infrastructure required to provide seamless access to the CIC libraries' OPACs. The utility of this infrastructure will be demonstrated through user-initiated interlibrary loans and document delivery throughout the CIC. The VEL will enable the more than one-half million faculty, staff, and students to explore and take advantage of vast resources within the CIC. Inherent to the VEL project is the addition of an expanded set of electronic resources to the VEL pool of information resources. Ultimately, the CIC-EJC will be an integral part of the VEL.

The VEL has provided the impetus for the CIC libraries to sponsor numerous working groups and projects. The Task Force on the CIC Electronic Collection, which oversees the CIC-EJC, is one of these groups. Each CIC library has appointed an Electronic Resources Officer to coordinate local participation in the various projects related to building the VEL. The Task Force on Preservation and Digital Technology is exploring both digitization of materials held by the libraries and preservation of original electronic materials using digital technology. The CIC Electronic Text Group is developing a core collection of encoded humanities texts and planning for networked access among the CIC libraries. Sharing expertise among CIC library computer specialists is a central component of the E-Text project, with group members specializing in applying text encoding standards, building search engines, developing collections, and training colleagues at other CIC institutions. Groups have just been appointed to address issues around geographic information systems and government document electronic resources. All these separate and overlapping projects provide a strong environment for collaborative research and work.

Serials and Electronic Material Management

Georgia State University is seeking an energetic, knowledgeable and visionary librarian to serve as Serials and Electronic Acquisitions Librarian. Georgia State University has an annual serials budget of approximately $3 million dollars for both print and electronic resources.

It is a full participant in GALILEO, which provides substantial online information sources, and in consortial purchases with other research libraries. Pullen Library seeks a person with serials experience for a faculty rank (non-tenure) position to manage all aspects of electronic serials acquisition, oversee the efficient operation of the Serials Unit and to serve as Assistant Department Head. The position reports to the

Head of the Acquisitions Department and will have administrative responsibility for the Acquisitions Department in the absence of the department head.

Responsibilities: The successful candidate will be responsible for, but are not limited to: coordinating the purchase and licensing of all electronic materials; overseeing all aspects of serials acquisitions including ordering, receipt, invoicing, claiming, binding, vendor assessment, and other serials-related functions; coordinating the work of the serials unit with the other appropriate areas to ensure efficient workflow and communication; serving as Assistant Department Head; and participating in university and professional activities including research and publication.

Required: ALA-accredited master's degree in library science plus two years serials experience. Computer skills. Experience supervising or organizing the work of others. PREFERRED: Experience with electronic resources including negotiating contracts and licenses for electronic resources. Some budget management experience. Experience working in an integrated automated environment, preferably Voyager. Excellent communications skills. Attention to detail. Strong analytical and problem solving skills. Demonstrated interest in professional and research activities.

Library and University Environment: Georgia State University (GSU) is a dynamic urban institution located in downtown Atlanta with an enrollment of approximately 25,000 students. The close relationship that exists between the university and its surrounding business, government and cultural communities makes GSU unique in the University System of Georgia and distinctive among universities in the South.

The William Russell Pullen Library houses over 1,300,000 volumes, subscribes to more than 8,000 serials, and is a Federal Document Depository with more than 850,000 government documents. Its growing Media Center has holdings of approximately 12,000 audio, video, and multimedia materials. The carefully selected collections are designed to serve varied research and instructional needs at the undergraduate and graduate levels of the university community. Library services are supported by GIL (GALILEO Interconnected Libraries) with integrated functions for OPAC acquisitions, cir culation systems and serials control, including a system-wide union catalog.

The University System of Georgia has a statewide system known as GALILEO providing equal access to electronic resources and other materials for libraries throughout the state. Pullen Library is a member of the Association of Southeastern Research Libraries; the Southeastern Library Network (SOLINET), and the Atlanta Regional Con! sortium for Higher Education, consisting of fourteen academic and research libraries serving nineteen institutions in the greater Atlant metropolitan area.

Materials Management

The Materials Management department is responsible for acquiring new library materials, preparing them for placement on the shelves, and maintaining the periodicals and serials collection. The Acquisitions Unit orders, receives, and pays for library materials. Acquisitions staff add records to the Foley Center's on-line catalog for materials which are on order. They also coordinate the selection of gifts donated to the library. Once received and paid for, new materials are routed to the Cataloging Unit. Cataloging staff search an international database to obtain cataloging records. They review records for accuracy and add holdings to the database so that other libraries will know which materials are contained in the Foley Center collection.

The cataloging records are then loaded into the Foley Center's on-line catalog. Cataloging staff physically process the materials and deliver them to the Public Services department for shelving. The Serials Unit is responsible for maintaining subscriptions and standing orders for materials such as magazines, scholarly journals, newspapers, government documents, and microforms. Serials staff also check in current issues of periodicals and prepare them for binding. They bind some volumes in-house in the Bindery located on the lower level of the Foley Center; they ship other volumes to a bindery outside of the Spokane area. Government Documents Processing: As a depository library, the Foley Center is responsible for maintaining collections of both state and federal government documents.

Preservation

Preservation is a branch of library and information science concerned with maintaining or restoring access to artifacts, documents and records through the study, diagnosis, treatment and prevention of decay and damage.

It should be distinguished from conservation which refers to the treatment and repair of individual items to slow decay or restore them to a usable state. Conservation is occasionally used interchangeably with preservation, particularly outside the professional literature.

History

Antecedents: Although preservation as a formal profession in libraries and archives dates from the twentieth century, its philosophy and practice has roots in many earlier traditions. In library science, preservation is treated as an active and intentional process, as opposed to the passive sense of preservation that might be applied to paleontological or archaeological finds. The survival of these items is a matter of chance, from an information science perspective, while the preservation of them after their discovery is a matter of intentional activity.

Human record-keeping arguably dates back to the cave painting boom of the upper paleolithic, some 32,000-40,000 years ago. More direct antecedents are the writing systems that developed in the 4th millennium B.C. Written record keeping and information sharing practices, along with oral tradition, sustain and transmit information from one group to another. This level of preservation has been supplemented over the last century with the professional practice of preservation and conservation in the cultural heritage community.

1. Oral tradition or oral culture, the transmission of information from one generation to the next without a writing system.
2. Antiquarian practices, including scribal practice, burial practice, the libraries at Pergamum, Alexandria and other ancient archives.
3. Medieval practices, including the scriptorium and relic collection
4. Renaissance and the changing conception of artists and works of art
5. Enlightenment and the Encyclopedists
6. Romantic movement's imperative to preserve

Significant Events

- 1933: William Barrow introduces the field of conservation to paper deacidification when he publishes a paper on the acid paper problem. In later studies, Barrow tested paper from American books made between 1900 and 1949 and learned that after forty years the books had lost on average 96 percent of their original strength; after less than ten years, they had already lost 64 percent. Barrow determined that this rapid deterioration was not the direct result of using wood-pulp fibers, since rag papers of this period were also aging rapidly, but rather due to the residual sulfuric acid produced in both rag and wood pulp papers. Manufacturing methods used after 1870 employed sulfuric acid for sizing and bleaching the paper. Earlier papermaking methods left the final product only mildly alkaline or even neutral. Such paper has maintained its strength for 300 to 800 years, despite sulfur dioxide and other air pollutants. Barrow's 1933 article on the fragile state of wood pulp paper predicted the life expectancy, or "LE," of this paper was approximately 40-50 years. At that point the paper would begin to show signs of natural decay, and he concluded that research for a new media on which to write and print was needed.

- 1966: The Flood of the River Arno in Florence, Italy damaged or destroyed millions of rare books and lead to the development of restoration laboratories and new methods in conservation. Instrumental in this process was conservationist Peter Waters, who lead a group of volunteers, called "mud angels", in restoring thousands of books and papers. This event awakened many historians, librarians, and other professionals to the importance of having a preservation plan. Many consider this flood to be one of the worst disasters since the burning of the Alexandria Library in ancient Rome. It spurred a resurgence in the profession of preservation and conservation worldwide.
- 1987: Terry Saunders releases the film Slow Fires: On the Preservation of the Human Record which examines paper embrittlement resulting from acid decay
- 1989: March 7 ["Commitment Day"] Major US print publishers convene at NYPL to endorse a community-wide commitment to utilizing ISO 9706 certified permanent durable paper in order to combat the acid paper epidemic.

Significant People in the History of Preservation

- William Barrow (1904 – 1967) was an American chemist and paper conservator, and a pioneer of library and archives conservation. He introduced the field of conservation to paper deacidification through alkalization.
- Paul N. Banks (1934-2000) was Conservator and Head of the Conservation Department at the Newberry Library from 1964 to 1981, and published regularly on bookbinding, book and paper conservation and problems related to conservation. He designed and implemented a curriculum for Columbia University's School of Library Science that dealt directly with preservation training.
- Pamela Darling, author and historian, was Preservation Specialist for the Association of Research Libraries. Her works include materials to aid libraries in

establishing their own comprehensive preservation programmes.

- Carolyn Harris worked as head of Columbia University Libraries' Preservation Division from 1981 until 1987, where she worked closely with Paul Banks. She published extensive research throughout her career, especially dealing with mass deacidification of wood-pulp paper.
- Peter Waters, former Conservation Officer at the Library of Congress in Washington, DC, worked in the areas of disaster recovery and preparedness, and the salvaging of water-damaged paper goods.
- Nicholson Baker is a contemporary American novelist and author of *Double Fold*, a criticism of libraries' destruction of paper-based media.
- Patricia Battin, as the first president of the Commission on Preservation and Access, worked to organize a national campaign both for the use of alkaline paper in publishing companies and for a national programme of preservation microfilming.
- John F. Dean, Preservation and Conservation Librarian at Cornell University, has made contributions towards improving preservation efforts in developing countries. Specifically, Dean has created online tutorials for library conservation and preservation in Southeast Asia and Iraq and the Middle East.

The Paul Banks and Carolyn Harris Preservation Award for outstanding preservation specialists in library and archival science, is given annually by the Association for Library Collections & Technical Services, a subdivision of the American Library Association. It is awarded in recognition of professional preservation specialists who have made significant contributions to the field. Banks/Harris award winners:

- Sally Buchanan 2001-Buchanan received the award in recognition of years of service in the preservation field while an associate professor at the University of Pittsburgh School of Information Science

- Ellen McCrady 2002-From 1975 to 2004, McCrady edited and published the "Abbey Newsletter", covering important information for preservation professionals. She also conducted research regarding papermaking and acid testing.
- John F. Dean 2003-Since its inception in 1985, Dean has led the Department of Preservation and Conservation at Cornell University.
- Jan Merrill-Oldham 2004-As the Malloy-Rabinowitz Preservation Librarian at Harvard University, Merrill-Oldham oversees the Weissman Preservation Center and the Preservation and Imaging Department.
- Paul Conway 2005-Conway is an associate professor in the University of Michigan School of Information and has worked with Yale and Duke University after beginning his career at the Gerald R. Ford Presidential Library. His research and educational work focuses primarily on digital preservation and electronic media.
- Gary Frost 2006-Currently the University Conservator at the University of Iowa Libraries, Frost has been an educator and practitioner in the field of library preservation for almost 40 years. Frost is actively involved in library preservation and maintains an online blog at Futureofthebook.com.
- Walter Henry 2007-Henry, a conservator at the Stanford University Libraries and Academic Information Resources, is the creator of Conservation OnLine and the Conservation DistList.
- Janet Gertz 2008-Director for Preservation, Columbia University Libraries has been chair of ALCTS' Preservation and Reformatting Section (PARS). She has taught, spoken and published widely on topics ranging from traditional library preservation, disaster preparedness, commercial binding, and preservation microfilming to digital preservation, audio preservation, preservation metadata and large-scale mass digitization. She is an adjunct faculty member in the Palmer School of Library and Information Science, Long Island

University, and has been a guest lecturer at Rutgers' Preservation Institute and at Queen's College.

Practices

Care and Handling:

1. Exhibitions
2. Circulating collections
3. Special collections

Environmental Controls

Environmental controls are necessary to facilitate the preservation of organic library materials and are especially important to monitor in rare and special collections. Key environmental factors to watch include temperature, relative humidity, pests, pollutants, and light exposure.

In general, the lower the temperature is, the better it is for the collection. However, since books and other materials are often housed in areas with people, a compromise must be struck to accommodate human comfort. A reasonable temperature to accomplish both goals is 65-68UF however, if possible, film and photography collections should be keep in a segregated area at 55UF.

Books and other materials take up and give off moisture making them sensitive to relative humidity. Very high humidity encourages mold growth and insect infestations. Low humidity causes materials to lose their flexibility. Fluctuations in relative humidity are more damaging than a constant humidity in the middle or low range. Generally, the relative humidity should be between 30-50% with as little variation as possible, however recommendations on specific levels to maintain vary depending on the type of material, i.e. paper-based, film, etc.

The Image Permanence Institute provides a downloadable calculator to assist in determining the ideal indoor temperature when taking into account the outdoor dew point. This calculator also provides information on the risk on condensation and how many days to mold based on the entered scenario.

Pests, such as insects and vermin, eat and destroy paper and the adhesive that secures book bindings. Food and drink in libraries, archives, and museums can increase the attraction of pests. An Integrated Pest Management system is one way to control pests in libraries.

Particulate and gaseous pollutants, such as soot, ozone, sulfur dioxide, oxides of nitrogen, can cause dust, soiling, and irreversible molecular damage to materials. Pollutants are exceedingly small and not easily detectable or removable. A special filtration system in the building's HVAC is a helpful defense. Exposure to light also has a significant effect on library materials. It is not only the light visible to humans that can cause damage, but also ultraviolet light and infrared radiation. Measured in lux or the amount of lumens/m^2, the generally accepted level of illumination with sensitive materials is limited to 50 lux per day. Materials receiving more lux than recommended can be placed in dark storage periodically to prolong the original appearance of the object.

Recent concerns about the impact of climate change on the management of cultural heritage objects as well as the historic environment has prompted research efforts to investigate alternative climate control methods and strategies that include the implementation of alternative climate control systems to replace or supplement traditional high-energy consuming HVAC systems as well as the introduction of passive preservation techniques.

Decision Making and Criteria

Making a proper decision is an important factor before starting preservation practices. Decision making for preservation should be made considering significance and value of materials. Significance is considered to have two major components: importance and quality. "Importance" relates to the collection's role as a record, and "quality" covers comprehensiveness, depth, uniqueness, authenticity and reputation of the collection. Moreover, analyzing the significance of materials can be used to uncover more about their meaning. Assessment of significance can also aid in documenting the provenance and context to argue the case for grant funding for the object and collection.

Forms of significance can be historically, culturally, socially, or spiritually significant. In the preservation context, libraries and archives make decisions in different ways. In libraries, decision-making likely targets existing holding materials, where as in archives, decisions for preservation are often made when they acquire materials. Therefore, different criteria might be needed on different occasions. In general, for archive criteria, the points include: 1) the characteristics of a record (purpose, creator, etc.); 2) the quality of the information in the record; 3) the record in context (part of a series or not); 4) potential use and possible limitations; and 5) the cost against the benefits from its existence. For library criteria, the following are evidence of significance: 1) uniqueness, 2) irreplaceability, 3) high level of impact – over time or place, 4) high level of influence, 5) representation of a type, and 6) comparative value (rarity, completeness, integrity relative to others of its kind).

Selection

Since the 1970s, the Northeast Document Conservation Center has stated that the study of understanding the needs of the library is inherently important to the survival of archives and libraries. In order for the preservation of a collection to survive for a long time it is important that a systematic preservation plan is in place. The first step in planning a preservation programme is to assess the institution's existing preservation needs. This process entails identifying the general and specific needs of the collection, establishing priorities, and gathering the resources to execute the plan.

Because budget and time limitations require priorities to be set, standards have been established by the profession to determine what should be preserved in a collection. Considerations include existing condition, rarity, and evidentiary and market values. With non-paper formats, the availability of equipment to access the information will be a factor (for example, playback equipment for audio-visual materials, or microform readers). An institution should determine how many, if any, other repositories hold the material, and consider coordinating efforts with those that do.

Institutions should establish an environment conducive to preservation changes, involve staff, and create an understanding among administration and staff. The first steps an institution should implement, according to the NEDCC, are to establish a policy that defines and charts the course of action and create a framework for carrying out goals and priorities. There are three methods for carrying out a preservation survey: general preservation assessment, collection condition surveys, and an item-by-item survey.

Selection for treatment determines the survival of materials and should be done by a specialist, whether in relation to an established collection development policy or on an item by item basis. Once an object or collection has been chosen for preservation, the treatment must be determined that is most appropriate to the material and its repository. If the information is most important, reformatting or creation of a surrogate is a likely option. If the artifact itself is of value, it will receive conservation treatment, ideally of a reversible nature.

Research and Testing

With old media deteriorating or showing their vulnerabilities and new media becoming available, research remains active in the field of conservation and preservation. Everything from how to preserve paper media to creating and maintaining electronic resources is being explored by students and professionals in library and information science. The two main issues that most libraries tend to face are the rapid disintegration of acidic paper and water damage (due to flooding, plumbing problems, etc). Therefore, these areas of preservation, as well as new digital technologies, receive much of the research attention.

The American Library Association has many scholarly journals that publish articles on preservation topics, such as *College and Research Libraries, Information Technology and Libraries,* and *Library Resources and Technical Services.* Scholarly periodicals in this field from other publishers include *International Preservation News, Journal of the American Institute for Conservation*, and *Collection Management* among many others.

Ethics

Conservators should refer to the AIC Code of Ethics and Guidelines for Practice, which states that the conservation professional must "strive to attain the highest possible standards in all aspects of conservation."

Ethics will play an important role in many aspects of the conservator's activities. When choosing which objects are in need of treatment, the conservator should do what is best for the object in question and not yield to pressure or opinion from outside sources.

Preservation of Cultural Objects

One instance in which these decisions may get tricky is when the conservator is dealing with cultural objects. The AIC Code of Ethics and Guidelines for Practice has addressed such concerns, stating "All actions of the conservation professional must be governed by an informed respect for cultural property, its unique character and significance and the people or person who created it." This can be applied in both the care and longterm storage of objects in archives and institutions.

The AIC Code of Ethics and Guidelines for Practice also states: "While recognizing the right of society to make appropriate and respectful use of cultural property, the conservation professional shall serve as an advocate for the preservation of cultural property." This statement speaks to the conservator's need to balance his or her duty to conserve objects and maintain a collection with society's right to have access and use of objects for their own cultural/religious purposes. While it is obvious that a member of a religion should be able to have access to an object or text that has spiritual value to them, it would be against the conservator's ethics to then allow that object to incur damage from such use. The conservator should make sure that the care of the object is kept in mind when access to an object is granted. The object should remain in the best condition possible not only so it is preserved for prosperity, but also so that it can be studied by researchers and by members of the cultural or religious group that created it.

It is important that preservation specialists to be respectful of cultural property and the societies that created it, it is also important for them to be aware of international and national laws pertaining to stolen items. The AIC Code of Ethics and Guidelines for Practice also states that:

> *"The conservation professional should be cognizant of laws and regulations that may have a bearing on professional activity. Among these laws and regulations are those concerning the rights of artists and their estates, occupational health and safety, sacred and religious material, excavated objects, endangered species, human remains, and stolen property."*

In recent years there has been a rise in nations seeking out artifacts that have been stolen and are now in museums. In many cases museums are working with the nations to find a compromise to balance the need for reliable supervision as well as access for both the public and researchers.

Conservators are not just bound by ethics to treat cultural and religious objects with respect, but also in some cases by law. For example, in the United States, conservators must comply with the Native American Graves Protection and Repatriation Act (NAGPRA). The First Archivists Circle, a group of Native American archivists, has also created Protocols for Native American Archival Materials. The non-binding guidelines are suggestions for libraries and archives with Native American archival materials.

With all these issues of respect and cultural sensitivity to consider, conservation and preservation issues are sure to arise. The care of cultural and sacred objects often affects the physical storage or the object. For example, sacred objects of the native peoples of the Western United States are supposed to be stored with sage to ensure their spiritual well being. The idea of storing an object with plant material is inherently problematic to an archival collection because of the possibility of insect infestation. When conservators have faced this problem, they have addressed it by using freeze-dried sage, thereby meeting both conservation and cultural needs.

Some individuals in the library science community have explored the possible moral responsibility to preserve all cultural phenomena, in regards to the concept of monumental preservation. Other advocates argue that such an undertaking is something that the indigenous or native communities that produce such cultural objects are better suited to perform. Currently, however, many indigenous communities are not financially able to support their own archives and museums. Still, indigenous archives are on the rise in the United States.

Preservation and the Library as a Sacred Institution

- In her book "Sacred Stacks: The Higher Purpose of Libraries and Librarianship," Nancy Kalikow Maxwell discusses how libraries are capable of performing some of the same functions as religion. Many librarians feel that their work is done for some higher purpose. The same can be said for preservation librarians. One instance of the library's role as sacred is to provide a sense of immortality: with the ever changing world outside, the library will remain stable and dependable. Preservation is a great help in this regard. Through digitization and reformatting, preservation librarians are able to retain material while at the same time adapting to new methods. In this way, libraries can adapt to the changes in user needs without changing the quality of the material itself. Through preservation efforts, patrons can rest assured that although materials are constantly deteriorating over time, the library itself will remain a stable, reliable environment for their information needs. Another sacred ability of the library is to provide information and a connection to the past. By working to slow down the processes of deterioration and decay of library materials, preservation practices help keep this link to the past alive.

Regional Centers

- The Conservation Center for Art and Historic Artifacts in Philadelphia, PA. CCAHA is a non-profit conservation laboratory specializing in the treatment of art and historic artifacts on paper. The Center also trains museum and library professionals in disaster planning, records and archives management.

- The Northeast Document Conservation Center in Andover, MA. Since its inception in 1973, the Center has instructed institutions and organizations, as well as librarians, conservators, preservationists and museum professionals in preservation care and procedures. From 1995 to 2007, NEDCC presented its School for Scanning conference eleven times in cities across the United States. The school takes a leading role for digital preservation.
- The Southeastern Library Network is a not-for-profit membership cooperative of libraries and other information organizations in the southeastern United States. Established in 1973, as the largest regional library network in the U.S., SOLINET provides a variety of preservation education programmes and workshops.

Format of Writing Bibliography: APA Standard and MLA Standard

Background

APA style, or APA format are the terms commonly used to describe the writing style guidelines which are developed, maintained, and periodically revised and updated by the American Psychological Association (APA).

The American Psychological Association came into being in its current form through the 1945 amalgamation of a number of different psychological societies and organizations which existed in the U.S.A. at that time, at both the national and state levels. The APA currently has almost 160,000 members and is the largest association of psychologists in the world.

Over the years, the APA has developed a standard for writing style that is now widely used by writers in the social sciences, education, business and psychology. Accordingly, the APA documentation style is now used throughout the world, in both business and academia.

The APA's writing style is documented in its manual entitled:

Publication Manual of the American Psychological Association, Fifth Edition (2001).

The APA's *Publication Manual* covers all aspects of the writing and publishing process including: organizing, writing, formatting, keying, and submitting a manuscript for publication. It provides detailed guidance on editorial style as well as on the appropriate standards for publishing research in accordance with ethical principles of scientific publishing.

There is often considerable confusion when teachers, students, editors and researchers use the terms "APA style" or APA format". To clear up that confusion I am including three paragraphs below from the APA website.

"When editors or teachers ask you to write in "APA style," they do not mean writing style. They are referring to the editorial style that many of the social and behavioral sciences have adopted to present written material in the field. Editorial style consists of rules or guidelines that a publisher observes to ensure clear and consistent presentation of written material. Editorial style concerns uniform use of such elements as:

- punctuation and abbreviations
- construction of tables
- selection of headings
- citation of references
- presentation of statistics
- as well as many other elements that are a part of every manuscript

The American Psychological Association has established a style that it uses in all of the books and journals that it publishes. Many others working in the social and behavioral sciences have adopted this style as their standard as well.

Please note that when researchers talk about APA style, they may be referring to APA's system of citations in text and reference format.

If you are unsure, you should clarify with your instructor or editor how they define "APA style." APA's style rules and guidelines are set out in a reference book called "The Publication Manual of the American Psychological Association."

APA Rules

APA documentation style (in similar fashion to MLA style) calls for "in-text" citations of sources of information to be listed within the text where they are referenced, rather than in footnotes and endnotes, as some systems require.

To assist those who would rather not wade through APA's 439 page Publication Manual, I have broken down and summarized the APA Rules for the Preparation of Manuscripts into three distinct sections as follows:

1. Overall APA Paper Format Rules
2. APA Rules For In-Text Citation of Sources
3. Compiling and Formatting the APA Reference List

Each of the above sections contains a link to an actual sample pages of of the formats being discussed. You can access this APA Rules Page at:

Basic APA Rules-Paper Format, Citations, and Samples

APA Software

StyleEase for APA Style is powerful software that automatically formats your APA paper for you. From title page to bibliography, StyleEase does it all, right from the MS-Word toolbar. Handles simple papers to major dissertations with equal ease. *If your paper is due soon, StyleEase will save the day.*

References in APA-standard

Documentation of Sources: It is important to document sources of information used in theses, reports and other papers, for several reasons. Written academic work normally builds upon previously published research and we refer to others' theories, formulations, arguments and empirical data. Readers must be able to locate your original sources of information in order to judge or confirm your work independently. In addition, it is necessary to distinguish between what is your own and what originally comes from others. If you don't document your sources you may be accused of plagiarizing. It is thus important to acknowle dge other authors' contributions, both from an ethical and an academic perspective.

References, Citations and Quotes

Three important terms used in the documentation of information sources are: references, citations and quotes.

Reference – a bibliographic description of a document which is placed after the main text. A reference includes information about the author, title, year, and publisher. References are listed alphabetically in a bibliography, also called reference list. All document types, both printed and electronic, are in the same list. References to the same author are listed chronologically, with the oldest on top.

Citation (also called in-text citation) – information in the main text which identifies the source. All citations point to references in the bibliography, and all references in the bibliography correspond to citations in the main text. The information in citations is enclosed in parentheses. The author's name can be integrated into the main text and thereby excluded from the parentheses.

Quotations

A quotation (also called quote) is a direct, word-for-word, reproduction of a source. Never quote out of context.

Short Quote: When you quote a source, the citation should include the page number, for example:

"The library is the heart of the school for both students and staff" writes Nierenberg et al. (2009).

or

"The library is the heart of the school for both students and staff" (Nierenberg et al., 2009).

Long Quote (longer than 3 lines): Long quotes should be indented, with a smaller font, with white space above and below, and without quotation marks. For example:

Torras and Sætre (2008) write that:

When Parts of a Quote are Excluded: If you cut out part of a quote, fill in with 3 dots ... or 3 dots in parentheses (...), for example:

Nierenberg et al. maintain that "the library is the heart of the school for ... staff" (2009).

Translated Quotation: You can translate quotes from other languages. Follow the rules for quoting sources and write "own translation" at the end of the citation, for example:

According to Dag Østerberg (1996), "many of our actions involve changing the materials which surround us: building roads, houses, equipment, signs, weapons, etc." (p. 136, own translation).

Quotations with Italics: If *italics* are found in the original text, it should also be italicized in the quotation. If you want to italicize text which isn't originally in italics, write [italics added] just after the italicized text.

APA-style: There are many different styles for handling references. The main differences are with punctuation and the order of information in the reference. Common for all styles is that they have a consistent method for handling references, and that they include the documentation necessary to identify the source. Never mix reference styles – once you've chosen one style, you must use it consistently throughout the entire paper.

Hedmark University College recommends that students and staff use the **APA**-style (American Psychological Association). This is a so-called author/year-system, where all references are collected at the end of the document. Footnotes should only be used to supply additional information which isn't a part of the main text. The collection below provides examples of how citations and references to different sources should be formatted in the APA-style. Many of the examples used below are fictitious.

MLA System: Parenthetical Author-Page References (humanities)

This streamlined format gives author and page in parentheses within the text of the paper, then sets out full references in a Works Cited (or Works Consulted) list. Developed by the Modern Language Association, it is now widely accepted in the humanities. The 2003 edition of the *MLA Handbook for Writers of Research Papers* gives detailed advice and examples on such matters as spacing of notes and Works Cited entries. It contains very useful sections on citing non-print sources such as films, paintings, sound recordings, and Internet sources. It's available in all campus libraries and at U of T Bookstores. See also the MLA website for recommendations on details of referring to non-print sources. The University of California at Berkeley provides a handy summary of the MLA system. Or try the University of Auckland's interactive guide for constructing references in MLA style.

NOTE: In listing a Web page as a source, include the date you read the page as well as the URL. That information lets your reader judge whether he or she is seeing the same version of the Web page you looked at. See also our note on Electronic Sources.

Example: When Hamlet protests to his mother, "Leave wringing of your hands" (III.iv.35), he is naming a universally recognizable gesture. As Smith says, similar broad physical movements are "still the most direct way of indicating inner turmoil" (960). Zygmundi confirms their continuing usefulness in contemporary productions of other sixteenth-century plays. Renaissance audiences would have recognized hand-wringing as a signal for inner distress (Brown, *Renaissance Stage* 111), specifically for a condition that the Elizabethan author Reynolds named "ague of the spirits" (qtd. in Mahieu 69). Poor sight lines in Elizabethan theatres also required highly visible body movements (Smith 964). In her new book, Brown attempts to show that such gestures are related to stylized movements from religious ceremonies, among other influences (Brown, *Ritual* 90). She argues that acting methods responded to both the physical conditions of the theatres and the audience's cultural expectations (Brown, *Ritual* 14).

Annotated Bibliography

An annotated bibliography is a bibliography that gives a summary of the research that has been done. It is still an alphabetical list of research sources. In addition to bibliographic data, an annotated bibliography provides a brief summary or annotation. The purpose of annotations is to provide the reader with a summary and an evaluation of the source. In order to write a successful annotation, each summary must be concise. An annotation should display the source's central idea(s) and give the reader a general idea of what the source is about. An annotation should include the complete bibliographic information for the source. It should also include some or all of the following:

- An explanation about the authority and/or qualifications of the author.
- Scope or main purpose of the work.
- Any detectable bias.
- Intended audience and level of reading
- A summary comment

An annotation should be between 100 to 200 words, ideally.

Indicative Annotations

This type of annotation defines the scope of the source, lists the significant topics and explains what the source is about. In this type of entry, there is no attempt to give actual data such as hypotheses, proofs, etc.

Informative Annotations

This type of annotation is a summary of the source. An informative annotation should include the thesis of the work, arguments or hypotheses, proofs and a conclusion.

Evaluative Annotations

This type of annotation assesses the source's strengths and weaknesses—how the source is useful and how it is not. Simply put, an evaluative annotation should evaluate the source's usefulness.

Combination Annotations

Most annotated bibliographies contain combination annotations. This type of annotation will summarize or describe the topic, and then evaluate the source's usefulness.

Writing Styles

No matter which writing style is used for annotations, all entries should be brief. Only the most significant details should be mentioned. Information that is apparent in the title can be omitted from the annotation. In addition, background materials and any references to previous work are usually excluded.

Telegraphic

A telegraphic writing style gets the information out quickly and concisely. Maintaining clarity, complete and grammatically correct sentences are not necessary.

Complete Sentences

A **complete** sentences writing style utilizes coherent sentences that are grammatically correct. Subjects and conjunctions are not eliminated even though the tone may be terse. Long and complex sentences are to generally be avoided.

Paragraph

A paragraph writing style utilizes a full, coherent paragraph. This can sometimes be similar to the form of a bibliographic essay. Complete sentences and proper grammar must be used.

Purpose

There are three main purposes behind writing an annotated bibliography. Each purpose can serve anyone in a different manner, depending on what they are trying to accomplish.

Learning about a Topic

Writing an annotated bibliography is an excellent way to begin any research project. While it may seem easier to simply copy down bibliographical information, adding annotations will force the researcher to read each source carefully. An annotation requires the source to be critically analyzed, not simply read over.

Formulating a Thesis

Any form of research paper or essay will require some form of argument. This is called a thesis. A developed thesis needs to be debatable, interesting and current. Writing an annotated bibliography will give the researcher a clear understanding about what is being said about their topic. After reading and critically analyzing sources, the researcher will be able to determine what issues there are and what people are arguing about. From there, the researcher will be able to develop their own point of view.

To assist Other Researchers

Extensive and scholarly annotated bibliographies are sometimes published. The purpose of these annotated bibliographies is to provide a complete and comprehensive overview of any given topic. While any normal researcher may not get their own annotated bibliography published, it could be a good idea to search for previously published annotated bibliographies that are related to their topic.

Writing a Review Article

The major pulmonary and critical care journals publish morethan 5,000 articles every year. To read these would requiremore than 25 hours each week. Despite the surfeit of information,the average physician is starving for wisdom. The aim of scholarshipis to increase understanding, not just accumulate discrete facts.A stack of papers no more conveys wisdom than a pile of bricksmakes a house.

If new research is to improve patient care, reports need tobe fitted into the mosaic of existing knowledge. General medicaljournals, such as the *New England* or *Annals*, publish a muchhigher proportion of review articles than do subspecialty journals.But the audience for a subspecialty journal is different froma general medical journal. The first rule of writing is to identifyyour audience. Review articles that appeal to general physiciansare unlikely to satisfy subspecialists, who are expected tohave a more detailed and nuanced understanding of subjects intheir field.

The first step in writing a review article is selecting a suitablesubject. Authors of a review article in *AJRCCM* may pick a broadfield suited to a comprehensive overview in a

State-of-the-Art(1–14), encapsulate a surge of rapid progress in a PulmonaryPerspective (15–30), turn a searchlight on an overlookedsubject in a Critical Care Perspective (31–40), captureadvances in related fields in an Update in Nonpulmonary CriticalCare (41–53), convey practice pearls in a Clinical Commentary(54–63), share the secrets of scientific discovery ina How it *Really* Happened (64–78), or comment on a socialconundrum in an Occasional Essay (79–83). By definition,a review article does not include original data. Yet, the perspectiveshould be fresh and the synthesis unique. Authors must avoida rehash of views expressed in existing reviews.

When writing a state-of-the-art review, the author needs toamass and synthesize a huge number of original reports. Theskill is akin to that of a landscape artist. When ranging overa great sweep of scenery, the naked eye takes in millions ofshapes, shades, and textures. The painter reduces this complexityto a few hundred brush strokes through ruthless selection, intensifyingsome contours, ignoring others, and reordering and harmonizingthe relationships between elements. Great compositional skillis needed to place the elements in a coherent space, avoidingdiscontinuities and depth-of-field distortions, and constructa unified and expansive canvas that achieves realistic verisimilitude.

Likewise, the author of a comprehensive review article standsback to form a panoramic view of a broad field. He or she siftsthrough a mass of miscellaneous detail, selecting the most relevant,and omitting trifling reports and ephemeral fads. The valueof the article depends as much on the dross and minutiae omittedas on the pearls included. The author does not cover every reportin a field, because all are not of equal quality. In contrastto the deluge of references generated by a PubMed search, thegood review article serves as a quality filter, directing thereader to the most influential journal and book literature.An author's selection of primary and secondary literature alsoconveys the legitimacy of his or her framework.

One of the most difficult tasks in writing a review articleis finding the best structure because manuscripts do not followthe fixed formula (introduction, methods, results, discussion)of research reports. The structure should facilitate sequentialunfolding of ideas in a logical order. To avoid getting lostmid journey, readers need to know where an author is comingfrom and where he or she is going. The best structure may notbecome obvious until several drafts have been written; indeed,the failure to change the structure during the course of writingis a warning that it is likely wrong.

Taking the mass of raw reports, the author classifies, interpretsand integrates the material, shaping it into a compact productthat is more manageable for the reader. The author moves backand forth between the universal and the particular, alternatingbetween use of a telescope and a microscope. He or she selectsstudies that are especially insightful, and locates them inthe overall pattern. A major challenge is compression: how totake a tangled mass of facts, eliminate those that do not enhanceunderstanding, and weave the remaining threads into a seamlessfabric. The good review article is not a compendium of sequentialstudies in the manner of "Smith found this and Jones found that."Instead, the author integrates broad conceptual ideas into anarrative, and the primary investigators disappear into theprose.

Another challenge is how to write sentences that form a linearsequence, one connected to the next by a logical extension ofthought. Sustaining reader interest over the course of a longreview requires the skill of a storyteller. A good narrativepulls readers along without them noticing the tug.

Some journals classify narrative review articles as less reliableand of lower intellectual caliber than "systematic reviews"(84). The compulsive tracking down of every trial on a topicis imperative when writing a review article on the basis ofa metaanalysis of randomized clinical trials; it is also importantto tabulate numbers, inclusion and exclusion criteria, and othersuch detail of the trials. A scrupulous search system mightbe expected to limit bias, although vigilant peer review willafford greater reassurance against this flaw (85–88).The uniformity of the approach to writing such review articlesenables a formulaic presentation. But the compulsive retrievalof every original paper is only one essential when writing areview article (and the least challenging). A punctilious listingof every detail produces prose that is prolix. It may also detractrather than enhance understanding, which is based on being ableto see a forest among the trees. A catalog approach is ill suitedto communicating a deeper understanding of biological principlesgarnered from the commingling of molecular research in animalswith bedside studies of pathophysiologic mechanisms in patients.A catalog approach is inappropriate for subjects reviewed in*Nature Medicine, PNAS*, *JCI*—and most subjects reviewedin *AJRCCM*.

That a review article does not carry the epithet"systematic" is not to say it was written in a desultory mannerand the presentation chaotic. The skills in writing a narrativereview are more intellectual than mechanical. Teams of "systematicreviewers" of questionable provenance are no substitute forwisdom derived from years of marinating in a subject and reflectingon its complexities. The worth of the final product dependson the author's conceptual sophistication, power of apprehension,cogency of analysis, sense of proportion, skill in condensation,explanatory force, and felicity of exposition—qualitiesnot emphasized in "quantitative systematic reviews" (89–91).

A reader's best guide that a review article will be worth readingis a foreknowledge of the journal's peer-review standards (92).At *AJRCCM*, peer review starts when the author submits a letterof intent and an outline of a planned article. (Details of informationto include in a proposal are provided in our *Instructions forContributors*.) Proposals are reviewed anonymously by six ormore experts. Many proposals are declined, and authors gettinga green light are also given concrete recommendations for improvingthe planned manuscript. Completed manuscripts undergo rigorouspeer review and only the fraction satisfying the highest standardsis published. The criteria differ from those used for originalresearch reports. Referees of research reports focus on noveltyof a hypothesis, rigor of experimental design, soundness ofthe methodology, approach to data analysis, and plausibilityof the findings. With a review article, referees evaluate theimportance and relevancy of the subject, comprehensiveness ofthe author's coverage, emphasis given to individual studies,legitimacy of the analyses, new insights and ideas being offered,ability to synthesize and integrate disparate observations,and the cogency and lucidity of the prose.

Scientific journals rightly set great store on original research.But much research consists of mopping up operations (93), andthe amount of truly new information is less than we think. GeorgeStigler (94), the 1982 Nobel Laureate in Economics, pointedout that "originality is a more complicated virtue than mostdiscussion seems to recognize, and that its role in progressis not easy to state or assess." He continues that, "originalitymay also impair progress. Originality means difference, notimprovement, and one may invent new errors as well as new truths."Moreover, new truths do not emerge fully formed. Accordingly,review articles help advance science. Progress in science dependson a certain aging process, whereby earlier findings are reanalyzed,previously undetected ambiguities are identified, residues oftruth are extracted before a disproved theory is discarded,concepts are refined, and the range of applicability of newideas is identified. *AJRCCM* contributes to a bountiful harvestof research reports. We hope that our review series also speedup scientific fermentation.

Review Paper

The purpose of a review paper is to succinctly review recent progress in a particular topic. Overall, the paper summarizes the current state of knowledge of the topic. It creates an understanding of the topic for the reader by discussing the findings presented in recent research papers.

A review paper is not a "term paper" or book report. It is not merely a report on some references you found. Instead, a review paper synthesizes the results from several primary literature papers to produce a coherent argument about a topic or focused description of a field.

Examples of scientific reviews can be found in:

- Scientific American

- Science in the "Perspectives" and "Reviews" sections
- Nature in the "News and Views" section
- Compilations of reviews such as:

  Current Opinion in Cell Biology

  Current Opinion in Genetics & Development

  Annual Review of Plant Physiology and Plant Molecular Biology

  Annual Review of Physiology

  Trends in Ecology & Evolution
- Almost every scientific journal has special review articles.

You should read articles from one or more of these sources to get examples of how your paper should be organized.

Scientists commonly use reviews to communicate with each other and the general public. There are a wide variety of review styles from ones aimed at a general audience (e.g., *Scientific American*) to those directed at biologists within a particular subdiscipline (e.g., *Annual Review of Physiology*).

A key aspect of a review paper is that it provides the evidence for a particular point of view in a field. Thus, a large focus of your paper should be a description of the data that support or refute that point of view. In addition, you should inform the reader of the experimental techniques that were used to generate the data.

The emphasis of a review paper is interpreting the primary literature on the subject. You need to read several original research articles on the same topic and make your own conclusions about the meanings of those papers.

How to Write the Paper?

Overview of the Paper: Your paper should consist of four general sections:

- Introduction
- The body of the paper
- Conclusion and future directions
- Literature cited

Review articles contain neither a materials and methods section nor an abstract.

Organizing the Paper: Use topic headings. Do not use a topic heading that reads, "Body of the paper." Instead the topic headings should refer to the actual concepts or ideas covered in that section.

Book Review

A book review (or book report) is a form of literary criticism in which a book is analyzed based on content, style, and merit. It is often carried out in periodicals, as school work, or online. Its length may vary from a single paragraph to a substantial essay. Such a review often contains evaluations of the book on the basis of personal taste. Reviewers, in literary periodicals, often use the occasion of a book review for a display of learning or to promulgate their own ideas on the topic of a fiction or non-fiction work. At the other end of the spectrum, some book reviews resemble simple plot summaries.

General

The book review is assigned to develop analytical skills. First, the reviewer has to depict the content, regardless of the type of novel, a historical or critical book. In the subsequent narration the goal of the book reviewer is to discuss the content of the book and provide analysis of what he/she had read, and deduce if the author managed to reveal the core, whether he/she kept to the thesis or properly achieved the purpose of the book. The last thing the reviewer has to do is to speculate on the topic him/herself. The book reviewer should also undertake through their own research to discuss the theme, assess the authors ability to express and explore this theme, and provide an opinion of the novel.

The determination of the book review is to communicate to the readers mind the ideas and sensations book reviewer experienced while researching the content, in this way explaining the reader what exact meaning the author presumed to transmit, or what did the reviewer experienced while during the reading. The book reviewer, then, stands as reporter, who informs the third party of the events, as an analyst, who makes judgments basing them on own experience, and as the observer from the side, who pretends to act as the reader him/herself should do by expressing own opinion, desires and expectations.

Making book review implies some special skills, as well as obliges with some precise responsibilities. Professional reviewer has not just to read and scrutinize the text, but to realize concealed, implied meaning the author obviously had dropped hints about. Skilled book reviewers' explanations make the reader feel this "that is just what I thought" sensation. The reviewer must also state the main points of the reviewed book. While some aspects are less meaningful, others are have to be marked out as prerogative issues. The task is even more complicated as the writer could unintentionally imply the idea the reviewer of the book can notice.

Then, the book reviewer has to decide upon authors points validity. The reviewer has to be the judge and say "did the writer persuade the audience, or were his/her evidences not sufficient and weak." The reviewer here makes judgment on the adequacy of the book topic to the content.

The book review is also the expertise of the contents authenticity. By comparing the reviewed book to other materials in the given category the reviewer work implies potential danger for those writers, who admit plagiarism. If the reviewer finds the book authentic and, perhaps, unique, the points and attitudes of the reviewer are discussed.

Textbooks

In reviewing a textbook, the reviewer has a different set of considerations. Unlike the language in a monograph, that in a textbook must be no technical and jargon must be avoided. The reader will be a student, not a peer of the scientist who wrote the book. Technical terms will be used, of course, but each should be carefully defined at first use. The function of the book reviewer is to determine whether the subject of the text is treated clearly, in a way that is likely to enable students to grasp and to appreciate the knowledge presented. The textbook reviewer has one additional responsibility. If other texts on the same subject exist, which is usually the case; the reviewer should provide appropriate comparisons.

Imprint Information

At the top of a book review, the reviewer should list complete imprint information. The usual order is as follows: title of the book, edition (if other than the first), name of author(s) or editor(s), publisher, place (city in which the publisher is located), year of publication, number of pages, and list price of the book. Conventionally, well-known cities are not followed by state or country names. A publisher located in New York is listed "New York" not "New York, NY" and London is listed as "London" not "London, U.K."

Professional Book Review

Books, as well as professional book reviews are important in all professions, but they are especially important in the sciences, which defines the specialization of the book reviewer. That is because the basic unit of scientific communication, the primary research paper, is short (typically five to eight printed pages in most fields) and narrowly specific. Therefore, to provide a general overview of a significant slice of science, professional writers of scientific books organize and synthesize the reported knowledge in a field into a much larger, more meaningful package. In other words, new scientific knowledge is made meaningful by sorting and sifting the bits and pieces into book reviews to provide a larger picture. Thus, the individual plants and flowers, and even the weeds, become a landscape.

Scientific, technical, and medical books are of many types, let alone reviews and overviews. In broad categories, they can be considered as monographs, reference books, textbooks, and trade books. Because there are significant differences among these four types, a professional book reviewer should understand the distinctions.

How to Find Reviews of a Given Book?

Some book reviews are available on the Internet, but not most and perhaps not the most important. There are many special journals devoted to book reviews and they are indexed in special databases such as *Book review Index*, but many more book reviews can be found in newspaper databases and in scholarly databases such as *Arts and Humanities Citation Index*, *Social Sciences Citation Index* and discipline specific databases. Ask the librarian about how to identify reviews of the books which reception you would like to study. Among the reviews of a given book there may be one that changes your view of that book.

Problems with Book Reviews

Principally book reviews are good sources for evaluating the quality of books. Sometimes, however, book reviews have been considered problematic. Katz (1985-1986) found that there are too few critical book reviews. This is also documentated by Novick (1988) in the field of history. Typically are book reviews in scholarly journals of a much higher quality than book reviews in newspapers.

Preparing Abstract and Indexes for Teacher Education Journals

While abstracts are not required in grades K-4 they are encouraged. They are strongly recommended for 5th Grade to 8th grade students, as abstracts are required for those nominated for the Discovery Channel Young Scientist Challenge (DCYSC). Selections for this nomination are based upon a well written abstract in addition to the science they have done.

An abstract is a brief (250 words or less), written discussion/ summary of your Science Project. It includes:

- The Project Title,
- The purpose of your project/ experiment: An introductory statement explaining the reason for the research, or a statement of the problem, hypothesis or question
- A summary/description of the procedures, emphasizing the key points or steps
- The results and observations made
- Conclusions of your investigation, and it may also include any possible research applications or goals.

- If there is space, you may also include where this will take you next.

Abstracts are helpful to the judges to understand more about the student's ability to write succinctly and show the degree of understanding of the project. Abstracts should never exceed 250 words. For the students in grades 5, 6, 7 and 8, the abstract will play considerably more importance than in the K-4 grades. It is a good learning tool and should be encouraged at all grade levels, even Kindergarten, but in the lower grades its absence will not downgrade a project. Its presence, however, could be the tie breaker. Abstracts are a good learning device at even the Kindergarten level. A Kindergarten abstract may only have 20 words, but he/she is learning how to tell their science story. As the student progresses in grade level, that ability to communicate with the written word becomes more and more important. Abstracts should be edited for correct spelling and grammar. Even the best writers and scientists have their work edited. A mentor, parent or teacher should review and help by editing your abstract AFTER you have written it.

DO NOT send abstracts to SARSEF. Bring your abstracts with you to set up for SARSEF at the Tucson Convention Center. They may be placed either on the table in front of the project or affixed to the display board (recommended).

The Sample High School Abstract below is Copied from the Science Service Link

The colour coding below in the Sample abstract indicates Purpose of the Experiment, Procedures Used, Observation/ Data/Results, and Conclusions as explained below:

Purpose of the Experiment

- An introductory statement of the reason for investigating the topic of the project.
- A statement of the problem or hypothesis being studied

Procedures Used

- A summarization of the key points and an overview of how the investigation was conducted.

- An abstract does not give details about the materials used unless it greatly influenced the procedure or had to be developed to do the investigation.
- An abstract should only include procedures done by the student. Work done by a mentor (such as surgical procedures) or work done prior to student involvement must not be included.

Observation/Data/Results

- This section should provide key results that lead directly to the conclusions you have drawn.
- It should not give too many details about the results nor include tables or graphs.

Conclusions

- Conclusions from the investigation should be described briefly.
- The summary paragraph should reflect on the process and possibly state some applications and extensions of the investigation.

Sample Abstract

Effects of Marine Engine Exhaust Water on Algae: This project in its present form is the result of bioassay experimentation on the effects of two-cycle marine engine exhaust water on certain green algae. The initial idea was to determine the toxicity of outboard engine lubricant. Some success with lubricants eventually led to the formulation of "synthetic" exhaust water which, in turn, led to the use of actual two-cycle engine exhaust water as the test substance.

Toxicity was determined by means of the standard bottle or "batch" bioassay technique. Scenedesmus quadricauda and Ankistrodesmus sp. were used as the test organisms. Toxicity was measured in terms of a decrease in the maximum standing crop. The effective concentration-50% (EC 50) for Scenedesmus quadricauda was found to be 3.75% exhaust water; for Ankistrodesmus sp. 3.1% exhaust water using the bottle technique.

Anomalies in growth curves raised the suspicion that evaporation was affecting the results; therefore, a flow-through system was improvised utilizing the characteristics of a device called a Biomonitor. Use of the Biomonitor lessened the influence of evaporation, and the EC 50 was found to be 1.4% exhaust water using Ankistrodesmus sp. as the test organism. Mixed populations of various algae gave an EC 50 of 1.28% exhaust water. The contributions of this project are twofold. First, the toxicity of two-cycle marine engine exhaust was found to be considerably greater than reported in the literature (1.4% vs. 4.2%). Secondly, the benefits of a flow-through bioassay technique utilizing the Biomonitor was demonstrated.

Index (Database)

A database index is a data structure that improves the speed of operations on a database table. Indexes can be created using one or more columns of a database table, providing the basis for both rapid random look ups and efficient access of ordered records. The disk space required to store the index is typically less than that required by the table (since indexes usually contain only the key-fields according to which the table is to be arranged, and excludes all the other details in the table), yielding the possibility to store indexes in memory for a table whose data is too large to store in memory.

In a relational database an index is a copy of part of a table. Some databases extend the power of indexing by allowing indexes to be created on functions or expressions. For example, an index could be created on upper(last_name), which would only store the upper case versions of the last name field in the index. Another option sometimes supported is the use of "filtered" indexes, where index entries are created only for those records that satisfy some conditional expression. A further aspect of flexibility is to permit indexing on user-defined functions, as well as expressions formed from an assortment of built-in functions.

Indexes may be defined as unique or non-unique. A unique index acts as a constraint on the table by preventing duplicate entries in the index and thus, the backing table.

Index Architecture

Index architectures can be classified as clustered or non-clustered.

Unclustered

An Unclustered index is structured in a way that doesn't correspond to the order of the actual data records. It resembles the words index at the back of a book. For this reason, it will perform worse than clustered indexes on ranged searches where the result set is large, since each result could cost an additional I/O-operation to get the actual data record. One can have any number of these kinds of indexes, since all that is required is the space to store the index itself—one does not copy the actual data to create a new index.

Clustered

Clustering re-orders the data block in the same order as the index, hence it is also an operation on the data storage blocks as well as on the index. A phone book ordered by last name resembles a clustered index in its structure and purpose. Exact operation of database systems vary, but because storing the row data more than once is never done in practice (since it is usually too expensive), the row data can only be stored in one order physically. Therefore, only one clustered index can be created on a given database table. Clustered indexes can greatly increase access speed, but usually only where the data is accessed sequentially in the same or reverse order of the clustered index, or when a range of items are selected.

Since the physical records are in this sort order on disk the next row item in the sequence is immediately before or after the last one, and so fewer data block reads are required. The primary feature of a clustered index is therefore the ordering of the physical data rows in accordance with the index blocks that point to them. Some databases separate the data and index blocks into separate files, while others intermix the two different types of data blocks within the same physical file(s). Databases that use the latter scheme may be said to store the actual data in the leaf node of the index, whereas, in fact there is still a distinction between the index and the data block, and the data blocks can be traversed without using the index by way of a link list that links the data blocks in order.

Index Implementations

Indexes can be implemented using a variety of data structures. Popular indexes include balanced trees, B+ trees and hashes.

In Microsoft SQL Server, the leaf node of the clustered index corresponds to the actual data, not simply a pointer to data that resides elsewhere, as is the case with a non-clustered index. Each relation can have a single clustered index and many unclustered indexes.

Column Order

The order in which columns are listed in the index definition is important. It is possible to retrieve a set of row identifiers using only the first indexed column. However, it is not possible or efficient (on most databases) to retrieve the set of row identifiers using only the second or greater indexed column.

For example, imagine a phone book that is organized by city first, then by last name, and then by first name. If you are given the city, you can easily extract the list of all phone numbers for that city. However, in this phone book it would be very tedious to find all the phone numbers for a given last name. You would have to look within each city's section for the entries with that last name. Some databases can do this, others just won't use the index.

Applications and Limitations

Indexes are useful for many applications but come with some limitations. Consider the following SQL statement: SELECT first_name FROM people WHERE last_name = 'Smith';. To process this statement without an index the database software must look at the last_name column on every row in the table (this is known as a full table scan). With an index the database simply follows the b-tree data structure until the Smith entry has been found; this is much less computationally expensive than a full table scan.

Consider this SQL statement: SELECT email_address FROM customers WHERE email_address LIKE '%@yahoo.com';. This query would yield an email address for every customer whose email address ends with "@yahoo.com", but even if the email_address column has been indexed the database still must perform a full table scan. This is because the index is built with the assumption that words go from left to right. With a wildcard at the beginning of the search-term the database software is unable to use the underlying b-tree data structure. This problem can be solved through the addition of another index created on reverse (email_address) and a SQL query like this: SELECT email_address FROM customers WHERE reverse (email_address) LIKE reverse('%@yahoo.com');. This puts the wild-card at the right-most part of the query (now moc.oohay@%) which the index on reverse(email_address) can satisfy.

Types

Bitmap Index: A bitmap index is a special kind of index that stores the bulk of its data as bit arrays (bitmaps) and answers most queries by performing bitwise logical operations on these bitmaps. The most commonly used index, such as B+trees, are most efficient if the values it indexes do not repeat or repeat a relatively smaller number of times. In contrast, the bitmap index is designed for cases where the values of a variable repeat very frequently. For example, the gender field in a customer database usually contains two distinct values: male or female. For such variables, the bitmap index can have a significant performance advantage over the commonly used trees.

Dense Index: A dense index in databases is a file with pairs of keys and pointers for every record in the data file. Every key in this file is associated with a particular pointer to *a record* in the sorted data file. In clustered indices with duplicate keys the dense index points *to the first record* with that key.

Sparse Index: A sparse index in databases is a file with pairs of keys and pointers for every block in the data file. Every key in this file is associated with a particular pointer *to the* *block* in the sorted data file. In clustered indexes with duplicate keys the sparse index points *to the lowest search key* in each block.

Covering Index: In most cases an index is used to quickly locate the data record(s) from which the required data is read. In other words, the index is only used to locate data records in the table and not to return data.

A covering index is a special case where the index itself contains the required data field(s) and can return the data.

Consider the following table (other fields omitted):

ID	Name	Other Fields
12	Plug	...
13	Lamp	...
14	Fuse	...

To find the Name for ID 13 an index on (ID) will be useful, but the record must still be read to get the Name. However, an index on (ID, Name) contains the required data field and eliminates the need to look up the record.

A covering index can dramatically speed up data retrieval but may itself be relatively large due to the additional keys, which slows down data insertion & update. To reduce such index size some systems allow non key fields to be included in the index. Non key fields are not themselves part of the index ordering but only included at the leaf level, allowing for a covering index with less overall index size.

UNIT-IV

LIBRARY NETWORK

Library Automation

This Library has the distinction of being the first University Library in India to have fully automated all its house keeping operations.

- The Library has started its automation activity in the year 1989, by procuring a PC-AT Intel 80286 with 4mb RAM, 80mb Hard disk, MS-DOS operating system.
- Initially some programmes were developed in dbase III+. In this process, the data for the new books became available in machine readable form. The database was created for searching by author, title, subject and call number. Simultaneously catalogue cards were printed on the continuous card stationery and monthly list of additions to the library was also generated using dot matrix printer.

Integrated Library Operations with Libsys

- During the year 1990, an integrated library application software (LIBSYS) was procured using XENIX as operating system. All the new book records available in machine readable form under dbase III+ were converted into the LIBSYS software package. XENIX is a multi-user operating system on which LIBSYS: an integrated library application software provided facilities for acquisition, cataloguing, circulation and serial control and OPAC (online public access catalogue) to provide quick search of books to the users.

- During the year 1991, the hard-disk was upgraded from 80MB to 200MB and again upgraded in 1993 its systems by acquiring a new PC 80486 system with 3 VT-220 terminals and UNIX operating system.
- During the year 1994, with the special grant from the UGC under modernization of library facilities, the library acquired a mini computer system DEC Alpha 2000 model with 6 GB hard disk, 16 numbers of 80386 PCs, 4 multimedia printers, 7 drive CD-ROM network server. Library has started using Bar-code technology at the circulation desk for issue and return transactions.
- By February 1995, the library could convert all the book records i.e. 2, 35,000 volumes of data base by entering the data from the shelf list catalogue cards and was made available for campus wide access across the Local Area Network (LAN) for the benefit of users in various Schools/Departments.

Automation and Digital Library with Vtls Software and Sun Microsystems

- During 2001, the Library switched over to VTLS software package for Library Automation and Digital Library. A Cyber Storage System (DF-1000) with facility for 400 GB hard disk storage to capture digital data from the CD/DVDs was made available for network access.

Online Public Access Catalog (OPAC)

- Library has replaced its card catalogue with Online Public Access Catalogue (OPAC) terminals for users in the central lobby of the Library and 4 + 3 terminals near the stack/ reading areas. The Library database consists of all the books, back volumes of periodicals, current journals and theses & dissertations.
- Users can search the database by author, title, classification number, subject, Journal title, Accession Number to know whether a book/document is there in the Library or not, its status with reservation facility if the book is issued out. Users can also access the new

books list from OPAC. Multimedia links are provided to enable users access digitized text of Thesis and few books and web pages of Journals to access Table of Contents, Abstracts and also the Full text. Library initiated linking the scanned pages of Table of Contents to Language Journals and few Indian Journals, where publishers are not providing such links.

Digital Library

A digital library is a library in which collections are stored in digital formats (as opposed to print, microform, or other media) and accessible by computers. The digital content may be stored locally, or accessed remotely via computer networks. A digital library is a type of information retrieval system.

The *DELOS Digital Library Reference Model* defines a digital library as:

> *An organization, which might be virtual, that comprehensively collects, manages and preserves for the long term rich digital content, and offers to its user communities specialized functionality on that content, of measurable quality and according to codified policies.*

The first use of the term *digital library* in print may have been in a 1988 report to the Corporation for National Research Initiatives The term *digital libraries* was first popularized by the NSF/DARPA/NASA Digital Libraries Initiative in 1994. The older names electronic library or virtual library are also occasionally used, though *electronic library* nowadays more often refers to portals, often provided by government agencies.

Types of Digital Libraries

The term *digital library* is diffuse enough to be applied to a wide range of collections and organizations, but, to be considered a digital library, an online collection of information must be managed by and made accessible to a community of users. Thus, some web sites can be considered digital libraries, but far from all. Many of the best known digital libraries are older than the web including Project Perseus, Project Gutenberg, and ibiblio. Nevertheless, as a result of the development of the internet and its search potential, digital libraries such as the European Library and the Library of Congress are now developing in a Web-based environment. Public, school and college libraries are also able to develop digital download websites, featuring eBooks, audiobooks, music and video.

A distinction is often made between content that was created in a digital format, known as born-digital, and information that has been converted from a physical medium, e.g., paper, by digitizing. The term hybrid library is sometimes used for libraries that have both physical collections and digital collections. For example, American Memory is a digital library within the Library of Congress. Some important digital libraries also serve as long term archives, for example, the ePrint arXiv, and the Internet Archive.

Academic Repositories

Many academic libraries are actively involved in building institutional repositories of the institution's books, papers, theses, and other works which can be digitized or were 'born digital'. Many of these repositories are made available to the general public with few restrictions, in accordance with the goals of open access, in contrast to the publication of research in commercial journals, where the publishers often limit access rights. Institutional, truly free, and corporate repositories are sometimes referred to as digital libraries.

Digital Archives

Archives differ from libraries in several ways. Traditionally, archives were defined as:

1. Containing primary sources of information (typically letters and papers directly produced by an individual or organization) rather than the secondary sources found in a library (books, etc);
2. Having their contents organized in groups rather than individual items;
3. Having unique contents.

The technology used to create digital libraries has been even more revolutionary for archives since it breaks down the second and third of these general rules. The Oxford Text Archive is generally considered to be the oldest digital archive of academic physical primary source materials.

Digital Preservation

Project Gutenberg, Google Book Search, Windows Live Search Books(shutdown), Internet Archive, Cornell University, The Library of Congress World Digital Library, The Digital Library at the University of Michigan, and Carnegie Mellon University's Million Book Project are considered leaders in the field of digital library creation and management.

The Future

Large scale digitization projects are underway at Google, the Million Book Project, MSN, and Yahoo!. With continued improvements in book handling and presentation technologies such as optical character recognition and ebooks, and development of alternative depositories and business models, digital libraries are rapidly growing in popularity as demonstrated by Google, Yahoo!, and MSN's efforts. Just as libraries have ventured into audio and video collections, so have digital libraries such as the Internet Archive.

Searching

Most digital libraries provide a search interface which allows resources to be found. These resources are typically deep web (or invisible web) resources since they frequently cannot be located by search engine crawlers. Some digital libraries create special pages or sitemaps to allow search engines to find all their resources. Digital libraries frequently use the Open Archives Initiative Protocol for Metadata Harvesting (OAI-PMH) to expose their metadata to other digital libraries, and search engines like Google Scholar, Google, Yahoo! and Scirus can also use OAI-PMH to find these deep web resources.

There are two general strategies for searching a federation of digital libraries:

1. distributed searching, and
2. searching previously harvested metadata.

Distributed searching typically involves a client sending multiple search requests in parallel to a number of servers in the federation. The results are gathered, duplicates are eliminated or clustered, and the remaining items are sorted and presented back to the client. Protocols like Z39.50 are frequently used in distributed searching. A benefit to this approach is that the resource-intensive tasks of indexing and storage are left to the respective servers in the federation. A drawback to this approach is that the search mechanism is limited by the different indexing and ranking capabilities of each database, making it difficult to assemble a combined result consisting of the most relevant found items.

Searching over previously harvested metadata involves searching a locally stored index of information that has previously been collected from the libraries in the federation. When a search is performed, the search mechanism does not need to make connections with the digital libraries it is searching-it already has a local representation of the information.

This approach requires the creation of an indexing and harvesting mechanism which operates regularly, connecting to all the digital libraries and querying the whole collection in order to discover new and updated resources. OAI-PMH is frequently used by digital libraries for allowing metadata to be harvested. A benefit to this approach is that the search mechanism has full control over indexing and ranking algorithms, possibly allowing more consistent results. A drawback is that harvesting and indexing systems are more resource-intensive and therefore expensive.

Construction and Organization

Frameworks: A digital library can be built around specific repository software. The best known examples of this are DSpace, Èprints, Fedora, dLibra(Poland), and Greenstone Digital Library Software.

The Reference Model for an Open Archival Information System (OAIS) provides a framework to address Digital preservation.

Other formal frameworks include the DELOS Reference Model(Agosti, et al., 2006) and the Streams, Structures, Spaces, Scenarios, Societies (5S) formal framework (Gonçalves, Fox, Watson, & Kipp, 2004)

Digitization: In the past few years, procedures for digitizing books at high speed and comparatively low cost have improved considerably with the result that it is now possible to plan the digitization of millions of books per year for creating digital libraries.

Advantages: The advantages of digital libraries as a means of easily and rapidly accessing books, archives and images of various types are now widely recognized by commercial interests and public bodies alike. Traditional libraries are limited by storage space; digital libraries have the potential to store much more information, simply because digital information requires very little physical space to contain it. As such, the cost of maintaining a digital library is much lower than that of a traditional library. A traditional library must spend large sums of money paying for staff, book maintenance, rent, and additional books. Digital libraries do away with these fees. Both types of library require cataloguing input to allow users to locate and retrieve material. Digital libraries may be more willing to adopt innovations in technology providing users with improvements in electronic and audio book technology as well as presenting new forms of communication such as wikis and blogs; conventional libraries may consider that providing online access to their OPAC catalogue is sufficient. An important advantage to digital conversion is increased accessibility to users. There in also availability to individuals who may not be traditional patrons of a library, due to geographic location or organizational affiliation.

- *No Physical Boundary:* The user of a digital library need not to go to the library physically; people from all over the world can gain access to the same information, as long as an Internet connection is available.
- *Round the Clock Availability:* A major advantage of digital libraries is that people can gain access to the information at any time, night or day.

- *Multiple Access:* The same resources can be used simultaneously by a number of institutions and patrons. This may not be the case for copyrighted material: a library may have a license for "lending out" only one copy at a time; this is achieved with a system of digital rights management where a resource can become inaccessible after expiration of the lending period or after the lender chooses to make it inaccessible (equivalent to returning the resource).
- *Information Retrieval:* The user is able to use any search term (word, phrase, title, name, subject) to search the entire collection. Digital libraries can provide very user-friendly interfaces, giving clickable access to its resources.
- *Preservation and Conservation:* Digitization is not a long-term preservation solution for physical collections, but does succeed in providing access copies for materials that would otherwise fall to degradation from repeated use. Digitized collections and born-digital objects pose many preservation and conservation concerns that analog materials do not. Please see the following "Problems" section of this page for examples.
- *Space:* Whereas traditional libraries are limited by storage space, digital libraries have the potential to store much more information, simply because digital information requires very little physical space to contain them and media storage technologies are more affordable than ever before.
- *Added Value:* Certain characteristics of objects, primarily the quality of images, may be improved. Digitization can enhance legibility and remove visible flaws such as stains and discoloration.

Problems

Digital Preservation: The work needed to ensure that digital content is maintained and accessible into the future is beginning to be addressed: see digital preservation. Technological standards change over time and forward migration must be a constant consideration of every library. Migration is a means of transferring an unstable digital object to another more stable format, operating system, or programming language. Migration allows the ability to retrieve and display digital objects that are in danger of becoming extinct.

This is a rather successful short-term solution for the problem of aging and obsolete digital formats, but with the ever-changing nature of computer technologies, migration becomes this never-ending race to transfer digital objects to new and more stable formats. Migration is also flawed in the sense that when the digital files are being transferred, the new platform may not be able to capture the full integrity of the original object. There are countless artifacts sitting in libraries all over the world that are essentially useless because the technology required to access the source is obsolete. In addition to obsolescence, there are rising costs that result from continually replacing the older technologies. This issue can dominate preservation policy and may put more focus on instant user access in place of physical preservation.

Copyright and Licensing

Some people have criticized that digital libraries are hampered by copyright law, because works cannot be shared over different periods of time in the manner of a traditional library. The republication of material on the Web by libraries may require permission from rights holders, and there is a conflict of interest between them and publishers who may wish to create Web versions of their content for commercial purposes.

There is a dilution of responsibility that occurs as a result of the spread-out nature of digital resources. Complex intellectual property matters may become involved since digital material isn't always owned by a library. The content is, in many cases, public domain or self-generated content only. Some digital libraries, such as Project Gutenberg, work to digitize out-of-copyright works and make them freely available to the public. An estimate of the number of distinct books still existent in library catalogues from 2000BC to 1960, has been made.

The Fair Use Provisions (17 USC § 107) under copyright law provide specific guidelines under which circumstances libraries are allowed to copy digital resources. Four factors that constitute fair use are purpose of use, nature of the work, market impact, and amount or substantiality used.

Some digital libraries acquire a license to "lend out" its resources. This may involve the restriction of lending out only one copy at a time for each license, and applying a system of digital rights management for this purpose.

Metadata Creation

The ability to find works of interest in large libraries is directly related to how well they are catalogued. While cataloguing electronic works digitised from a libraries' existing holding may be as simple as copying moving a record for the print to the electronic item, with complex and born-digital works require substantially more effort. While full text search can be used for some searches, there are many common catalog searches which can't be performed using full text, including:

- finding texts which are the translation of other texts
- linking texts published under pseudonyms to the real author (Samuel Clemens and Mark Twain, for example)
- differentiating non-fiction from parody (The Onion from The New York Times, for example)

Electronic Library

Unique Attributes

The Electronic Library is devoted to the applications and implications of new technology, automation, digitisation, the Internet, user interfaces, and networks in all types of libraries, information centres and museums throughout the world as well as the development of software and hardware for such applications. It provides a vehicle for the latest research and ongoing developments in today's digital library and information environments in different countries, and offers practical advice, useful information and descriptions of specific applications around the globe.

Key Benefits

Subscribers enjoy access to:

- International contributions
- Comment on existing and developing systems and technologies
- First hand user experience of techniques and applications
- Practical information on the application of digital technology
- Analysis of underlying trends and their likely effects

Coverage

The Electronic Library covers a broad range of topics including:

- Libraries and the web
- The digital library
- Software and hardware developments
- Library networking and automation – integrated library systems, OPACs
- User interfaces – web usability
- Internet access and use
- E-books and e-journals
- E-governance and e-readiness
- Online and distance learning

Key Journal Audiences

- Senior Library Managers
- Collection Development Officers
- Acquisitions Librarians
- Reference Librarians

The Electronic Library is indexed and abstracted in:

- CINAHL
- Computer Science Index
- Current Awareness Abstracts
- Current Contents/Social and Behavioral Sciences

- Emerald Management Reviews
- The Informed Librarian
- Information Management & Technology Abstracts
- Information Science & Technology Abstracts
- INSPEC (Electrical & Electronics Abstracts)
- Internet and Personal Computing Abstracts
- ISI Alerting Services
- Journal Citation Reports/Social Sciences Edition
- Library and Information Science Abstracts
- Library, Information Science and Technology Abstracts
- Scopus
- Social Sciences Citation Index
- Social SciSearch
- Referativnyi Zhurnal
- Compendex
- Paperchen (CPX)
- Library Literature and Information Science
- zetoc

Virtual Library

"*Virtual reality* (VR) is an environment that is simulated by a computer. Most virtual reality environments are primarily visual experiences, displayed either on a computer screen or through special stereoscopic displays, but some simulations include additional sensory information, such as sound through speakers or headphones. Some advanced and experimental systems have included limited tactile feedback."

Given this definition of VR a virtual library could be a library environment simulated by a computer. An example is the Book House System developed by Annelise Mark Pejtersen.

Another definition of a virtual library is synonymous with a digital library:

"Virtual Library *means library without walls. The resources are available in digital format, there is no paper, microforms etc. The resources are locally held or accessed through computer networks."*

"The World Wide Web Virtual Library *was the first index of content on the World Wide Web. It was started by Tim Berners-Lee, the creator of HTML and the Web itself, in 1991 at CERN in Geneva."*

ERNET (Education and Research Network)

ERNET (Education and Research Network) has made a significant contribution to the emergence of networking in the country. It practically brought the Internet to India and has built up national capabilities in the area of net-working, especially in protocol software engineering. It has not only succeeded in building a large network that provides various facilities to the intellectual segment of Indian society—the research and education community, it has over the years become a trendsetter in the field of networking. UNDP has lauded ERNET as one of the most successful programmes it has funded. The Govt. of India has committed itself to further strengthen the project by including it in the 9th Plan with the allocation of funds and by creation of a new organisational set-up in the form of a Society. The Science community of the country has also recognized ERNET's contribution—both for infrastructure services as well as for R&D. The Scientific Advisory Committee to the Cabinet has adopted ERNET as the platform for launching an S&T network in the country.

How it Began?

ERNET was initiated in 1986 by the Department of Electronics (DoE), with funding support from the Government of India and United Nations Development Programme (UNDP), involving eight premier institutions as participating agencies—NCST (National Centre for Software Technology) Bombay, IISc (Indian Institute of Science) Bangalore, five IITs (Indian Institutes of Technology) at Delhi, Bombay, Kanpur, Kharagpur and Madras, and the DoE, New Delhi. ERNET began as a multi protocol network with both the TCP/IP and the OSI-IP protocol stacks running over the leased-line portion of the backbone. Since 1995,however, almost all traffic is carried over TCP/IP.

The Objectives of ERNET Indfia

ERNET operations, i.e. providing state-of-the-art communication infrastructure and services to Academic and Research institutions, Govt. organisations, NGOs, private sector R&D organisations, and various other non-commercial organisations;

Research and development;

Training and Consultancy;

Content development.

Achievements

Foundation of national capability building in the area of computer networking laid through:

Setting up of a chain of core groups at the participating agencies with a minimal setof lab facilities and creation of skilled manpower to carry out R&D.

Generating man power at different levels.

Making the world of standards (TCP/IP, OSI etc.) well understood.

Providing an insight into emerging issues such as ATM networks, networked multi-media, and information infrastructure.

Network infrastructure and services set up, including:

Installation, maintenance and operation of large Campus LANs.

Design, commissioning and testing of SATWAN hub and the installation of VSATs.

Seamless interconnection of LAN-WAN segments, & multi-protocol capability provided.

Provision of the whole range of Internet services.

Deployment of TDM/TDMA based VSAT network for Internet access.

DELNET

DELNET was started at the India International Centre Library in January 1988 and was registered as a society in

1992. It was initially supported by the National Information System for Science and Technology (NISSAT), Department of Scientific and Industrial Reseach, Government of India. It was subsequently supported by the National Informatics Centre, Department of Information Technology, Ministry of Communications and Information Technology, Government of India and The Ministry of Culture, Government of India.

DELNET has been established with the prime objective of promoting resource sharing among the libraries through the development of a network of libraries. It aims to collect, store, and disseminate information besides offering computerised services to users, to coordinate efforts for suitable collection development and also to reduce unnecessary duplication wherever possible.

INFLIBNET

Information and Library Network (INFLIBNET) Centre is an Autonomous Inter-University Centre (IUC) of University Grants Commission, Government of India, involved in creating infrastructure for sharing of library and information resources and services among Academic and Research Institutions. INFLIBNET works collaboratively with Indian university libraries to shape the future of the academic libraries in the evolving information environment.

Introduction

Information and Library Network (INFLIBNET) Centre is an autonomous Inter-University Centre of the University Grants Commission (UGC) of India. It is a major National Programme initiated by the UGC in 1991 with its Head Quarters at Gujarat University Campus, Ahmedabad. Initially started as a project under the IUCAA, it became an independent Inter-University Centre in 1996.

INFLIBNET is involved in modernizing university libraries in India and connecting them as well as information centres in the country through a nation-wide high speed data network using the state-of-art technologies for the optimum utilisation of information. INFLIBNET is set out to be a major player in promoting scholarly communication among academicians and researchers in India

Objectives

The primary objectives of INFLIBNET are:

To promote and establish communication facilities to improve capability in information transfer and access, that provide support to scholarship, learning, research and academic pursuit through cooperation and involvement of agencies concerned.

To establish INFLIBNET: Information and Library Network a computer communication network for linking libraries and information centres in universities, deemed to be universities, colleges, UGC information centres, institutions of national importance and R & D institutions, etc. avoiding duplication of efforts.

Functions

In order to fulfill the broad objectives, INFLIBNET will do the following:

Promote and implement computerisation of operations and services in the libraries and information centres of the country, following a uniform standard.

Evolve standards and uniform guidelines in techniques, methods, procedures, computer hardware and software, services and promote their adoption in actual practice by all libraries, in order to facilitate pooling, sharing and exchange of information towards optimal use of resources and facilities.

Evolve a national network interconnecting various libraries and information centres in the country and to improve capability in information handling and service. Provide reliable access to document collection of libraries by creating on-line union catalogue of serials, theses/dissertations, books, monographs and non-book materials (manuscripts, audio-visuals, computer data, multimedia, etc.) in various libraries in India.

Provide access to bibliographic information sources with citations, abstracts etc. through indigenously created databases of the Sectoral Information Centres of NISSAT, UGC Information Centres, City Networks and such others and by establishing gateways for on-line accessing of national and international databases held by national and international information networks and centres respectively.

Develop new methods and techniques for archival of valuable information available as manuscripts and information documents in different Indian Languages, in the form of digital images using high density storage media.

Optimise information resource utilization through shared cataloguing, inter-library loan service, catalogue production, collection development and thus avoiding duplication in acquisition to the extent possible.

Enable the users dispersed all over the country, irrespective of location and distance, to have access to information regarding serials, theses/dissertations, books, monographs and non-book materials by locating the sources wherefrom available and to obtain it through the facilities of INFLIBNET and union catalogue of documents.

Create databases of projects, institutions, specialists, etc. for providing on-line information service. Encourage co-operation among libraries, documentation centres and information centres in the country, so that the resources can be pooled for the benefit of helping the weaker resource centres by stronger ones.

Train and develop human resources in the field of computerised library operations and networking to establish, manage and sustain INFLIBNET.

Facilitate academic communication amongst scientists, engineers, social scientists, academics, faculties, researchers and students through electronic mail, file transfer, computer/ audio/video conferencing, etc.

Undertake system design and studies in the field of communications, computer networking, information handling and data management.

Establish appropriate control and monitoring system for the communication network and organise maintenance.

Collaborate with institutions, libraries, information centres and other organisations in India and abroad in the field relevant to the objectives of the Centre.

Create and promote R&D and other facilities and technical positions for realising the objectives of the Centre.

Generate revenue by providing consultancies and information services.

Do all other such things as may be necessary, incidental or conducive to the attainment of all or any of the above objectives.

Dr. Jagdish Arora is the Director of The Centre as on date.

Documentation Centre

A big library like NUEPA Library and Documentation Centre are situated in a building of the University covering 750 sq. meter of carpet area of three floors. It has a wide collection of more than 53500 volumes on educational planning and management including books, documents, government publications, annual reports, project reports, UNESCO, International Institute of Educational Planning (IIEP), World Bank and International Monetary Fund (IMF) publications. It has about 4141 bound volumes of journals. In addition, the library has audio-visual facilities containing about 380 items of non-book material such as Audio cassettes, Video cassettes, Films, Micro films, Microfiches and CD-ROMs on education and its allied disciplines. Users can view video films from the library collection in audio-visual room. The library subscribes to more than 250 journals and magazines both national and international in the core area of education, planning and management.

NUEPA's Documentation Centre comprises of a unique collection of the Central and State Governments' publications such as Census of India, State Census Reports, State Gazetteers, Statistical Handbooks of States, All India Educational Surveys, Economic Survey, State Economic Surveys, State Educational Plans, Five Year Plans, NUEPA Research Studies, NUEPA Occasional Paper Series, NUEPA Training Programme Reports,

Annual Reports of various Ministries, International Institute of Educational Planning (IIEP), Paris. Moreover, it holds a rich collection of theses and dissertations on International Diploma in Educational Planning and Administration (IDEPA) and Diploma in Educational Planning and Administration (DEPA). Documentation Centre subscribes to 25 national and regional newspapers and maintains the press clippings for the use of faculty and other users.

It has computerized all its operations by using an integrated software LibSys 4.0. Moreover, the Library and Documentation Centre are equipped with electronic databases like Educational Resources and Information Centre (ERIC), Census of India and Internet facilities. The Library and Documentation Centre have a membership of DELNET (Developing Library Network) to promote the sharing of resources at national and international level.

Moreover, the Library and Documentation Centre have developed an online library that provides access to more than 200 full-text Indian and foreign journals, national and international indexing databases, current contents of periodicals, newspapers and full-text reports both national and international.

It has air-conditioned facility, which provides conducive environment for the readers of the library and documentation centre. The Library and Documentation Centre have the reading cum reference room that having the capacity of more than 75 readers on three floors. It meets the information needs of faculty, researchers and participants of workshops, seminars and training programmes conducted by NUEPA time to time.

NASSDOC

National Social Science Documentation Centre (NASSDOC), was established in 1969 as a Division of the ICSSR with the objective to provide library and information support services to researchers in social sciences; those working in academic institutions, autonomous research organisations, policy making, planning and research units of government departments, business and industry etc. NASSDOC also provides guidance to libraies of ICSSR Regional Centres and ICSSR supported Research Institutes.

Facilities Available at NASSDOC

i. Documentation Library and Reference Service;
ii. Collection of unpublished doctoral dissertations, research project reports, current and old volumes of social science journals of Indian and foreign origin;
iii. Literature Search Service from printed and digital databases, i.e CD-ROMS, floppies, Online database etc;
iv. Compilation of short bibliographies on request;
v. Study grant to doctoral students for collection of research material from various libraries located in different parts of India;
vi. Financial assistance is provided for taking up bibliographical and documentation projects;
vii. Document Delivery Service is provided by procuring books and journals on Inter-library loan or by photocopying the documents;
viii Short-term training courses are organized for the research scholars, social scientists, librarians and IT professionals to acquaint them with the latest information and communication technology;and
ix. Cyber Cafe, to facilitate access to internet resources on social sciences.

INSDOC

Indian National Scientific Documentation Centre (INSDOC) is a premier organisation dealing with library, documentation and information science, technology, services and systems. It is a national laboratory under the Council of Scientific and Industrial Research (CSIR) providing information and documentation services both at the national and the international level. INSDOC's activities fall under five broad categories:

1. Services, Products and Publications
2. Projects in Competency Areas

3. National Information Resource
4. Education and Training
5. International Collaboration

Since its inception in 1952, INSDOC has been providing information services that aim at fulfilling the information needs of researchers and scientists in the country. Over the years, INSDOC has designed several information products and services for the corporate and business sector as well. Keeping pace with technological developments, new information products are being brought out on CD-ROMs and floppies and many services are being offered on networks like the Internet.

INSDOC's competency areas include: Library automation, Library networks, Computer networking, Electronic libraries, CD-ROM networking, Design and development of databases, Access to international information sources, On-line system, Feasibility studies, and Design, establishment and operational management of library-cum-information centres.

INSDOC houses the National Science Library that acts as a major information resource centre in the country in the area of Science and Technology and a strong reference collection in general S&T aspects. It receives over 3,320 periodicals both Indian and foreign. A significant number of these periodicals are received in electronic form in CD-ROMs. An Electronic Library Division is set up with facilities to access information from CD-ROMs.

INSDOC has a strong academic and training programme. As part of the academic programme INSDOC offers a Master's level programme in Information Science called Associateship in Information Science. INSDOC also conducts regular short-term courses and attachment training programmes on various topics, including the application of computers and information technology in the field of library, documentation and information. To support its academic and training programme, INSDOC has set up an information technology laboratory which is equipped with the state of the art computer and networking facilities to ensure high quality education and training to the students.

INSDOC works closely with counterpart institutions in other countries to bring about global information exchange. INSDOC is associated with the activities of International Federation for Information and Documentation (FID), International Federation of Library Associations(IFLA) and the Documentation Centre of the South Asian Association for Regional Co-operation(SAARC).

Wide dissemination of S&T information is an important aim of INSDOC. For this purpose, it has a network of regional centres located at Bangalore, Calcutta and Chennai to provide information services in these regions. In addition, INSDOC's services are available through Communications Research Consultants, Calcutta for the Eastern and North-Eastern regions of the country.

A team of about 300 personnel comprising scientific, technical and administrative staff handling the programmes of INSDOC. Over 120 persons of the staff are graduates or post-graduates in science, engineering or computers. Many of them have specialised in Library, Documentation of Information Science.

Objectives

- To meet the information needs of scientific research organisations, universities, government establishment, industries and individuals.
- To harness information technology applications in information management with particular reference to modernising libraries and information centres.
- To act as a single point access for science and technology information generated in India.
- To develop human resources in the areas of library, documentation and information science, technology, management, systems, services, products and marketing.
- To act as a facilitator in furthering economic, social, industrial, scientific and commercial development by providing timely access to relevant and accurate information.

- To collaborate with international information agencies to evolve as an integral part of the globalisation process in the field of information and documentation.

Internet

The Internet is a global network of interconnected computers, enabling users to share information along multiple channels. Typically, a computer that connects to the Internet can access information from a vast array of available servers and other computers by moving information from them to the computer's local memory. The same connection allows that computer to send information to servers on the network; that information is in turn accessed and potentially modified by a variety of other interconnected computers. A majority of widely accessible information on the Internet consists of inter-linked hypertext documents and other resources of the World Wide Web (WWW). Computer users typically manage sent and received information with web browsers; other software for users' interface with computer networks includes specialized programmes for electronic mail, online chat, file transfer and file sharing.

The movement of information in the Internet is achieved via a system of interconnected computer networks that share data by packet switching using the standardized Internet Protocol Suite (TCP/IP). It is a "network of networks" that consists of millions of private and public, academic, business, and government networks of local to global scope that are linked by copper wires, fiber-optic cables, wireless connections, and other technologies.

WWW

The World Wide Web (commonly abbreviated as "the Web") is a system of interlinked hypertext documents accessed via the Internet. With a Web browser, one can view Web pages that may contain text, images, videos, and other multimedia and navigate between them using hyperlinks. Using concepts from earlier hypertext systems, the World Wide Web was started in 1989 by the English physicist Sir Tim Berners-Lee, now the

Director of the World Wide Web Consortium, and later by Robert Cailliau, a Belgian computer scientist, while both were working at CERN in Geneva, Switzerland. In 1990, they proposed building a "web of nodes" storing "hypertext pages" viewed by "browsers" on a network, and released that web in December.

Connected by the existing Internet, other websites were created, around the world, adding international standards for domain names & the HTML language. Since then, Berners-Lee has played an active role in guiding the development of Web standards (such as the markup languages in which Web pages are composed), and in recent years has advocated his vision of a Semantic Web.

The World Wide Web enabled the spread of information over the Internet through an easy-to-use and flexible format. It thus played an important role in popularizing use of the Internet. Although the two terms are sometimes conflated in popular use, *World Wide Web* is not synonymous with *Internet*. The Web is an application built on top of the Internet.

History

The underlying ideas of the Web can be traced as far back as 1980, when, at CERN in Switzerland, Sir Tim Berners-Lee built ENQUIRE (a reference to *Enquire Within Upon Everything*, a book he recalled from his youth). While it was rather different from the system in use today, it contained many of the same core ideas (and even some of the ideas of Berners-Lee's next project after the World Wide Web, the Semantic Web).

In March 1989, Berners-Lee wrote a proposal which referenced ENQUIRE and described a more elaborate information management system. With help from Robert Cailliau, he published a more formal proposal (on November 12, 1990) to build a "Hypertext project" called "WorldWideWeb" (one word, also "W3") as a "web of nodes" with "hypertext documents" to store data. That data would be viewed in "hypertext pages" (webpages) by various "browsers" (line-mode or full-screen) on the computer network, using an "access protocol" connecting the "Internet and DECnet protocol worlds".

The proposal had been modeled after EBT's (Electronic Book Technology, a spin-off from the Institute for Research in Information and Scholarship at Brown University) Dynatext SGML reader that CERN had licensed. The Dynatext system, although technically advanced (a key player in the extension of SGML ISO 8879:1986 to Hypermedia within HyTime), was considered too expensive and with an inappropriate licensing policy for general HEP (High Energy Physics) community use: a fee for each document and each time a document was changed.

A NeXT Computer was used by Berners-Lee as the world's first Web server and also to write the first Web browser, WorldWideWeb, in 1990. By Christmas 1990, Berners-Lee had built all the tools necessary for a working Web: the first Web browser (which was a Web editor as well), the first Web server, and the first Web pages which described the project itself.

On August 6, 1991, he posted a short summary of the World Wide Web project on the alt.hypertext newsgroup. This date also marked the debut of the Web as a publicly available service on the Internet.

The first server outside Europe was set up at SLAC in December 1991.

The crucial underlying concept of hypertext originated with older projects from the 1960s, such as the Hypertext Editing System (HES) at Brown University—among others Ted Nelson and Andries van Dam—Ted Nelson's Project Xanadu and Douglas Engelbart's oN-Line System (NLS). Both Nelson and Engelbart were in turn inspired by Vannevar Bush's microfilm-based "memex," which was described in the 1945 essay "As We May Think".

Berners-Lee's breakthrough was to marry hypertext to the Internet. In his book *Weaving The Web*, he explains that he had repeatedly suggested that a marriage between the two technologies was possible to members of *both* technical communities, but when no one took up his invitation, he finally tackled the project himself. In the process, he developed a system of globally unique identifiers for resources on the Web and elsewhere: the Uniform Resource Identifier.

The World Wide Web had a number of differences from other hypertext systems that were then available. The Web required only unidirectional links rather than bidirectional ones. This made it possible for someone to link to another resource without action by the owner of that resource. It also significantly reduced the difficulty of implementing Web servers and browsers (in comparison to earlier systems), but in turn presented the chronic problem of link rot. Unlike predecessors such as HyperCard, the World Wide Web was non-proprietary, making it possible to develop servers and clients independently and to add extensions without licensing restrictions.

On April 30, 1993, CERN announced that the World Wide Web would be free to anyone, with no fees due. Coming two months after the announcement that the Gopher (protocol) protocol was no longer free to use, this produced a rapid shift away from Gopher and towards the Web. An early popular Web browser was ViolaWWW, which was based upon HyperCard.

Scholars generally agree that a turning point for the World Wide Web began with the introduction of the Mosaic Web browser in 1993, a graphical browser developed by a team at the National Center for Supercomputing Applications at the University of Illinois at Urbana-Champaign (NCSA-UIUC), led by Marc Andreessen. Funding for Mosaic came from the U.S. *High-Performance Computing and Communications Initiative*, a funding programme initiated by the *High Performance Computing and Communication Act of 1991*, one of several computing developments initiated by U.S. Senator Al Gore. Prior to the release of Mosaic, graphics were not commonly mixed with text in Web pages, and its popularity was less than older protocols in use over the Internet, such as Gopher and Wide Area Information Servers (WAIS). Mosaic's graphical user interface allowed the Web to become, by far, the most popular Internet protocol.

The World Wide Web Consortium (W3C) was founded by Tim Berners-Lee after he left the European Organization for Nuclear Research (CERN) in October, 1994. It was founded at the Massachusetts Institute of Technology Laboratory for Computer Science (MIT/LCS) with support from the Defense

Advanced Research Projects Agency (DARPA)—which had pioneered the Internet—and the European Commission.

Internet for Teacher Educators

More than eight out of ten teachers (84 percent) believe that computers and access to the Internet improve the quality of education, according to a survey by education technology nonprofit NetDay, and 75 percent of teachers said the Internet is an important tool for finding new resources to meet new standards.

Two-thirds of teachers, however, agree the Internet is not well integrated into their classrooms and only 26 percent of them feel pressure to use it in learning activities.

NetDay also found that nearly every teacher has access to the Internet at his or her school and 80 percent of classrooms have computers that are online. Seventy-seven percent of teachers agree that teachers without Internet access in the classroom are at a disadvantage.

Teachers cite multiple uses for the Internet, but most primarily see its potential as a research tool, and say it has not changed the way they teach. Forty-eight percent of teachers say the Internet has become an important tool for teaching over the last two years, yet across every demographic group of teachers, half or more use the Internet at school for less than 30 minutes a day.

Other findings from NetDay's survey include:

- 78 percent of teachers cited lack of time as the number one reason for not logging on to the Internet
- 46 to 50 percent list lack of equipment, speed of access or lack of technical support as hindering their use of online resources
- 44 percent of teachers cite lack of knowledge about how to use the Internet, and 32 percent list lack of leadership from the principal or administrators as reasons for not logging on.

NetDay's research suggests the critical challenge ahead is to find ways to help teachers go beyond the research functions of the Internet. Most teachers do not use the Internet in daily activities such as communication with students, parents and other teachers, or for organizational activities. Sixty-seven percent of teachers believe the Internet is not well integrated into their classroom. Those teachers most likely to use the Internet and say it is well integrated into their classrooms are sixth through eighth grade teachers.

Less than half of teachers use the Internet when building new lessons or engaging in classroom projects (42 percent), and an even greater number (62 percent) do not update lesson plans with material found online. Teachers in private and parochial schools engage in technology integration more often than teachers in public schools. Fifty-two percent of private and parochial teachers use the Internet for class projects and for updating lesson plans; compared to 40 percent of public school teachers who use the Internet for these activities.

Nearly three-quarters (73 percent) of teachers say they do not feel pressure to use the Internet in classroom instruction or the curriculum.n Of those teachers who reported feeling pressure, 54 percent say district administrators, colleagues and peers are the source of that pressure. Only 10 percent say the pressure comes from principals. The lack of pressure that teachers feel from principals suggests the need for more guidance to help principals learn how to best utilize technology to support education. In addition, learning how to provide leadership on educational technology is a new development area for many principals.

Internet Training and Support for Teachers

How do teachers prepare to guide their students wisely and effectively in using the Internet, a medium to which they are just gaining access? Teachers have received little preparatory support for using computers as they exist today. Of 219 teachers consulted in a recent Canadian needs assessment (McLeod, 1995), 118 teachers believed they required more computer instruction. Training has often focused primarily on technical matters and needs to deal as well with pedagogical concerns (Bennett, 1993; Siegel, 1995). An integrated support programme using carefully trained peer mentors is described by MacArthur, Pilato *et al.* (1995). A well-rounded programme of preparation is matched to school resources and curriculum and includes technical and pedagogical training, examining what other teachers have done, ready access to guide materials, opportunities for peer collaboration, and ongoing support from experienced classroom teachers, librarians, support staff, and principals.

Training, support, and professional development activities only have value when the technical infrastructure is in place. Ministries of education and school boards are trying to install the resources needed for Internet use at the same time that education budgets in many provinces are being reduced. Fournier and MacKinnon (1994) suggest that one new, fully networked computer be provided for each four students every three years—a goal far beyond the current reach of most school boards—but the authors acknowledge that simply having networked computers in place and working well will not ensure proper use. Once teachers are aware of the potential of the Internet, they are keen to include its use in their repertoire of teaching techniques, but they do not have time to mess about unproductively without guidance. They need enough equipment to provide convenient access, and they need support that is well adapted to their teaching situation.

Often the most effective training and support comes from teachers themselves. About one third of the teachers consulted in McLeod's study (1995) indicated that they were teaching computer skills to their colleagues. The new medium can be of considerable service to teachers in seeking and offering peer support (Bascia, 1994, 1995). Using email and computer conference systems, teachers request information and guidance from distant and often unknown colleagues and publish resources and notes on their experience. In this way, they take initiative and responsibility for their own professional development. In Ontario, approximately 40,000 of the province's 130,000 teachers have accounts on the Education Network of Ontario (1995), part of an initiative of the Ontario Teachers Federation called "Creating a Culture of Change" (Bascia 1994,

1995). In Newfoundland nearly all teachers have access to STEM~Net, "a high-quality computer network for educators in Newfoundland and Labrador... to support teaching, curriculum and professional development activities related to their work" (TILE, 1994). Canada's SchoolNet is encouraging peer support though a moderated list, inclass@schoolnet.carleton.ca, and through the SchoolNet Grass Roots Project, which offers modest funding in exchange for reports of successful telecommunications-based learning projects. All of these programmes and systems help teachers help themselves in exchanging information, in questioning underlying assumptions, and in realigning values and practice.

In addition to knowing how to use Internet resources and knowing what is available, teachers need to figure out how to organize the classroom depending on the resources available, how to plan, develop, undertake, and assess telecommunications-based activities and projects, how to justify their work to parents and the public, and how to collaborate on all of this with colleagues. Much of this they can figure out on their own once they have initial support and guidance, based on well-developed ministry and board policy. Excellent guides have been written by experienced teachers on planning, organizing, and conducting telecommunications-based projects in schools (Walker, 1994; Andres & Rogers, 1995). Warren (1995) advises paying attention to the aim, rationale, context, objectives, participant requirements, time line, student assessment and project evaluation, contact information, logistics, and follow-up. Little work has been done in the area of assessment and evaluation of telecommunications-based learning; the author is supervising an M.Ed. thesis that is a case study on such work.

In faculties of education, where access to Internet resources is provided to all teacher candidates, it is possible, with considerable effort, to establish habits of using the new media. At York University, all teacher candidates are given access to a computer conference system which they use extensively for peer-moderated discussion of the practicum. That discussion spills over into course work and helps to keep the whole B. Ed. programme moving ahead (Crossland & Egnatoff, 1996). In some teacher education programmes, teacher candidates are able to provide leadership in the use of computers during their practicum simply because they have had more opportunity to work with computers. Faculties are also working diligently to use telecommunications to support close collaboration with schools in the preparation of new teachers. These efforts are the beginning of a continuum of professional development for both new and experienced teachers, including faculty instructors themselves.

A recent survey report (Crossland & Egnatoff, 1996), provides information on the availability, organization, content, and scope of various Canadian teacher professional development programmes emphasizing telecommunications and information technology. In some cases, programmes of support are related to work on distance education, for which instructors need special preparation. The British Columbia Open Learning Agency has programmes that include a three-day residential training programme coupled with on-site or telecommunications-based support. The Open Learning Agency views professional development as the teacher's responsibility and staff development and training the responsibility of the organization. Some provinces have major networks designed to increase communication and peer-mediated professional development and support. The survey of such programmes was conducted to set in context a particular pilot programme, the SchoolNet Support Teachers Pilot Project.

The SchoolNet Support Teachers Pilot Project

The SchoolNet Support Teachers Pilot Project was a collaborative experiment in supporting teachers wishing to enrich their students' learning through the use of new telecommunications tools and resources (Egnatoff, 1996). The project began in September 1995 as a four-month pilot to provide training and professional development for interested teachers. The sponsors—SchoolNet and six school boards—extended the project for the entire 1995-96 school year.

The project employed a "SchoolNet Support Teacher" in each of six urban-region school boards of which two were francophone and four anglophone, and three were public and three Roman Catholic separate. These boards varied greatly in size, computer resources, and support, but were all highly committed to making the project work well. The project had four distinguishing characteristics:

- Most of the teacher training—technical and pedagogical—in the project was done by certified teachers;
- The SchoolNet Support Teachers were newly certified teachers, having just graduated from a faculty of education;
- Most of the training was done on site, in the schools, during the school day, and was related directly to the work of the teachers;
- The support teachers worked in close cooperation with board administrative personnel to expand or establish sustainable on-site professional development programmes in keeping with board plans for the educational use of telecommunications.

For the work to be sustained, it was felt that the project needed to address four areas of concern:

- development of teacher knowledge, skills, and attitudes;
- curriculum integration;
- school-level site-based planning; and
- board-level planning.

The SchoolNet Support Teachers were expected to deal primarily with the first three areas of concern. Board-wide matters were to be a concern for the project team to address as a whole, with the guidance of PARTNERS, an organization contracted as project facilitator.

The entire project had three objectives:

- to establish a pilot project in an urban region having several school boards;
- to evaluate the effectiveness of the project; and
- to promote similar projects nationally.

The work of the support teachers included many tasks of the sort normally done by coordinators, special assignment teachers, and resource teachers. One of the SchoolNet Support Teachers conducted a detailed survey of computer resources, use, knowledge, and needs which the board used to assess and reconsider its resource allocation. With varying emphasis, all support teachers introduced teachers—in hands-on workshops, presentations, and small-group or individual tutorials—to the Internet and to various ways of working on it; developed guides to Internet use; developed acceptable use policies; taught in the classroom along with the regular classroom teachers; trained teachers who would later train their peers; started teachers and classes on Internet projects; collaborated across boards to share resources; made presentations to parents, board officials, and trustees to bring the work into focus and to assure continuing support; and provided reports for the author's evaluation study.

Findings from the evaluation study of the first half of the project attest to its success. The success was due in part to the work of PARTNERS, a coordinating agency that drew together all the stakeholders to plan and coordinate the work and that ensured that the results were well known to the public and to those who set and implement board policy. The success was due in equal measure to the high degree of collaboration of teachers, principals, coordinators, SchoolNet staff, and, most important, the SchoolNet Support Teachers themselves.

The promotion phase of the project began just prior to the writing of this paper. Organizers of a related project in Alberta that began in the spring of 1996 studied the SchoolNet Support Teachers Pilot Project and adapted its approach. Several other variations are under development elsewhere in Canada.

Findings of the Evaluation Study

Partnership was a key to the success of the project. The project grew out of the agenda of the Training, Research, and Evaluation committee of Canada's SchoolNet National Advisory Board, which represents government, business, and educational stakeholders. PARTNERS invited the boards to collaborate and worked behind the scenes to ensure that the project ran smoothly at all stages.

The SchoolNet Support Teachers began with little specialized training, but quickly learned on the job, took initiative, and were very soon providing strong leadership. Collaboration emerged naturally within a few weeks of startup, taking the form of sharing resource documents, discussing solutions to common problems, and sharing accomplishments and approaches in bimonthly meetings.

The coordinators and support teachers worked very well together, often learning from and with each other, and working side by side. Having indefinite plans turned out to be an advantage because it required the support teachers to take ownership of their work. Even though the support teachers quickly became quite independent, they nevertheless kept the coordinators well-informed of the work. Several coordinators were in attendance at any given project meeting. The support teachers worked very much for the board, with only minimal direction or guidance from SchoolNet staff.

The support teachers conducted their own research and kept their own records of teacher progress according to the needs of the boards. Report writing helped them see what they had accomplished and sharing those reports gave them a sense of being part of an enterprise whose significance went beyond the boundaries of the individual boards. In the words of one superintendent, the support teachers helped get the board vision "over the mountain" from board office to classroom.

Initially, it was expected that after a few weeks of training and support, some teachers would be ready to use telecommunications as part of curriculum projects, a strong wish of the SchoolNet staff. For most participants, a focus on projects had to be postponed until the infrastructure was more secure and until basic skills and knowledge were more highly developed. Project work was more evident in the second term.

The support teachers found that the teachers they encountered were keen to use telecommunications when infrastructure development, training, and support were well coordinated. In one board especially, knowing that new equipment was coming and that the network would be connected was a strong motivator. Participating teachers all agreed that it was very important to have support from a qualified teacher when it came to working with classes and planning learning activities. Teachers also agreed on the value of sustained support rather than isolated workshops.

Many telecommunications activities worked well because the support teachers, like all dedicated teachers, did a lot of work behind the scenes. This included preparing guide materials for teachers, editing HTML documents produced by students, arranging for Internet access services, assisting with software installation and LAN setup, and keeping up an email dialogue with teachers and students.

Evidence of sustainability began to appear towards the end of the second month, even though it seemed clear that the boards would not be able to support a SchoolNet Support Teacher on their own, especially given impending layoffs due to government cutbacks. The project very quickly took on a life of its own. Once the basic design was established in consultation with the partners, all the players pulled their weight and did their own work. Because board leaders were involved, and because the support teachers were self-starters, the researchers were able very quickly to focus on the research without worrying about project management or animation. Many expectations were realized without deliberate planning. That happened in large measure because there was a commonly understood purpose.

Online Search of Teacher Education Database

Training Provided by Online Training Directory Online Research Techniques is a seven day online course.

This course will help you develop online research skills and gain knowledge on Grolier Online and GaleNet resources.

This course is offered by a State Accredited University and offers State Board Continuing Education credits for Michigan teachers.? If you are located in a state other than Michigan, please check to see if your State Board will honour the Continuing Education Credit.? The course provider will be happy to provide you with appropriate documentation.

This course is designed for K12 teachers but the concepts and examples will translate for any online course developer.

Search Engines

A Web search engine is a tool designed to search for information on the World Wide Web. The search results are usually presented in a list and are commonly called *hits*. The information may consist of web pages, images, information and other types of files. Some search engines also mine data available in newsbooks, databases, or open directories. Unlike Web directories, which are maintained by human editors, search engines operate algorithmically or are a mixture of algorithmic and human input.

History

Before there were web search engines there was a complete list of all webservers. The list was edited by Tim Berners-Lee and hosted on the CERN webserver. One historical snapshot from 1992 remains. As more and more webservers went online the central list could not keep up. On the NCSA Site new servers were announced under the title "What's New!" but no complete listing existed any more.

The very first tool used for searching on the (pre-web) Internet was Archie. The name stands for "archive" without the "v." It was created in 1990 by Alan Emtage, a student at McGill University in Montreal. The programme downloaded the directory listings of all the files located on public anonymous FTP (File Transfer Protocol) sites, creating a searchable database of file names; however, Archie did not index the contents of these sites.

The rise of Gopher (created in 1991 by Mark McCahill at the University of Minnesota) led to two new search programmes, Veronica and Jughead. Like Archie, they searched the file names and titles stored in Gopher index systems. Veronica (Very Easy Rodent-Oriented Net-wide Index to Computerized

Archives) provided a keyword search of most Gopher menu titles in the entire Gopher listings. Jughead (Jonzy's Universal Gopher Hierarchy Excavation and Display) was a tool for obtaining menu information from specific Gopher servers. While the name of the search engine "Archie" was not a reference to the Archie comic book series, "Veronica" and "Jughead" are characters in the series, thus referencing their predecessor.

In June 1993, Matthew Gray, then at MIT, produced what was probably the first web robot, the Perl-based World Wide Web Wanderer, and used it to generate an index called 'Wandex'. The purpose of the Wanderer was to measure the size of the World Wide Web, which it did until late 1995. The search engine Aliweb appeared in November 1993. Aliweb did not use a web robot, but instead depended on being notified by website administrators of the existence at each site of an index file in a particular format.

JumpStation (released in December 1993) used a web robot to find web pages and to build its index, and used a web form as the interface to its query programme. It was thus the first WWW resource-discovery tool to combine the three essential features of a web search engine (crawling, indexing, and searching) as described below. Because of the limited resources available on the platform on which it ran, its indexing and hence searching were limited to the titles and headings found in the web pages the crawler encountered.

One of the first "full text" crawler-based search engines was WebCrawler, which came out in 1994. Unlike its predecessors, it let users search for any word in any webpage, which has become the standard for all major search engines since. It was also the first one to be widely known by the public. Also in 1994 Lycos (which started at Carnegie Mellon University) was launched, and became a major commercial endeavor.

Soon after, many search engines appeared and vied for popularity. These included Magellan, Excite, Infoseek, Inktomi, Northern Light, and AltaVista. Yahoo! was among the most popular ways for people to find web pages of interest, but its search function operated on its web directory, rather than full-text copies of web pages. Information seekers could also browse the directory instead of doing a keyword-based search.

In 1996, Netscape was looking to give a single search engine an exclusive deal to be their featured search engine. There was so much interest that instead a deal was struck with Netscape by 5 of the major search engines, where for $5Million per year each search engine would be in a rotation on the Netscape search engine page. These five engines were: Yahoo!, Magellan, Lycos, Infoseek and Excite.

Search engines were also known as some of the brightest stars in the Internet investing frenzy that occurred in the late 1990s. Several companies entered the market spectacularly, receiving record gains during their initial public offerings. Some have taken down their public search engine, and are marketing enterprise-only editions, such as Northern Light. Many search engine companies were caught up in the dot-com bubble, a speculation-driven market boom that peaked in 1999 and ended in 2001.

Around 2000, the Google search engine rose to prominence. The company achieved better results for many searches with an innovation called PageRank. This iterative algorithm ranks web pages based on the number and PageRank of other web sites and pages that link there, on the premise that good or desirable pages are linked to more than others. Google also maintained a minimalist interface to its search engine. In contrast, many of its competitors embedded a search engine in a web portal.

By 2000, Yahoo was providing search services based on Inktomi's search engine. Yahoo! acquired Inktomi in 2002, and Overture (which owned AlltheWeb and AltaVista) in 2003. Yahoo! switched to Google's search engine until 2004, when it launched its own search engine based on the combined technologies of its acquisitions.

Microsoft first launched MSN Search (since re-branded Live Search) in the fall of 1998 using search results from Inktomi. In early 1999 the site began to display listings from Looksmart blended with results from Inktomi except for a short time in 1999 when results from AltaVista were used instead. In 2004, Microsoft began a transition to its own search technology, powered by its own web crawler (called msnbot).

As of late 2007, Google was by far the most popular Web search engine worldwide. A number of country-specific search engine companies have become prominent; for example Baidu is the most popular search engine in the People's Republic of China.

How Web Search Engines Work?

A search engine operates, in the following order:

1. Web crawling
2. Indexing
3. Searching

Web search engines work by storing information about many web pages, which they retrieve from the WWW itself. These pages are retrieved by a Web crawler (sometimes also known as a spider) — an automated Web browser which follows every link it sees. Exclusions can be made by the use of robots.txt. The contents of each page are then analyzed to determine how it should be indexed (for example, words are extracted from the titles, headings, or special fields called meta tags). Data about web pages are stored in an index database for use in later queries. Some search engines, such as Google, store all or part of the source page (referred to as a cache) as well as information about the web pages, whereas others, such as AltaVista, store every word of every page they find.

This cached page always holds the actual search text since it is the one that was actually indexed, so it can be very useful when the content of the current page has been updated and the search terms are no longer in it. This problem might be considered to be a mild form of linkrot, and Google's handling of it increases usability by satisfying user expectations that the search terms will be on the returned webpage. This satisfies the principle of least astonishment since the user normally expects the search terms to be on the returned pages. Increased search relevance makes these cached pages very useful, even beyond the fact that they may contain data that may no longer be available elsewhere.

When a user enters a query into a search engine (typically by using key words), the engine examines its index and provides a listing of best-matching web pages according to its criteria, usually with a short summary containing the document's title and sometimes parts of the text. Most search engines support the use of the boolean operators AND, OR and NOT to further specify the search query. Some search engines provide an advanced feature called proximity search which allows users to define the distance between keywords.

The usefulness of a search engine depends on the relevance of the **result set** it gives back. While there may be millions of webpages that include a particular word or phrase, some pages may be more relevant, popular, or authoritative than others. Most search engines employ methods to rank the results to provide the "best" results first. How a search engine decides which pages are the best matches, and what order the results should be shown in, varies widely from one engine to another. The methods also change over time as Internet usage changes and new techniques evolve.

Most Web search engines are commercial ventures supported by advertising revenue and, as a result, some employ the practice of allowing advertisers to pay money to have their listings ranked higher in search results. Those search engines which do not accept money for their search engine results make money by running search related ads alongside the regular search engine results. The search engines make money every time someone clicks on one of these ads.

Revenue in the web search portals industry is projected to grow in 2008 by 13.4 percent, with broadband connections expected to rise by 15.1 percent. Between 2008 and 2012, industry revenue is projected to rise by 56 percent as Internet penetration still has some way to go to reach full saturation in American households. Furthermore, broadband services are projected to account for an ever increasing share of domestic Internet users, rising to 118.7 million by 2012, with an increasing share accounted for by fiber-optic and high speed cable lines.

Search Techniques

Guidance for getting good results with online searching, whether you are using the library catalog, research databases, or the web.

- *Keyword searching*
  - o How it works
  - o Advantages of keyword searching
  - o Choosing keywords
  - o Combining keywords with connectors
  - o Searching for phrases
  - o Truncation
  - o Common words
- *Subject heading searching*
  - o How it works
  - o Advantages of subject heading searching
  - o Choosing subject headings
- *Natural language searching*
  - o How it works
  - o Advantages of natural language searching
- *Refining your search strategy*
  - o Limit your search results
  - o Select different search terms
  - o Try a different type of search
  - o Try a different resource
  - o Ask a librarian for suggestions

Security Search Techniques: Baggage

DVD Format: Searching baggage is far more complex than simply opening it up to see what is inside. Proper practices and procedures need to be followed to comply with the law and to avoid an oversight that might create a security breach or worse, lead to a catastrophe.

The ISPS Code explicitly states that "In liaison with the port facility, the ship should ensure that designated secure areas are established in which inspections and searching of persons, baggage (including carry-on items), personal effects, vehicles and their contents can take place." Security Search Techniques: Baggage examines the most important features of conducting successful searches. The video presents how to prepare for the search, how to conduct a thorough search and how to respond if contraband or prohibited items are discovered.

The first step in a thorough search begins with the establishment of identity and an examination of credentials. The importance of posting a search policy is explored. Coordinating with the port facility and establishing a secure area for searches are shown to be critical elements in the process. Reference is made to the Ship Security Plan as the primary document for appropriate levels of search at various ship security levels. Dealing with unaccompanied baggage is described.

The methods demonstrated in Security Search Techniques: Baggage are based on what is required in the ISPS Code and the expertise of Ravi Shankar, security consultant to some of the largest shipping companies in the world. Security Search Techniques: Baggage allows your crew to see a thorough and careful baggage search, to hear from an industry expert why such care must be taken, and to understand what needs to be done to prevent unauthorized or illegal items from gaining access to your ship.

What you will learn:

- Establishing a secure search area
- The importance of the Ship Security Plan
- What to do with unaccompanied baggage
- Proper response to finding contraband

Search Techniques

Free Text Search: The most simple search involves a free text search. This is based on a word or phrase of your choice appearing anywhere in the source material. Most bibliographic databases have their own individual controlled language which is composed of keywords. These are organised in a structured hierarchy (Thesaurus). This demonstrates the relationship between them, and enables the user to include all the terms that are relevant to their search. The Thesaurus permits a more controlled and detailed search to be undertaken because keywords are used in the indexing of the database.

Boolean Logic

If the only thing you learn about effective searching is how to use Boolean logic, you will not go far wrong. Boolean logic breaks a subject down into concepts and uses "operators" such as:

AND – narrows down a search using a combination of terms

OR – broadens a search by searching for a number of different terms

NOT – narrows down a search by eliminating terms that are not associated with something you are trying to find

For example:

- Salmonella AND eggs will retrieve records that contain both terms
- Salmonella OR eggs will retrieve all records containing a reference to either salmonella or eggs
- Salmonella NOT eggs will retrieve records that contain Salmonella but have no reference to eggs

Boolean logic can be improved by "nesting" which involves the use of parentheses to combine several search requests, for example:

- (Salmonella OR Listeria) AND (chocolate OR eggs) will retrieve records on Salmonella and eggs, Salmonella and chocolate, Listeria and eggs, and Listeria and chocolate.

Not all search engines support Boolean logic but most academic resources (journals, bibliographic databases, reference works) will.

Some search engines will support phrase searching which looks for a specifc term. For example:

- "salmonella in eggs" will only find records with that exact term.

Proximity

Not all search engines recognise proximity operators but a few search engines will have advanced features where proximity searching can be deployed. The most common proximity operator is "NEAR" allowing you to specify two terms that can be found close together.

Wildcards

Wildcards are not supported by all search engines but can be used to represent a character or number of characters. They are useful when you are either not sure how to spell something or when you want to find records with different word endings. Different search engines use different symbols but the most common wildcards are "*" and "?". for example:

- poison* will retrieve all records that include poison, poisons, poisoned or poisoning
- col*r will retrieve all records that contain either colour or colour
- wom*n will retrieve all records that contain either woman or women

Field Searching

Electronic sources of information have a field structure. Not all sources use the same fields. You will therefore need adapt your search accordingly. Field searching is very precise and powerful but not all sources allow you to search in this way

Other Search Tools

Depending on the database or information resource you are using, you may be able to refine your search, save your search, set up search alerts which will run a search for you and email you the results on a regular basis. Search tools and user guides can be found either on your library website or may be made available by the resource provider. These are well worth using in order to get the most out of your searching.

UNIT-V

Information Literacy

Information Literacy for Teacher Education

"Critical thinking skills," "problem solving," "decision making": both the popular and professional literature use these phrases in reporting on skills that the K-12 curriculum must provide to equip students for the 21st century. All three of these phrases refer to cognitive skills that are necessary to create new knowledge and to learn how to learn. A recognition that learning how to learn is fundamental to economic and personal success in the information age has been cited by sources as diverse as Alvin Toffler and the Secretary's Commission on Achieving Necessary Skills (SCANS) and Goals 2000 reports (Doyle, 1994). This ability to learn how to learn is a key characteristic of those who are information literate; i.e., those who "know how to learn because they know how knowledge is organized, how to find information, and how to use information in such a way that others can learn from them" (American Library Association [ALA], 1989). If teachers are to use information so that others can learn from them, then teachers must be information literate. This Digest will discuss the concept of information literacy (the ability to access, evaluate, and use information from a variety of sources) and its relevance for teachers.

Rationale for Information Literacy for Teachers

The American Library Association Presidential Committee on Information Literacy recognized that the "information age is divorced from most teaching styles" (ALA, 1989). In its report, the ALA Presidential Committee called for a restructuring of the learning process in order to create a new information-age school characterized by interactive, self-initiated learning with the teacher as the guide to learning.

In March 1998, the National Forum on Information Literacy (NFIL), a broad-based association of over 65 national organizations, issued "A Progress Report on Information Literacy" in which they reported on the status of the recommendations of the 1989 report. Recommendation five from the 1989 report stated: "Teacher education and performance expectations should be modified to include information literacy concerns." Progress reported in 1998 on this recommendation was: "none" (National Forum, 1998). The lack of progress is especially notable given the changes in technology for accessing information in the intervening years. This increase in information technology has resulted in the development of new standards, which deal in whole or in part with information literacy skills for K-12 students, by other professional associations.

The International Society for Technology in Education National Educational Technology Standards Project (NETS) has begun a multi-year effort to "effectively support use of technology for teaching-learning and administration" (Thomas, 1998). Their first set of standards focuses on a technology foundation for students and includes the use of technology research tools "to locate, evaluate and collect information from a variety of sources" and to "evaluate and select information resources" (Thomas, 1998).

In June 1998, the American Association of School Librarians (AASL) and the Association for Educational Communications and Technology released "Information Literacy Standards for Student Learning," which addresses issues in information literacy, independent learning, and social responsibility, as a guide for "school library media specialists and other K-12 educators as they cultivate and refine their students' information literacy skills in print, nonprint and electronic format" ("Information Literacy Standards," 1998). Teachers cannot prepare their students to be information literate unless they themselves understand how to find and use information.

The Commission on Higher Education of the Middle States Association of Colleges and Schools has been implementing standards for information literacy at the institutional level for some years. The association offers professional development workshops on this topic in conjunction with its national meetings.

This need to know not just content but also the process of learning is supported not only by the exploding amount of information but also by new understandings of cognitive science. Recent studies in cognitive science refute the notion that content comes before process, recognizing that the process of accessing, evaluating, and using information is integral to understanding content. The information-literate teacher will also be able to select and use resources most appropriate to multiple intelligences and learning styles (Warmkessel & McCade, 1997).

Guidelines for Information Literacy for Teachers

The two major professional associations for librarians who work with preservice teachers and inservice teachers have each developed guidelines and position statements on what information-literate teachers need to know. The Education and Behavioral Sciences Section (EBSS) of the Association of College and Research Libraries (ACRL) places emphasis on conceptually based skills for searching, retrieving, and evaluating information for learners who are undergraduate students, graduate students, practitioners, and researchers. The EBSS identifies a sequence of skills that begins with understanding that the generation and communication of knowledge in education includes recorded and unrecorded sources and formats that differ in publication cycles and authority.

The process of intellectual access includes the development of a strategy for locating information that takes into consideration the different terminologies and organization of access tools such as databases, Internet resources, and print materials. This intellectual access is improved by an understanding of the citation, URL, or other bibliographic representation for information sources, which then guides the educator to physical access and evaluation of information sources. Lastly, the EBSS skills highlight the importance of the collaborative roles of teachers and library media specialists in developing assignments that will provide opportunities for K-12 students to refine their own information literacy skills (Libutti & Gratch, 1995, pp. 123-26).

The American Association of School Librarians issued a 1995 position paper on information competencies that stresses application rather than concepts. The paper recognizes the different roles of the administrator and the teacher in providing the integration of information literacy into the curriculum, supporting collaboration in planning and teaching among teachers and school library media specialists, and providing access to and using resource-based learning experiences, as well as notes the value of literature and technology as resources for student learning.

Models for Teachers' Information Literacy

Programmes in information literacy for teachers range from individual workshops for both preservice and inservice teachers to course-related and course-integrated instruction. This breadth in programme development and focus is illustrated in "Teaching Information Retrieval and Evaluation Skills to Education Students and Practitioners: A Casebook of Applications" (Libutti & Gratch, 1995). Ten case studies of teaching and learning situations for preservice and inservice teachers provide lesson plans and objectives, a session narrative, and a reflection on each case.

These cases present reflective examples of programmes that present instruction on such topics as resource-based teaching for student teachers, Internet searching for graduate education students, and conducting a literature review in preparation for a test critique. The cases develop these diverse themes in programmes that range from a one-hour workshop to a semester course. Common themes emerging from these cases that are important to those developing information literacy programmes for teachers are the heterogeneity of graduate students in education, the breadth and complexity of information resources in education, the impact of the World Wide Web on the need for exploration and evaluation, and a needed emphasis on teaching how to search for information using a variety of strategies. The development of an integrated information literacy programme for preservice teachers is described by Miner, whose programme was focused on "preparing prospective teachers for ongoing self-renewal in terms of life-long learning" (1992). This programme at Brigham Young University began with independent workshops and, through revision based on the needs of student teachers, moved to a full-course, integrated programme. Key to the success and growth of this programme was the development of integrated course activities that would "fulfill course objectives at the same time they enhanced the planned development of. .. information literacy" (Miner, 1992).

O'Hanlon has provided a model for information literacy for teachers that emphasizes collaborative and problem-solving activities relevant to the student teacher. This model offers a guided design, which is based on Bloom's Taxonomy, and approximates real-life experience while modeling efficient practice in locating appropriate information sources (O'Hanlon, 1988).

Conclusion

Professional associations for K-12 and higher education have recognized the importance of information literacy to the teaching-learning process. However, integration of information literacy into teacher preparation and development has not occurred. In moving towards this goal, the "Progress Report on Information Literacy" identified two specific courses of action. The first is "to encourage leaders in school reform movements to incorporate information literacy skills into their efforts" and the second is "to partner with national teacher education organizations to get information literacy on their agendas" (National Forum, 1998). Teacher educators, teachers, and others interested in preparing K-12 students to be information literate can move forward by reflecting upon and adapting existing models.

User and Their Information Needs

Apart from information retrieval there is virtually no other area of information science that has occasioned as much research effort and writing as 'user studies'. Within user studies the investigation of 'information needs' has been the subject of much debate and no little confusion. The aim of this paper is to attempt to reduce this confusion by devoting attention to the definition of some concepts and by proposing the basis for a theory of the motivations for information-seeking behaviour.

Information

Part of the difficulty with 'information needs' lies with the troublesome concept 'information'. Numerous definitions have been evolved, seeking to distinguish, for example, among 'data', 'information' and 'knowledge', and recently there have been attempts at a single concept of information for information science.

However, the problem seems to lie not so much with the lack of a *single* definition as with a failure to use a definition appropriate to the level and purpose of the investigation. The word 'information' is used, in the context of user-studies research, to denote a *physical entity* or phenomenon (as in the case of questions relating to the number of books read in a period of time, the number of journals subscribed to, etc.), the *channel of communication* through which messages are transferred (as when we speak of the incidence of oral versus written informa-tion), or *the factual data,* empirically determined and presented in a document or transmitted orally.

The situation is further complicated by the fact that distinctions may or may not be made among 'facts', 'advice' and 'opinion'. The distinction, of course, is that the first of these is assumed (not always correctly) to be free of value judgements, whereas value judgements almost certainly affect advice and opinion.

These multiple uses of the term 'information' cause confusion because researchers sometimes fail to distinguish between one sense and another, or simply leave the reader to discover which sense is meant by reading the paper or report. Even then it is sometimes unclear which of the senses the researcher had in mind when setting the research objectives.

User Studies

Figure presents a way of thinking of the field, 'user studies'; its aim is not to 'model' information-seeking behaviour but to draw attention to the interrelationships among concepts used in the field. The figure suggests that information-seeking behaviour results from the recognition of some need, perceived by the user. That behaviour may take several forms: for example, the user may make demands upon formal systems that are customarily defined as information systems (such as libraries, on-line services, Prestel or information centres), or upon systems which may perform information functions in addition to a primary, non-information function (such as estate agents' offices or car sales agencies, both of which are concerned with selling, but which may be used to obtain information on current prices, areas of 'suitable' housing, or details of cars that hold their secondhand value).

Alternatively, the user may seek information from other *people,* rather than from systems, and this is expressed in the diagram as involving 'information exchange'. The use of the word 'exchange' is intended to draw attention to the element of reciprocity, recognized by sociologists and social psychologists as a fundamental aspect of human interaction. In terms of information behaviour, the idea of reciprocity may be fairly weak in some cases (as when a junior scientist seeks information from a senior but hierarchically equal colleague) but in other cases may be so strong that the process is inhibited, as when a subordinate person in a hierarchy fears to reveal his ignorance to a superior.

In any of the above cases of information-seeking behaviour, 'failure' may be experienced: this is indicated in the diagram for the use of systems but, of course, it may also be experienced when seeking information from other people.

Whatever the source of the information it will at some point be 'used', if only in the sense of being evaluated to discover its relationship to the user's need. That 'use' may satisfy or fail to satisfy the need and, in either event, may also be recog-nized as being of potential relevance to the need of another person and, conse-quently, may be 'transferred' to such a person.

Although all of these areas are of potential interest to the field of user studies, attention has been given in the past chiefly to the demands people make upon formal information systems. Curiously, information use (which ought to point most directly to the needs experienced by people) is one of the most neglected areas; and 'information exchange' as defined here has tended to fall within the sphere of interest of sociologists and organizational theorists rather than within that of information scientists.

'Information' in the figure may be understood in any of the senses mentioned earlier. Thus, in information exchange, an individual may be looking for facts, advice or opinions, and may receive any of these either in writing or orally. Sometimes the channel itself may be of overriding significance, as when orally given advice may be *preferred* over anything in writing. Again, a user may be interested in a specific document as a physical entity, as in the expression of a need to view variant copies of an incunabulum. In information transfer it may be a fact, an opinion or a piece of advice that is transferred orally, or a physical document 'containing' the fact, opinion or advice may be given to another person. We can choose to study the facts, ideas, advice or opinions, or the nature and distribution of the documentary 'containers'. In any event, when the term 'user study' is employed the specific sub-field should be specified, and the aspect or aspects of 'information' under consideration should be defined.

Information Needs

Within the field of user studies the investigation of 'information needs' has presented seemingly intractable problems. If we date user studies from 1948 and the Royal Society Scientific Information Conference, with its several surveys of users' information-seeking behaviour, then the progress towards some theoretical understanding of the concept of 'information need' has been slow. This fact is recognized by virtually every commentator on the subject from Menzel and Paisley through the various authors in the ARIST volumes, to Ford's review of 1977. As well as drawing attention to this fact, the authors have tried to discover why it is so and have generally concluded that the reason lies in inadequate methodology and the failure to do research that is 'cumulative'. Attention has also been paid to the definitional problem of 'information need' and the difficulty of separating the concept from 'wants', 'expressed demand', 'satisfied demand' and so on. However, while much of this work is very useful, the problem remains generally unresolved.

Partly, this is the result of a failure to identify the context within which information needs investigations are carried out. Figure is an attempt to show some of the possible contexts. It is difficult in any two-dimensional diagram to convey the complexity of the 'real' world and abstract elements of that real world. The 'universe of knowledge', for example, is an abstract concept which embraces all knowledge-related objects, events and phenomena and, as such, clearly interacts with the 'physical universe'.

To show the complex interactions of the physical and abstract universes, however, would involve a multi-dimensional diagram which would be extremely difficult, if not impossible, to express upon a sheet of paper. Accepting that difficulty, however, the 'user's life world' can be defined as the totality of experiences centred upon the individual as an information user. Within this life-world one important sub-world will be the world of work, within which will exist various 'reference groups' with which the user identifies: fellow professionals, the peer group within an organization and so on.

The user will be in contact with a variety of 'information systems', only one of which is shown in the diagram, hence the indicated overlap with the user and his life-world. Within the information system two subsystems are shown: the 'mediator' (generally a living system, i.e. a human being) and the 'technology', used here in the general sense of whatever combination of techniques, tools and machines constitute the information-searching subsystem.

The information system must have access to various 'embodiments of know-ledge', phrased in this general way to indicate that such embodiments may be documents or living people.

The lettered paths on the diagram are intended to show some of the possible search paths that may be used by the information seeker directly or used on his behalf by the information system and its subsystems. The paths are not comprehensive of all possible search paths; however, they do identify four relevant groups:

- paths a, b, c and d identify search strategies by a user independent of any information system, and will be referred to as 'Category A' paths;
- paths e and f identify search paths involving either a mediator or an information system's technology (manual card file, computer terminal etc.) – Category B paths;
- paths g, h and i identify search strategies employed by a mediator to satisfy a user's demand for information– Category C; and
- paths j and k identify strategies employed by a sophisticated technology on behalf of either the user or the mediator – Category D. As an example of this latter category, a system could be envisaged in which a computer network could be searched at the initiative of any computer which is a member of that system. The network might include files of knowledge in the process of creation, such as research data files, computer conference files etc.

If we choose to investigate any of these categories of search strategies we are clearly investigating 'information-seeking behaviour' rather than the user's *need* for information. Equally clearly, our motives for investigating search processes may be to make inferences about need, or it may be to uncover facts relating to *other* variables related to the design, development or adaptation of information systems.

Thus, we may wish to investigate Category A strategies to discover whether they are undertaken in ignorance of formal information systems, or because they are more efficient (for example, simply in terms of speed of delivery of a response) or more effective (for example, in terms of the quality of the information pro-vided, or its currency). Such studies may never address the central question of 'information need', that is, *why* the user decides to seek information, what purpose he believes it will serve and to what use it is actually put when received. However, the data derived from such studies may be of considerable use in dis-covering whether it is possible to redesign existing formal information systems so that they are more efficient or more effective.

Similarly, the search processes involved in Categories B and C may be studied to find out how efficiently the mediator, or the 'technology', is performing, and Category D searches may be studied for similar reasons. As noted above, the study of information-seeking behaviour can stand on its own as an area of applied research where the motive for the investigation is prag-matically related to system design and development. A different motivation is involved if we wish to understand *why* the information seeker behaves as he does. This is an area of *basic* research and, although the resulting knowledge may have practical applications, there is no *necessity* that it should.

However, many (if not most) 'information scientists' are practitioners in information work or information systems management, and they look to studies of information 'needs' for guidance on aspects of systems design, development and operation. A confusion then arises between what is *intended* by information needs research and what is *expected* of such research. As a consequence, basic research may fail to be funded because referees do not find in the proposals indi-cations of potential practical applications which were never intended by the researcher.

There is another confusion, possibly more basic, in the association of the two words 'information' and 'need'. This association imbues the resulting concept with connotations of a basic 'need' qualitatively similar to other basic 'human needs'. However, if we examine the literature on human needs we find that this concept is divided by psychologists into three categories:

- physiological needs, such as the need for food, water, shelter etc.;
- affective needs (sometimes called psychological or emotional needs) such as the need for attainment, for domination etc.;
- cognitive needs, such as the need to plan, to learn a skill etc.

It will be quickly recognized that these three categories are interrelated: physiological needs may trigger affective and/or cognitive needs; affective needs may give rise to cognitive needs; and problems relating to the satisfaction of cognitive needs (such as a failure to satisfy needs, or fear of disclosing needs) may result in affective needs (for example, for reassurance). These interrelation-ships are shown in which suggests that, as part of the search for the satisfaction of these needs, an individual may engage in information-seeking behaviour. Indeed, it may be advisable to remove the term information needs' from our professional vocabulary and to speak instead of information-seeking towards the satisfaction of needs'.

This is not to suggest that some affective or cognitive need will *immediately* 'trigger' the. response of information-seeking. Many factors other than the existence of a need will play a part: the importance of satisfying the need, the penalty incurred by acting in the absence of full information, the availability of information sources and the costs of using them, and so forth. Many decisions are taken with incomplete information or on the basis of beliefs, whether we call these prejudices, faith or ideology. So, information-seeking may not occur at all, or there may be a time delay between the recognition of the need and the in-formation-seeking acts; or, in the case of affective needs, neither the need nor its satisfaction may be consciously recognized by the actor; or a cognitive need of fairly low salience may be satisfied by chance days, months or even years after it has been recognized, or the availability of the information may bring about the recognition of a previously unrecognized cognitive need. These factors are crudely represented in personal, interpersonal and environmental barriers to information-seeking.

If we take the earlier analysis of the ways in which the word 'information' is used we can see that the different senses are more or less related to the above needs. Thus– the factual data, or subject content, of a document may satisfy cognitive needs, and this is the usual sense in which we think about the use to which information is put. The attempts at single definitions of 'information' are also couched solely in cognitive terms. For example, Belkin notes that his concept of an information recipient's 'anomalous state of knowledge' leads to 'an explicitly cognitive view of the situation with which information science is concerned' and Wersig's view of information as reduction in the uncertainty involved in problematic situations similarly connotes cognitive changes in the recipient of a communication. However, as Hollnagel writes:

> *'Information science is concerned with the use of information by humans. ... And it is concerned specifically with the way in which humans search for information, systematically as well as unsystematically. The basis for information science is therefore to be found in our experience of using and searching for information...'.*

Because the situations in which information is sought and used are *social* situations, however, purely cognitive conceptions of information need are probably adequate for some research purposes in information science, but not for all. Information may also satisfy affective needs, such as the need for security, for achievement, or for dominance;

- the channel of communication, particularly the choice of oral channels over written channels, may well be guided by affective needs as much, if not more than, by cognitive needs. For example, in seeking information from a superior, someone may be more interested in being recognized and accepted as a particular kind of person than in the actual subject content of the message; in other words, he may be seeking approval or recognition. The oral transfer of information to others may also be done for affective reasons; for example, to establish dominance over others by reminding them that you are better informed and, therefore, in some sense superior;

– the physical document may satisfy an affective need, as when someone collects rare bindings, or illustrated books, because of their beauty. Under extreme circumstances documents may serve physiological needs, as when the tramp on the park bench covers himself with newspapers to avoid freezing to death.

If, as suggested here, the full range of human, personal needs is at the root of motivation towards information-seeking behaviour, it must also be recognized that these needs arise out of the roles an individual fills in social life. So far as specialized information systems are concerned, the most relevant of these roles is 'work role', that is, the set of activities, responsibilities etc. of an individual, usually in some organizational setting, in pursuit of earnings and other satisfactions.

At the work-role level it will be clear that the performance of particular tasks, and the processes of planning and decision-making, will be the principal generators of cognitive needs; while the nature of the organization, coupled with the individual's personality structure, will create affective needs such as the need for achievement, for self-expression and self-actualization. The particular pattern of needs and the resulting form of information-seeking behaviour will be a function of all of these factors, plus factors such as the organizational level at which a role is performed and the 'climate' of the organization.

Again, the search for determining factors related to needs and information-seeking behaviour must be broadened to include aspects of the environment within which the work-role is performed. The immediate work-environment and its 'climate' has been mentioned above, but the socio-cultural environment, and the physical environment, will all have an impact in particular ways. The relationships will be too numerous to detail here, but examples can be given:

- the economic climate and the differential stratification of resources will define some work environments as 'information-poor' and others as 'information-rich', with consequent effects upon the probability of information-seeking behaviour and the choice of channel of communication;

- the political system may define certain types of information as forbidden to particular groups (including the general public) and, consequently, the non-availability of this material may affect performance in specific work roles;
- the physical environment will have a clear effect upon the nature of some categories of tasks and upon the consequent cognitive needs. For example, questions emerging out of drilling for oil in the North Sea are likely to differ in many cases from those that emerge out of drilling in Saudi Arabia.

The probable interrelationships among personal needs and these other factors, the aim of which is to suggest that when we talk of users' 'information needs' we should not have in mind some conception of a fundamental, innate, cognitive or emotional 'need' for information, but a conception of in-formation (facts, data, opinion, advice) as one means towards the end of satisfying such fundamental needs. In the past a great deal of user studies research has suffered from a concentration on the *means* by which people discover information (often analysed in terms of the information researcher's view of how the user *ought to* have been seeking information) rather than upon the *ends* served by the information-seeking behaviour.

It is this bias in past research that has led to dissatisfaction with the results of user studies research, since the service implications of the results have been far from clear. There are, of course, exceptions; the Baltimore study of the information needs of the ordinary citizen avoided the means versus ends trap by building the interview schedule around the idea of problems experienced in everyday life, for which information-seeking using formal information systems might or might not be appropriate. What emerges from the Baltimore study is certainly compatible with the view presented in this paper but, again, information needs are presented in largely cognitive terms (although the existence of non-cognitive barriers is recognized) and the affective dimension of the user's situation is lacking.

Consequences

The analysis presented above is not intended to be merely definitional; the aim is to suggest that the analysis may be used as a springboard to research based upon a wider, holistic view of the information user. In such a wider view the individual would be perceived not merely as driven to seek information for cognitive ends, but as living and working in social settings which create their own motivations to seek information to help satisfy largely affective needs. There would need to be a consequent shift in the focus of research from an examination of the information sources and systems used by the information-seeker to an exploration of the role of information in the user's everyday life in his work organization or social setting.

The consequences of a shift in focus could be fundamental for information research in at least three respects. First, there are consequences for the methods to be employed in research. The vast majority of studies of 'information needs' has been conducted under a relatively crude conception of the 'scientific method', using self-completed questionnaires as the main data-collection instrument. Social researchers of many kinds have become disenchanted with this model of research and are turning increasingly to a consideration of 'qualitative research' either as a complete alternative to quantitative research or, at least, as a pre-liminary.

The methods employed in qualitative research overlap to some extent those of traditional 'quantitative' research in the social sciences in that they include interviewing, but qualitative research is likely to use less formally struc-tured interviewing procedures and may, in addition, use methods such as observa-tion, free-flowing discussion, and the analysis of documents (personal or organizational) and conversational analysis. Under one school of thought, 'Qualitative research ... is concerned with developing concepts rather than applying pre-existing concepts', and given the state of theory in information science (that is, its undeveloped state) it can well be argued that 'developing concepts' is what is needed. Qualitative research seems particularly appropriate to the study of the needs underlying information-seeking behaviour because: our concern is with uncovering the facts of the everyday life of the people being investigated;

- by uncovering those facts we aim to understand the needs that exist which press the individual towards information-seeking behaviour;
- by better understanding of those needs we are able better to understand what meaning information has in the everyday life of people; and
- by all of the foregoing we should have a better understanding of the user and be able to design more effective information systems.

The second consequence for information research of the proposed shift in focus is that, before a generally applicable theory of information-seeking be-haviour can be evolved, the context of the research must be narrowed so that crucial determining factors can be identified and analysed. There can be little use, for example, in a national survey of the 'information needs' of any group (chemists, botanists, economists etc.) if members of these groups are undertaking widely differing kinds of tasks in totally different organizations with varying levels of information provision. If we wish to uncover the determining factors of behaviour we must do so by first undertaking in-depth studies of well-defined categories of persons, developing explanatory concepts and then testing these concepts in related but different settings.

The third consequence for research would be a need to widen our conceptual perspectives of the user and his behaviour. It seems unlikely that information-seeking behaviour can be explained by purely 'information' concepts. Belkin notes that, 'The most commonly proposed information concept for information science... is that of Shannon... This is hardly surprising, since Shannon's information concept is almost the only formalized, mathematical, and successfully implemented concept ever proposed for any purpose'. However, the communication model proposed by Shannon, with its elements: source, channel, message, coder, decoder, receiver and noise, was never intended as an information-science model nor as a behavioural science model, and, consequently, can tell us nothing about the information user and his needs. The concepts we need for explanation, or for development within our own emergent discipline, multi-discipline, or whatever it may be, need to be drawn from psychology, social psychology and sociology, as much as from communication theory.

There are other consequences for information science defined here as a multi-disciplinary field rather than as a single-discipline, theoretical science. Roberts has drawn attention to the need to pay more than lip-service to the suggestion that, in some respects at least, information science is a social science. The proposed shift of focus suggested here would support that proposition by insisting upon the more intelligent use of social research methods for the development of models from the point of view of the philosophy of social (rather than physical) science. It would require that such models pay more attention to the behavioural and organizational contexts of information-seeking than hitherto, and to the totality of types of information resources and information transfer mechanisms. Information science is likely to make more progress in this way than by seeking to evolve on the basis of physical science notions of a discipline alone.

An 'information science' firmly founded upon an understanding of information users in the context of their work or social life is also likely to be of more use to the information practitioner, by pointing the way to practical innovations in information services, and to potentially beneficial associations with other communication or information-related subsystems. It does little injustice to the historic record to suggest that information services have developed more by copying previously existing examples than by genuine analysis of the needs of potential users. In particular, the transfer of techniques from special libraries in science and technology to information units in the vastly different environments of public service bureaucracies, voluntary organizations, business concerns and central government, has been carried on without any serious questioning as to whether these different contexts of information provision require different means of service delivery or, indeed, whether information itself needs re-definition. An orientation towards the user in the true sense, that is, avoiding preconceptions about what *he or she* will perceive to be 'information', while concentrating upon the problems that create cognitive and/or affective needs, must result in a greater humility about the potential value of traditional information practices and a greater willingness to innovate and experiment.

The result of a more truly user-oriented, innovative, experimental information profession should be a reduction in the *marginality* of information service. Scientific research generally recognizes the significance of services which provide access to the external research literature, but when such services are adopted by different kinds of organization with little or no adaptation in the light of a proper analysis of the needs of users or of their relationship with organizational com-munication systems, information services become increasingly marginal to the organization's functioning. Evidence for this can be found in industry, where, when economic pressures have been intense, numerous special libraries and information systems have been abolished or subject to severe staff redundancies.

The answer to this does not lie simply in manoeuvring for a more central reporting position in the organization, but in analysing the *total* range of informa-tion services that may be appropriate to meeting the needs of members of the organization. In all probability this may mean closer association, to the point of merger, with other organizational subsystems that have an 'information' mission – indeed, as a result of developments in information technology, the trend has already begun.

There are, finally, consequences of all of the foregoing for 'information science' as a profession and for professional education in the field. No sooner had information science (in this professional sense) emerged out of special librarianship, than it found what appeared to be the central ground occupied by computer scientists, system analysts, management information system designers, and most recently, data-base entrepreneurs. Soon, office automation through word-processors and other applications of micro-technology will be extending their influence into areas information scientists as practitioners have believed to be theirs. The only sensible response to this is a widening of the concept of the 'information profession' and an acceptance of the need for consultation and co-operation with other groups, the better to serve the needs of the information user. That there is potential for this can be seen in the increased disenchantment with crudely designed management information systems and the increased awareness that, in designing such systems, the technology involved is only part of the total system, and that the user, hitherto somewhat neglected, is an important element.

As for the impact on professional education, there are several things to consider. First, if the social situation of the user is as significant as suggested in this paper, and if the need for more care in the use of social research methods (both quantitative and qualitative) is accepted, then curricula should become more concerned with the social and organizational contexts of information-seeking and information use, and should pay more attention to general theories of com-munication (mass media, organizational, person-to-person), and to social research methods and their philosophical basis.

However, if a shift takes place towards a new information profession, revision of existing curricula in information science will not be enough and, certainly, the mere addition of one or two courses to a curriculum will be far from sufficient. The members of that wider profession will be drawn from many disciplines, and the most fruitful development (and, in these hard times, possibly the most cost-effective) could be the incorporation of 'information science' subjects into the graduate schools of a variety of different disciplines. With luck this could be achieved by designing joint programmes with other departments within a teaching institution, coupled with increased service teaching to undergraduate courses in particular fields. If this development does not take place, that is if planning does not begin now or in the near future, the result may be a gradual diminution of the role of schools of librarianship and information science in the education of the new information professional.

Acknowledgements

The ideas in this paper have been developed over a number of years– in fact, since wrestling with the concept of 'information need' with students at the University of Maryland in 1971! Oral presentations of earlier papers were made at an IBICT seminar in Rio de Janeiro and at a research seminar at Sheffield University Postgraduate School of Librarianship and Information Science, both in 1979, and I am grateful to the participants at these meetings for their discussion of the issues. Further, useful comments have been made on earlier drafts of this paper by three colleagues, Professor Wilfred Saunders, Norman Roberts and David Streat-field, and, most recently and very helpfully, by an anonymous referee. I am aware of the imperfections that remain, however, and accept full responsibility for them.

Access

Equity of access to information, information skills and information technology is crucial to both individuals and to our society as a whole. Students who do not have access to information skills instruction and information technologies will not have the skills they need to fully participate an economy increasingly based on information skills andproducts. Access to information is the foundation of our democratic processes. In the emerging information society, those who do not have the means and skills to access information will be powerless to participate effectively in our decision-making processes. School boards and schools must be committed to providing all students with a wide range of information, access to information technology and information skills training. This is important for all students, and crucial to the success of those who, because of background or economic circumstances, do not have access to information technologies in their homes.

Equity of access to information instruction and technologies in schools will help to overcome economic barriers to achievement. It will also help educators reduce other barriers that prevent some students from both imagining and realizing their potentials.

Information technologies can:

- Provide new learning opportunities to geographically isolated communities and individuals Distance education, satellite telecommunications, fibre optic networks, and other emerging technologies and education delivery programmes will make it possible for students throughout Ontario to have access to richer learning environments and expanded learning opportunities. These advances will also make it easier for all residents to pursue learning and knowledge, regardless of their age or where they live.
- Enhance instruction in French and other languages Information technologies will make it possible, through the sharing of resources, for Francophone students, native students and those students for whom English is a second language to have greater access to information, learning materials, instruction and support.
- Expand racial and ethnocultural perspectives By bringing new worlds of information into schools, information technologies and information skills training will give students of all races and ethnic backgrounds improved access to information and knowledge about their cultures and the opportunity to develop greater confidence in their cultural and racial identities.
- Enable students to work and express ideas in an environment relatively free of gender stereotyping and other biases In comparison with other forms of communication, electronic networks have the greatest potential for allowing students to interact without regard for gender. They also allow students with any impediments to social interaction to interact with others in ways that build confidence.
- Provide new opportunities for students with special needs and abilities Information technologies are easily

modified to meet the special needs of students with special hearing, visual, motor and learning needs. For example, computers can be adapted to synthesize a human voice to assist students with visual limitations or to respond to voice commands from students who have restricted movement. Computer work stations provide a non-threatening environments where students of all abilities and backgrounds can learn at their own paces and make mistakes without embarrassment. In the same regard, information technologies can accommodate students with advanced skills who wish to explore information far beyond the limitations of the classroom. The use of computers can also help teachers adapt their teaching strategies to the learning styles of individual students, whether they learn best through listening, watching or participating in activities.

These potentials can be realized only if school boards and schools are committed to equity of access to information technology and instruction, including implementation of technology-based solutions for meeting the special needs of individual students.

Evaluation

Evaluation is systematic determination of merit, worth, and significance of something or someone using criteria against a set of standards. Evaluation often is used to characterize and appraise subjects of interest in a wide range of human enterprises, including the arts, criminal justice, foundations and non-profit organizations, government, health care, and other human services.

Evaluation Standards and Meta-evaluation

Depending on the topic of interest, there are professional groups which look to the quality and rigor of the evaluation process.

The Joint Committee on Standards for Educational Evaluation has developed standards for educational programmes, personnel, and student evaluation. The Joint

Committee standards are broken into four sections: *Utility, Feasibility, Propriety,* and *Accuracy*. Various European institutions have also prepared their own standards, more or less related to those produced by the Joint Committee. They provide guidelines about basing value judgments on systematic inquiry, evaluator competence and integrity, respect for people, and regard for the general and public welfare.

The American Evaluation Association has created a set of Guiding Principles for evaluators. The order of these principles does not imply priority among them; priority will vary by situation and evaluator role. The principles run as follows:

- Systematic Inquiry: Evaluators conduct systematic, data-based inquiries about whatever is being evaluated.
- Competence: Evaluators provide competent performance to stakeholders.
- Integrity/ Honesty: Evaluators ensure the honesty and integrity of the entire evaluation process.
- Respect for People: Evaluators respect the security, dignity and self-worth of the respondents, programme participants, clients, and other stakeholders with whom they interact.
- Responsibilities for General and Public Welfare: Evaluators articulate and take into account the diversity of interests and values that may be related to the general and public welfare.

Furthermore, the international organizations such as the I.M.F. and the World Bank have independent evaluation functions. The various funds, programmes, and agencies of the United Nations has a mix of independent, semi-independent and self-evaluation functions, which have organized themselves as a system-wide UN Evaluation Group (UNEG), that works together to strengthen the function, and to establish UN norms and standards for evaluation.

There is also an evaluation group within the OECD-DAC, which endeavors to improve development evaluation standards. Evaluation is an in depth analysis of an answer, using for instance diagrams.

Evaluation Approaches

Evaluation approaches are conceptually distinct ways of thinking about, designing and conducting evaluation efforts. Many of the evaluation approaches in use today make truly unique contributions to solving important problems, while others refine existing approaches in some way.

Classification of Approaches

Two classifications of evaluation approaches by House and Stufflebeam & Webster can be combined into a manageable number of approaches in terms of their unique and important underlying principles.

House considers all major evaluation approaches to be based on a common ideology, liberal democracy. Important principles of this ideology include freedom of choice, the uniqueness of the individual, and empirical inquiry grounded in objectivity. He also contends they are all based on subjectivist ethics, in which ethical conduct is based on the subjective or intuitive experience of an individual or group. One form of subjectivist ethics is utilitarian, in which "the good" is determined by what maximizes some single, explicit interpretation of happiness for society as a whole. Another form of subjectivist ethics is intuitionist/ pluralist, in which no single interpretation of "the good" is assumed and these interpretations need not be explicitly stated nor justified.

These ethical positions have corresponding epistemologies—philosophies of obtaining knowledge. The objectivist epistemology is associated with the utilitarian ethic. In general, it is used to acquire knowledge capable of external verification (intersubjective agreement) through publicly inspectable methods and data. The subjectivist epistemology is associated with the intuitionist/pluralist ethic. It is used to acquire new knowledge based on existing personal knowledge and experiences that are (explicit) or are not (tacit) available for public inspection.

House further divides each epistemological approach by two main political perspectives. Approaches can take an elite perspective, focusing on the interests of managers and professionals. They also can take a mass perspective, focusing on consumers and participatory approaches.

Stufflebeam and Webster place approaches into one of three groups according to their orientation toward the role of values, an ethical consideration. The political orientation promotes a positive or negative view of an object regardless of what its value actually might be. They call this pseudo-evaluation. The questions orientation includes approaches that might or might not provide answers specifically related to the value of an object. They call this quasi-evaluation. The values orientation includes approaches primarily intended to determine the value of some object. They call this true evaluation.

When the above concepts are considered simultaneously, fifteen evaluation approaches can be identified in terms of epistemology, major perspective (from House), and orientation (from Stufflebeam & Webster). Two pseudo-evaluation approaches, politically controlled and public relations studies, are represented. They are based on an objectivist epistemology from an elite perspective. Six quasi-evaluation approaches use an objectivist epistemology. Five of them—experimental research, management information systems, testing programmes, objectives-based studies, and content analysis—take an elite perspective. Accountability takes a mass perspective. Seven true evaluation approaches are included. Two approaches, decision-oriented and policy studies, are based on an objectivist epistemology from an elite perspective. Consumer-oriented studies are based on an objectivist epistemology from a mass perspective. Two approaches—accreditation/certification and connoisseur studies—are based on a subjectivist epistemology from an elite perspective. Finally, adversary and client-centered studies are based on a subjectivist epistemology from a mass perspective.

Summary of Approaches

The following table is used to summarize each approach in terms of four attributes—organizer, purpose, strengths, and weaknesses. The organizer represents the main considerations or cues practitioners use to organize a study. The purpose represents the desired outcome for a study at a very general level. Strengths and weaknesses represent other attributes that should be considered when deciding whether to use the approach for a particular study. The following narrative highlights differences between approaches grouped together.

Pseudo-evaluation

Politically controlled and public relations studies are based on an objectivist epistemology from an elite perspective. Although both of these approaches seek to misrepresent value interpretations about some object, they go about it a bit differently. Information obtained through politically controlled studies is released or withheld to meet the special interests of the holder.

Public relations information is used to paint a positive image of an object regardless of the actual situation. Neither of these approaches is acceptable evaluation practice, although the seasoned reader can surely think of a few examples where they have been used.

Objectivist, Elite, Quasi-evaluation

As a group, these five approaches represent a highly respected collection of disciplined inquiry approaches. They are considered quasi-evaluation approaches because particular studies legitimately can focus only on questions of knowledge without addressing any questions of value. Such studies are, by definition, not evaluations. These approaches can produce characterizations without producing appraisals, although specific studies can produce both. Each of these approaches serves its intended purpose well. They are discussed roughly in order of the extent to which they approach the objectivist ideal.

Experimental research is the best approach for determining causal relationships between variables. The potential problem with using this as an evaluation approach is that its highly controlled and stylized methodology may not be sufficiently responsive to the dynamically changing needs of most human service programmes.

Management information systems (MISs) can give detailed information about the dynamic operations of complex programmes. However, this information is restricted to readily quantifiable data usually available at regular intervals.

Testing programmes are familiar to just about anyone who has attended school, served in the military, or worked for a large company. These programmes are good at comparing individuals or groups to selected norms in a number of subject areas or to a set of standards of performance. However, they only focus on testee performance and they might not adequately sample what is taught or expected.

Objectives-based approaches relate outcomes to prespecified objectives, allowing judgments to be made about their level of attainment. Unfortunately, the objectives are often not proven to be important or they focus on outcomes too narrow to provide the basis for determining the value of an object.

Content analysis is a quasi-evaluation approach because content analysis judgments need not be based on value statements. Instead, they can be based on knowledge. Such content analyses are not evaluations. On the other hand, when content analysis judgments are based on values, such studies are evaluations.

Objectivist, Mass, Quasi-evaluation

Accountability is popular with constituents because it is intended to provide an accurate accounting of results that can improve the quality of products and services. However, this approach quickly can turn practitioners and consumers into adversaries when implemented in a heavy-handed fashion.

Objectivist, Elite, True Evaluation

Decision-oriented studies are designed to provide a knowledge base for making and defending decisions. This approach usually requires the close collaboration between an evaluator and decision-maker, allowing it to be susceptible to corruption and bias.

Policy studies provide general guidance and direction on broad issues by identifying and assessing potential costs and benefits of competing policies. The drawback is these studies can be corrupted or subverted by the politically motivated actions of the participants.

Objectivist, Mass, True Evaluation

Consumer-oriented studies are used to judge the relative merits of goods and services based on generalized needs and values, along with a comprehensive range of effects. However, this approach does not necessarily help practitioners improve their work, and it requires a very good and credible evaluator to do it well.

Subjectivist, Elite, True Evaluation

Accreditation/ certification programmes are based on self-study and peer review of organizations, programmes, and personnel. They draw on the insights, experience, and expertise of qualified individuals who use established guidelines to determine if the applicant should be approved to perform specified functions. However, unless performance-based standards are used, attributes of applicants and the processes they perform often are overemphasized in relation to measures of outcomes or effects.

Connoisseur studies use the highly refined skills of individuals intimately familiar with the subject of the evaluation to critically characterize and appraise it. This approach can help others see programmes in a new light, but it is difficult to find a qualified and unbiased connoisseur.

Subjectivist, Mass, True Evaluation

The adversary approach focuses on drawing out the pros and cons of controversial issues through quasi-legal proceedings. This helps ensure a balanced presentation of different perspectives on the issues, but it is also likely to discourage later cooperation and heighten animosities between contesting parties if "winners" and "losers" emerge.

Client-centered studies address specific concerns and issues of practitioners and other clients of the study in a particular setting. These studies help people understand the activities and values involved from a variety of perspectives. However, this responsive approach can lead to low external credibility and a favorable bias toward those who participated in the study.kristen is cool.

Uses of Information

Fisheries policy and management objectives need to be based upon analyses of reliable data. Policy and management issues can be broadly divided into food security, socio-economic and environmental concerns, each of which need certain types of information for decision-making. While the precautionary approach could be used when information is insufficient, management in general should be based on the "best scientific information available" and this has important implications in terms of type, quantity and quality of data to be collected.

Policy and Management Objectives

"In order to ensure sustainable management of fisheries and to enable social and economic objectives to be achieved, sufficient knowledge of social, economic and institutional factors should be developed through data gathering, analysis and research."

It is essential to have adequate data to formulate a useful policy for the whole fisheries sector and effective management plans for particular fisheries. Fishery policies and management plans should address the fishery sector as a contributor to the food supply and economy at local and national levels, and as a critical component of the ecosystem. Hence, data collection should cover all aspects of a fishery, from the natural resources, via exploitation to the local consumers, industry and trade.

The formulation of detailed policies and management plans for fisheries are outside the scope of this document. However, some examples of common areas of concern for policy setting and management are given.

Fisheries Contribution to Food Supply

Food security is an over-riding concern for natural living resources policy-makers, planners and administrators, especially in many developing countries. Fish may be the major source of animal protein for many communities. Small island developing states are often particularly dependent on fish as a food source. It is essential to be able to quantify the dependence on fish as a food source, so that policies and management ensure sustainable use and sufficient access for dependent communities.

Fisheries Contribution to the Economy

For national and local policy-making and planning, it is essential to describe the contribution of fisheries to the economy. If managed effectively, fisheries are able to generate substantial economic benefits to the national and local economies. Assessments of the economic contribution of fisheries need to take into account the generation of income in the local community, of returns to the broader community and of foreign exchange from export earnings. Various countries also obtain revenue from charging fees to non-national fishing boats for access to the resource within their Exclusive Economic Zone (EEZ). This is a significant source of national income for many small island economies. In addition, assessments should include a measure of economic and social dependence. This requires estimates of the numbers of people employed in the harvest, processing and other sectors, and the total numbers dependent on fisheries for their livelihood (workers plus dependants).

Fisheries Impact on the Ecosystem

Fisheries reduce wild fish populations, decreasing the population sizes below that of the unexploited stock. This may not only affect the exploited population but also the interrelated species, which are predators, preys or species in competition with the target species for food resources. It is therefore important to monitor changes in the fish community as well as the exploited stock, to ensure the ecosystem is not damaged by the fishery. Catch, effort, discards and biological data are required to monitor the direct effects of exploitation, and fisheries-independent and environmental monitoring may also be necessary to track all ecological changes.

For inland fisheries, the creation and loss of habitat is often a determining factor in production. Seasonal and long term changes in the area of flooding need to be monitored alongside fishery activities to account for different factors influencing fish stocks. In some cases, special environmental monitoring may be necessary where an inland or marine fishery may cause significant changes to the underlying habitat. This is of special concern for conservation as habitat change is the primary cause of species extinction. Gears that have a physical impact on benthic habitats, such as bottom trawling and dredges, may require special monitoring.

The Precautionary Approach

The Code of Conduct for Responsible Fisheries emphasises the obligation on States to conserve stocks and avoid over-exploitation.

"The right to fish carries with it the obligation to do so in a responsible manner so as to ensure effective conservation and management of living aquatic resources." (CCRF 6.1)

To achieve this they are required to collect data so that decisions are based on the best scientific evidence available.

"Conservation and management decisions for fisheries should be based on the best scientific evidence available, also taking into account traditional knowledge of the resources and their habitat, as well as environmental, economic and social factors... States should assign priority to undertake research and data collection to improve knowledge of the fisheries..." (CCRF 6.4).

Fisheries management has so far generally failed to prevent overfishing and rehabilitate depleted resources. This has led to a reappraisal of the fisheries management process, including the basis for all management, the gathering and analysis of information.

One manifestation of this reappraisal is the requirement to adopt the precautionary approach to fisheries management. The precautionary approach requires fisheries managers to be cautious when the state of a resource is uncertain, such as when fishery data are insufficient or unreliable. The past practice in fisheries management has generally been that restrictive measures had to be justified by sound data, analysis and interpretation. Under the precautionary approach, the burden of evidence is reversed so that it is necessary to justify that it is safe for a fishery to proceed. In the absence of such evidence, the fishery is restricted to a minimum level. The precautionary approach is, therefore, a powerful incentive for the collection of reliable and relevant fisheries data.

The precautionary approach has been embodied in two important international initiatives: the UN Fish Stocks Agreement and the FAO Code of Conduct for Responsible Fisheries (Article 7.5).

"States should apply the precautionary approach widely.... The absence of adequate scientific information should not be used as a reason for postponing or failing to take conservation and management measures." (CCRF 7.51)

When data are insufficient, as in the case of new or exploratory fisheries, the Code provides that:

> *"States should adopt, as soon as possible, cautious conservation and management measures.... Such measures should remain in force until there are sufficient data to allow assessment of the impact of the fisheries on the long-term sustainability of the stocks." (CCRF 7.53)*

The 1995 UN Fish Stocks Agreement is a binding instrument, which applies the precautionary approach both on the high seas and within EEZs for straddling and highly migratory fish stocks. It specifies the roles and responsibilities for regional fisheries agencies and Flag States in the collection and exchange of data necessary to meet stock assessment requirements, and support management objectives for straddling and highly migratory fish stocks. Annex I of the Agreement, titled Standard Requirements for the Collection and Sharing of Data (see Annex 1), specifies the minimum data requirements for the conservation of fish stocks. Article 48 of the Agreement specifies that the Annexes to the Agreement may be revised from time to time based on scientific and technical considerations or may be elaborated by regional fishery organisations or arrangements. Importantly, Flag States are charged with ensuring that vessels flying their flag report the necessary fishery data, irrespective of where the vessels are fishing, and are required to verify those data.

Furthermore, the FAO Compliance Agreement, which is part of the Code of Conduct, states that all parties will provide information to assist in identifying those fishing vessels engaged in undermining international conservation and management measures.

How to Promote Information Products and Services?

Promotion—The Fourth 'P'

After an information product or service has been developed, the price for it has been determined, and the way to reach it to the clients, at the places, where they want it has been worked out, then, the potential clients must come to know of the product or service. Without this basic information or awareness, they cannot act. Therefore, the fourth 'P' in marketing, after product, price, and place, stands for *promotion,* i.e., the communication activity. The basic purposes of promotion are to:

- Attract and hold the attention of the clients (both potential and existing).
- Make the clients aware of the product or service and the organization providing it.
- Position the product or service and the organization in the minds of the potential clients in a unique and favourable manner.
- Motivate the clients to actually buy the product or service.
- Constantly reinforce the message on the clients.

S. Seetharama points out:

Promotion involves mechanisms by which the target groups are informed about the resources available, services and products offered by the library / information centre. Essentially, the purpose of promotional activities is said to be to communicate, to convince, and to compete. Therefore, the library's promotional packages need to be so designed as to achieve these objectives. In this context, the information collected in the market segmentation stage, would be useful.

Dr T. Viswanathan, Director of Indian National Scientific Documentation Centre (INSDOC), New Delhi, gave an example of what would happen if promotion was not done. Speaking at a workshop on 'Marketing of Information Products and Services' held by the Indian Institute of Management, Ahmedabad, and the International Development Research Centre, Canada, in February 1994, he pointed out that INSDOC's CAPS (Contents, Abstracts and Photocopies Services) could only achieve '50% of the target in the first two years.' (Jain *et al.*)

Promotion Methods

In general, promotion, as Philip Kotler points out, involves one or more, or all, of the following methods to reach the clients:

- Direct marketing
- Public relations
- Advertising
- Sales promotion
- Personal selling

The most relevant promotion methods for librarians and information managers are direct marketing, public relations, and advertising—in that order. For them, sales promotion and personal selling may not be much relevant. Fairs, trade shows, presentations, demonstrations, and meetings, which librarians and information managers do sometimes conduct, are more the direct marketing and public relations kind, rather than the sales promotion and personal selling variety.

Moreover, given that the nature of a library or an information centre is that of a social and service institution educating the clients becomes an important promotion tool, particularly about how to use the library and how to use the new information technology available in the library. Therefore, educational and training programmes may have to be organized for clients to help them make the best use of the library or the information centre, and of the new information technology.

Teaching, participating in educational programmes of academic institutions and community organizations and conducting short training programmes for clients become major promotion activities of librarians and information managers.

Libraries and information centres have to do promotion not only to their clients, but also, to their own staff and to the managers of their sponsoring organizations.

Without the internal bridges, the external promotion activity will not be effective.

Promotion Activities

Some of the relevant promotion activities for librarians and information managers under direct marketing, public relations, and advertising, (adapted from Kotler) are as follows:

Direct Marketing	*Public Relations*	*Advertising*
Catalogues	Press kits	Print and broadcast
Mailings	Speeches	ads
Telemarketing	Seminars	Packaging
fileetronic shopping	Annual reports	Packaging inserts
TV shopping	Charitable donations	Brochures and
Direct response:	Sponsorships	booklets
radio, magazine.	Publications	Posters and leaflets
and newspaper	Community relations	Directories
Kiosk shopping	Lobbying	Display signs
Free samples	News (events/	Point-of-purchase
	people/products)	displays
	Public interest articles	Audiovisuals
	in media	Symbols and logos

How to Develop a Communication Programme?

The First Level—Objectives, Target Segment, and Message

To develop a communication programme, first decide the objectives to be achieved, in a specific target market segment, and with what message.

Objectives	Target segment	Message

These three communication elements interact with one another. It is irrelevant with which element you begin. Which comes first is like the chicken and the egg question. Although the order does not matter, the iteration among the three elements and their matching does.

The objectives indicate the direction for action. They tell us where we want to reach, whether we are on the right track, and finally, whether we have reached where we wanted to. Any evaluation, during or at the end of the programme is possible, only, if clear objectives are available.

On the Need for Specifying Objectives, Kotler Writes

Once the target market and its characteristics are identified, the marketing communicator must decide on the desired audience response. The ultimate response, of course, is purchase and satisfaction. But the purchase behavior is the end result of a long process of consumer decision making. The marketing communicator needs to know how to move the target audience to higher states of readiness to buy.

The marketer can be seeking a *cognitive, affective,* or *behavioral* response from the target audience. That is, the marketer might want to put something into the consumer's mind, change the consumer's attitude, or get the consumer to act.

Therefore, to be effective, the objectives must be:

- Realistic to the situation and the organization.
- Specific and measurable.
- Prioritized.

The objectives, as Kotler points out, should specify for the market as a whole, and for each target audience the stage at which it is and the level to which it needs to be moved on the following dimensions:

Communication Goals: Percentage Target Audience			
Stages	*Hierarchy of Effects*	*Current Status (%)*	*Desired Status (%)*
Cognitive stage	Awareness		
	Knowledge		
Affective stage	Liking		
	Preference		
	Conviction		
Behaviour stage	Purchase		

Libraries and information centres cater to two different types of *markets,* i.e., individuals or households and organizations. The individual and organizational markets can be segmented on different criteria called bases of segmentation. General types of bases used for segmentation are as follows:

Individual	*Organizational*
Socio-cultural (social class, life style)	Industry (sector of the economy) Function (production, finance, marketing, HRD, staff/line, etc.)
Geographical (towns, states, nations, etc.)	Level of Managers flop, senior, middle, etc.)
Personal/Demographic (age, education, income, etc.)	Location (headquarter, branch, field, project, etc.)
Psychological (risk prone/averse, etc.)	

The understanding of the target segment should lead to the identification of the client who would be interested in the product or service and his/her motivations to buy it.

Having decided on the target audience and the objectives, the third decision to be taken is about the creation of a message for achieving these objectives. There are three steps in creating messages: generation of message options, evaluation and selection of an appropriate message, and execution of the message. Alternatively, messages can be generated around two dimensions: type of experience and type of reward (Maloney).

Type ofExperiences include: (i) end result of the use of the product/service (like value of time saved), (ii) in process benefit of the product/service (like time saved in locating literature), and (iii) benefit incidental to use (like learning to work on internet through an on-line information product).

Type of Reward could be: (i) rational (like time or value of time) and, (ii) emotional (like I use the least reference service).

By combining the two dimensions several types of messages can be created. The ultimate purpose is to generate message options which fit a situation. Artists/advertising people might do this creatively, rather than going through the above systematic route.

Whatever may be the method of creating messages, ultimately only one/two messages need to be selected for execution. You might like to evaluate the messages generated through research. Messages may be evaluated on parameters of desirability, believability, and uniqueness from the point of view of the target audience in the context of competing messages. Obviously, a message which is desirable, believable and also unique should be chosen. Usually, the options in message execution emerge through a combination of ideas, words, pictures, and promises. Broadly, the message execution can be classified on the basis of the senses they appeal to (presentation), and their tone.

Senses	*Tone*
Sight	Positive
Sound	Negative
Smell	Balanced
Taste	Emotive
Touch	Logical
Combination	Combination

In information products and services, sight, sound, and touch become very important. The buyer may like to experience the book (i.e. see it and touch it) before deciding to buy it. The social esteem and self-actualization needs may predominate in motivating a professional, or an educated adult, to buy an information product or service. Straightforward logical appeals (without any hype) would interest an educated adult. But a little bit of hype may be in order to attract the educated youth to join an educational or a training programme.

The test of a good message is that, it is both rational and emotive and that it moves the client towards the desired action. It is useful to test the message on a sample audience before implementing the promotional programme for achieving the objectives set. Talking about the designing of promotional messages in the publishing industry, Mr. Chin Saik Yoon of Southbound, Penang, Malaysia, said at the workshop:

A former director of marketing, with the Cambridge University Press in New York, wrote an interesting article on Scholarly Publishing, which has influenced many of my designs of promotional materials for the books I publish. He pointed out:

Librarians prize straightforward information. They dislike hyped-up promotion ... over designed and full of breathless superlatives. Such ads are thought to be misleading and wasteful. They are likely to be quickly passed over or chucked out by most librarians, who would rather see plain descriptive copy in simple format with full bibliographic data ... What does persuade librarians to invest their institutions' money in books and journals? Reviews and endorsements by established authorities are probably most important. It makes sense, since the acquisitions people can't be experts in all fields. They are fearful of drawing criticism for purchasing a 'bad' or non-authoritative publication and being accused of wasting money. Therefore, ads and promotion materials should ideally carry a review quote for every publication listed.... (Jain et al.*)*

The Second Level—Media, Time, and Place

At the second level, find the media which reaches the target audience at the time and place suitable for the objectives and the target audience. The iteration among these three items and between the objectives, target segment and message is important.

Media—Time—Place

For instance, if an advertisement in a newspaper is chosen as a medium, it is important to know that the time when the newspaper will be read depends on the convenience of the target audience. The page or pages which are read more often, or more carefully, depends on the reader's interests. For instance, managers, businessmen, and investors are more likely to read the business page than the other pages. Therefore, an advertisement placed on a business page is more likely to reach them than if it is on any other page. Similarly, an advertisement on TV during the cartoon programmes is more likely to reach children.

Often the choice of media lies, at the first cut, between mass media (like a newspaper), specialized media (like a computer magazine), or direct media (like letter through regular or electronic mail). Within the mass media, the choice is between print, radio, television, and internet. The choice is often decided by (i) which medium reaches the target audience, (ii) how fast, (iii) at which place, and (iv) at what cost.

The direct mail—both regular and electronic—is the cheapest medium. The next cheapest one is the print medium (mass and specialized) and then the radio. Television is the costliest medium and often unaffordable by libraries and information centres. However, special publicity or educational programmes of common interest to a mass audience could be presented on television, as part of public affairs programmes, to achieve high reach at low cost. Such programmes, may also be able to attract sponsorship of outside organizations.

Seetharama points out:

It is believed that 'word of mouth' campaigns are the best mechanisms for promoting the use of libraries. Alternate mechanisms include—direct contact with target groups either by mail or in person; indirect contact through the medium of brochures, pamphlets, posters, guides, handbooks, newspaper releases, advertisements, tape-slide shows, video, radio transmission, etc., exhibitions and demonstrations, etc. It should, however, be remembered that promotion activity is not a one-time affair but is a continuous process. Further, while each mechanism has its own advantages, it would be ideal if different approaches are adopted at different point of time. Perhaps, the most effective way is through the library staff who should be courteous, efficient, and possess the necessary knowledge and skill.

Some, however, believe that a very well directed user education programme (or user sensitizing programme, as it is often referred to nowadays) will promote better utilization of the library.

The consensus, among the participants of the Ahmedabad workshop, about low cost media was as follows:

> *... costs of promotion through mass media were extremely high. Therefore, librarians and information managers should develop budgets using the least costly media for ... marketing of products and services.*

The low cost and most frequently used media were direct mail and publicity, particularly for creating awareness among the target customers. CEIS [Caribbean Energy Information System] found that allowing a leading newspaper to publish an article of interest helped in generating tremendous awareness. Cards, logos, etc. could also be used for creating awareness. Advertising could be resorted to only in very limited areas.

Creation of awareness and interest was presently being done through catalogues, brochures, slide shows, exhibitions and fairs. Generating commitment and actual purchase was thought to be best influenced by word-of-mouth, the cheapest means of promotion. However, visits, seminars, and demonstration workshops were found to be useful in getting subscriptions to complex products and services and memberships.

Given the pressure on budget, selection of limited target audience was considered important. However, prioritization of target audience was not easy in the absence of knowledge about their status in the communications hierarchy. Also, sharp focusing of messages was required. Messages and their execution was different for different segments (Chin). The type of messages used were primarily product specific rather than emotive, which in some cases could play a significant role in creating interest, commitment, and purchase. One reason for lack of emotive messages was lack of understanding of what could be promised and fulfilled by the information.

It was proposed that media habits, usefulness of information, etc. be included in the information to be collected through research on buyer behaviour so as to decide appropriate messages and media. Scanning of academic literature on advertising and promotion would also help a great deal in fine tuning promotion (Chin). (Jain *et al.*)

Indicating that publicity could be helpful in promotion, Ashok Vijayavergiya, chief executive of INFUSE Inc, New Delhi, said at the workshop:

> *What we have earned in these years is decent press coverage. There were a couple of articles in the Financial Express, Business World, Economic Times, and some of the leading journals and magazines of India. That publicity has helped in getting wider awareness of our products and services. (Jain* et al.*)*

ICRISAT (International Crops Research Institute for the Semi-Arid Tropics) has undertaken more aggressive promotion methods, like travelling workshops, to market their products. Dr. L. J. Haravu, Senior Manager of the Library and Documentation Services of ICRISAT, explained its methods, as follows, at the workshop:

A number of travelling workshops have been conducted at user sites (research stations and academic institutions) in different countries of SAT. One or two information specialists have been going to user sites in a country to make presentations to potential end-users. Specifically, the workshops have the following objectives:

- o To improve the awareness of end-users to the value of information in general and to the products and services of the Library and Documentation Services (LDSD) and Semi-Arid Tropical Crops Information Service (SATCRIS) in particular!
- o To build contacts with libraries and documentation centres to (1) examine how they can be enlisted to act as switching centres or distribution channels for SATCRIS products and services, and (2) to encourage and develop exchange relationships encompassing documents, databases, and services.

The workshops are targeted to researchers, academicians, postgraduate students and research scholars, policy-makers, and intermediaries such as librarians and extensionists. The presentation highlights the rationale, purposes, and advantages of each service. The presentation is followed by a demonstration of searches of the SATCRIS database (using a subset mounted on a laptop computer under Micro CDS/ISIS) on topics of interest to the participants. Then the potential end-users are encouraged to enrol on the Selective Dissemination of Information (SDI) services or ask for a specific search.

Librarians and documentalists, among the participants, are encouraged to act as focal points or as channels of distribution for our services. Access tools (e.g. the International Agricultural Research Centres (IARC)—Union Catalogue of Serials) are made available to such libraries, and they are encouraged to utilize our document delivery and other services. Software developed at SATCRIS, which may be useful to the libraries visited, is also demonstrated and made available.

Travelling workshops have been conducted in nine countries of Africa and three countries of Asia. More than 40 user sites in these countries have been visited. About 800 participants have attended these workshops.

The workshops have contributed substantially in making potential users aware of our products and services and enrolling new users from these countries. Very importantly, the workshops and enrolment of new users have started a multiplier effect in these countries because satisfied users do 'advertise' our services with their peers.

Presentations and poster sessions are organized at ICRISAT whenever potential end-users congregate in regional or international workshops or seminars. We have found this useful in spreading the word about our services. A colour brochure explaining our services is given away to all visitors to ICRISAT and the LDSD. We have found, however, that presentation, followed by discussions and demonstration, is far more effective in generating interest and demand for our services than the brochure. (Jain *et al.*)

Elaborating at the workshop, the promotional activities that libraries and information centres could take up, Dr H. Arthur Vespry, consultant to the Library and Regional Documentation Centre at the Asian Institute of Technology, Bangkok, said:

You may consider publishing a newsletter. Certainly your annual report is a good way to attract the attention of your community.

Although it often involves extra work, libraries should not shy away from holding exhibits and displays. Use a display to show the benefits of using the library collection.

At all times, use your imagination. Displays need not be limited to within your library or information centre. You may well use a storefront or other locality, with the permission of the owner. Remember the local groups are always interested in displaying the work of their members, whether they be handicrafts, photographs, paintings, or faculty publications. The public relations value of all these activities, by raising customers' interests, may be very great.

We are supposed to be experts in the new information technology. We should therefore grasp these technologies and use them for our benefit. It is always possible to borrow equipment for audio-visual displays from a photographic centre in the community, and do a slide and sound presentation. The company lending the equipment could receive free advertisement. (Jain *et al.*)

Indicating how some kind of a joint venture could also be helpful for promoting one's activities, Dr Vespry pointed out that:

AGE [Asian Geotechnical Engineering Information Centre] is working with the international and regional geotechnical societies to forge closer links with the societies and to become a clearing house for them. This could make joint membership possible, and be beneficial to all parties. (Jain et al.*)*

Dr Vespry also cited the following promotional publications of the Regional Documentation Centre of the Asian Institute of Technology.

- Abstract bulletin
- Newsletter
- Primary journal

- Pocket guides
- Reprints
- Do-it-yourself manuals
- State-of-the-art reviews
- Children's book(s), comics
- Proceedings of conferences (on contract)
- Surveys, studies
- Literature surveys

Publication is one of our major activities at the RDC. We need to think in a commercial manner, and not be afraid to go out and seek advertisements to put in our publications.

Even when you are producing an 'academic' publication, you should try to include news items on projects, people, and happenings. Including these items gives your publication a more human aspect, and hence it is more readable, and more people are likely to subscribe. It is also a way of informing your readers of who you are and what you are doing. Remember, you are trying to gain funds to support yourselves. (Jain *et al.*)

At the Ahmedabad workshop, Ms Mona Whyte, Project Coordinator of CEIS, cited the following promotion activities of the CEIS:

- Publishing a newsletter.
- Establishing a marketing theme around which factors in sales talk can be built. The slogan is 'The One-Stop Shop' for information on energy in the Caribbean.
- Attending energy seminars, exhibitions, etc. where CEIS products have been displayed and more subscriptions solicited.
- Distributing announcement fliers for publications which are being marketed.
- Distributing a brochure on the network, including price lists.
- Developing a booklet on the detailed services at the National Focal Points.
- Approaching companies to encourage them to purchase large numbers of copies for distribution to educational

and youth institutions which are unable to presently subscribe.

- Obtaining endorsements of products and services from high level ministers and politicians.
- Encouraging leading journalists to critique articles published in the CEIS newsletter.
- Encouraging contributors of articles to CEIS to hold discussions about CEIS on radio programmes.
- Seeking advertisements in national, regional, and international publications.
- Exchanging advertisements on CEIS with those of other companies.
- Adding a section in the newsletter for comments which would allow for positive/negative feedback. (Jain *et al.*)

The Third Level—Evaluation

At the third level, think of *what, when,* and *how* you would like to *evaluate*. Keep in mind that:

- The evaluation will be as good as the clarity and concreteness of your objectives.
- The two major items of evaluation are message and media options.
- The two stages of evaluation are:
  - o Before the launch of the programme (to develop the objectives and fine tune media and messages).
  - o After the programme (to ascertain the results, assess the effectiveness of the promotion, and draw lessons for future campaigns).

For pre-launch evaluation of the message options for their effectiveness, the most commonly used research method is the focus group discussion. The post-launch evaluation of both media and message is done through survey research.

The Fourth Level—Budget

Finally, at the fourth level, determine whether the budget matches the decisions that you have taken in the first three levels.

Budget, as Kotler points out, is decided upon by:

- Affordable method
- Percentage-of-sales method
- Competitive parity method
- Objective-and-task method

The first method, *affordable method,* is what the organization thinks it can bear.

In the second, *percentage of sales method,* an arbitrary percentage of the sales is the reference point in many businesses. But for information products and services, the reference point could be the overall budget of the library or the information centre.

In the third, *competitive parity method,* the reference point is what the competitors are spending. If information products and services of other libraries and information centres are attracting more attention, the reference could be how much the others are spending on promotion.

Finally, the fourth method, the *objective-and-task method,* appears to be more rational. Having decided the objectives, the audience, the messages, the media, one has an idea of how much money is required to implement the communication programme.

In reality, a mix of all these methods are used. If the budget is not sufficient, either try to get an increase in the budget or rework the major items so as to fit in the available budget.

The four major items of promotion budget, in order of monetary value, are:

Media is the costliest item of a promotion budget. For developing the media budget through objective-task approach,

- Assess the current percentage of audience on each objective and what percentage of audience should be moved from the current to the desired level.
- Estimate the cost of moving the audience from the current to the desired level.

Advertising companies normally peg their fee to the media cost—usually 15 per cent of it. They charge for the cost of preparing the message and conducting the evaluation either as a percentage of the media cost, or separately. In addition, they charge the actual costs of copy creation, like photography and cover design, and actual costs of data collection and analysis.

In addition, there are administration costs like the time spent by the information managers on the development of the promotion programme, coordinating with the advertising agency, and mailing letters, brochures, etc. Sometimes, it is difficult to identify and categorise these costs. If well managed, these costs may remain insignificant as a part of the overall management costs. If not, these costs may become a long-term financial burden to the organization, irrespective of whether any promotion activity is undertaken or not on a regular annual basis. For instance, you may hire staff on a permanent basis for *ad hoc* jobs like doing mailing for a campaign.

Integration Through Iteration

The development of a communication programme is an iterative process rather than a linear one. The communication dimensions interact between themselves at each level and between the levels. They coalesce into one, to form the kaleidoscopic impression or image on the client.

To process the thought, iterative operation is necessary. But, to implement or to act, a linear or sequential matching of these elements is essential. Therefore, for the successful implementation of the communication programme, it would be useful to have a map by writing down the details at each stage and checking whether they make a meaningful whole.

Conclusion

Promotion of an information product or service is the essential communication process to let the prospective client or buyer become not only aware of the new products and services available, but also to motivate him/her to actually subscribe to the products or services. Therefore, promotion forms an essential fourth pillar among the four Ps of marketing.

What happens when promotion is lacking was explained at the workshop by Dr A. Lahiri, Joint Adviser of the Department of Scientific and Industrial Research, with reference to NISSAT (National Information System for Science and Technology) centres as follows:

> *Authorities are often found to say with much conviction (with a touch of ego) that they need not take pains to tell others what they can do for them; if somebody is interested in knowing things, let them take pains to find out for themselves; after all when somebody comes for assistance, they are not sent back disappointed (splash of ego indeed!).*

While the 'word of mouth' is the best means of communication, additional promotional efforts are indeed necessary. So far the centres have widely used brochures. National Information Centre on Leather Technology (NICLAI), Chennai and National Information Centre on Drugs and Pharmaceuticals (NICDAP), Lucknow print desk and pocket calendars, desk top engagement diary sheets, and posters. Few of them participate in the annual conventions of industries by putting up exhibition stalls. Unfortunately, none of these is done systematically; the hand-outs are also not circulated periodically. Earlier the NISSAT Newsletter had offered them free space to advertise their information products and services, but the response of the centres had been lukewarm, and therefore, the offer was discontinued.

In one case, the product/service was not appropriately defined. Since 1976, NISSAT has been trying to bring in and popularize the 'on-line technology' by setting up various facilities. All the while, the services were being promoted as 'on-line technology' in the brochures, talks, and in TV discussions without realizing that the potential users were not aware of the technology and the benefits that would accrue through its use. A concept test carried out by a well-known market researcher at the instance of NISSAT brought out the lacuna in communication. Since then, the services of NISSAT centres are being promoted as information services through international database facilities. While 'information service' goes well with people looking for information, the concept of 'international database facilities' reflects that it provides comprehensive state-of-the-art trends (and trendy touch of class at the same time). (Jain *et al.*).

Marketing of Information Product and Services to Teacher Community

A society that consumes and generates the most knowledge and information is the strongest society. The information industry has grown dramatically in services, revenue, and coherence over the last decade. Though the marketing of information services is a concept of comparatively recent origin, it has now emerged as an important area for libraries and information centers. Marketing covers those activities that connect the organization to those parts of its outside world that use, buy, sell or influence the outputs it produces and the benefits and services it offers (O'Shaughnessy). As Kotler points out, organizations such as museums, universities, libraries, and charities need to market their causes and their products to gain political and social support as well as economic support.

One of the major barriers to operating a profitable information business is the lack of business expertise among librarians and information scientists. Marketing is a comprehensive term that describes all the processes and interactions that result in satisfaction for users and revenue for the information firm.

Libraries and information centers have begun to realize that marketing of information products and services is an integral part of administration, especially as a means for improving user satisfaction and promoting the use of services by current and potential users. Three main factors, namely the information explosion, the technology revolution, and escalating library costs are responsible for encouraging the library profession to develop a marketing approach in its operations and services. Some information service managers feel that marketing is inimical to the nature of their activities. But with increased competition in the world of information, marketing is a factor for survival. At the same time, there is a common misconception that promotional activities alone constitute marketing.

Information Management (IM)

IM is managing the processes of selection, collection building, processing, controlling, and dissemination of information in an organization. IM can help an organization recognize and use the potentials of the resources of information and information technology. (Brenner) Librarians have a significant role to play in IM. Considering the IM cycle, one can find that librarians have a role to play in almost every step in the information-user matching process.

IM Cycle

Information Marketing

Basic Concepts and Definition: Marketing is planning and managing the organization's exchange relations with its clientele. It consists of studying the target market's needs, designing appropriate products and services, and using effective pricing, communication, and distribution to inform, motivate, and serve the market. The American Marketing Association defines marketing as those activities which direct the flow of goods and services, from production to consumption.

The following are vital concepts that will be discussed one by one:

- Marketing Activities
- Principles of Marketing Management
- Marketing Techniques
- Marketing Strategy
- Creating a Market

Marketing Activities

Market profiling is an important marketing activity, which is done to obtain marketing information. It is necessary to identify the market scope to formulate appropriate policies. Market profiling should consider:

- User affordability
- Extent of use
- Relevance of the service to users

- Repeat customers
- User preferences
- Staffing

Product planning is the marketing activity concerned with developing a product that satisfies customers. Management must decide:

- Who should be the user groups?
- To whom the information services/products should be targeted?
- What should be the services/products that can be produced and marketed to the different target groups?

Pricing is the marketing activity that determines the price of the product on the basis of costs as well as market factors such as distribution channels, discount structure, competitors' prices, ability or willingness of customers to pay, and so on.

The following are questions to ask during pricing.

- What are the costs involved in the generation of services and products?
- What factors need to be considered in arriving at costs?
- Should the information services/products be given free? If so, to whom and why?
- What would be the impact in relation to the value of a product, if given free?
- What should be the criteria for pricing?

Promotion is the activity that covers all aids to sales. Promotion stimulates demand and increases sales. Usually promotion moves the product toward the customers. It involves mechanisms that inform the target groups about the resources available, services and products offered by the libraries/ information centers.

Questions to ask regarding promotion:

- To whom is the promotional material directed?
- What is the message?
- What promotional mechanisms are available?

- What points are to be considered in the design of a promotional package?
- What is the role of the library staff in promotional activities?

Distribution is the marketing activity concerned with distributing the product from the manufacturer to the customer, making the product available and easy to buy. Following are the major channels of dissemination:

- Interpersonal delivery
- Group personal delivery
- Strategic placement
- In-house dissemination
- Local depositories
- Mass media
- Broadcasting
- Mail
- Telephone
- Computer network

Principles of Marketing Management: Modern library services should be based on the following marketing principles.

- The company must have an active attitude towards the market. It cannot expect customers to buy a product simply because it is produced. The management must actively study the market, persuade customers, promote the product, and organize distribution.
- Marketing should be given at least as much importance as other basic functions such as administration, production and finance.
- The marketing function must be "integrated". This means that the various marketing considerations must be taken into account in the decisions of all the managers, not only those directly concerned with sales.

Marketing Techniques: Management is required to control the application of a range of skills and techniques in marketing, generally derived from practical industrial experience and from modern social sciences such as economics, statistics and applied psychology. Marketing skills and techniques can be divided into four broad groups.

- Those used in order to obtain data about the market
- Those used to create and stimulate demand
- Those used to analyze costs and other marketing factors
- Other practical skills and techniques

Marketing Strategy: Not all enterprises can afford to use all the marketing techniques. Furthermore, different situations require different techniques.The marketing manager must be able to select those techniques that are necessary for a particular product in a particular situation. Therefore, successful marketing includes the art of deciding which techniques to use in different situations. Marketing strategy also means selecting various techniques in proper proportion and balance.

Creating a Market: The proper and active use of marketing techniques provide the possibility of creating a market. Here are three examples:

- Increasing the present volume of sales can create a market.
- Creating a market can mean waking up a sleeping market.
- Creating a market can involve creating a demand that did not exist at all.

Thus, the products are made and the market is created as a result of effective marketing strategy.

Professional Skills for Marketing

Library personnel require the following professional knowledge and skills for marketing information and library services:

- Perception of user needs and ability to obtain feedback from users
- Technical knowledge, such as ability to use the Internet
- Knowledge of various marketing strategies for promoting information skills

Factors which characterize the difficulties of marketing information services are:

- The relatively low level of knowledge and lack of agreement on user requirements, wants, and needs.
- The subsidized non-market environment in which most scientific and technical information products and services are used.
- The virtual impossibility of estimating the value contributed by information products and services to the efficiency and conduct of research and development and the advancement of scholarly pursuits
- The general economic unsophistication of those, mostly schooled in the humanities and the non-market-oriented library school environment, who purchase information products and services.

Hence the subjective concept of information makes marketing difficult. The value of information varies with the purpose and is also time and space dependent-hence, the difficulty in projecting the benefits of marketing information. There is also difficulty in estimating the contribution of information to R&D activity and to the advancement of scholarly pursuits. In addition, the reluctance of librarians and other information professionals to engage in marketing adds to the problems.

Conclusion

The library can be called an information market and the library user is a consumer of information. Information is a vital resource for national development. Increasing realization of the role of information has resulted in the establishment of information systems to provide a variety of information services and products. It is an essential step in the planning, designing, and use of such services and products for optimal use of information. Library acquisition, organization and dissemination must be based on the modern concept of marketing to achieve reader satisfaction. It must endeavor to nurture culture of customer service to enhance its image in the eyes of the users.

Bibliography

Aparac-Gazivoda, T & K, Dragutin: *Wounded Libraries in Croatia*, Zagreb, Croatian Library Association, 1993.

Bloss, Marjorie E.: *Guidelines for Union Lists of Serials*, Chicago: Resources and Technical Services Division, American Library Association, 1982.

Bosch, Stephen: *Guide to Selecting and Ccquiring CD-ROMs, Software, and Other Electronic Publications,* Chicago: American Library Association, 1994.

Boss, Richard W.: *Technical Services Functionality in Integrated Library Systems*. Chicago: American Library Association, 1995.

Buchanan, B.: *Theory of Library Classification*, London, Bingley, 1979.

Budd, John: *CEO Credibility: The Management of Reputation*, Turtle Publishing, 1993.

Chan, L.M.: *Library of Congress Subject Headings: Principles and Application*, Colo, Libraries Unlimited, 1995.

Chen, Dora Chiou-sen. *Serials Management: a Practical Guide*, Chicago, American Library Association, 1995.

Comaromi, J.P.: *Dewey Decimal Classification and Relative Index: Devised by Melvil Dewey*, Albany, Forest Press, 1989.

Danton, J. Periam: *The Dimensions of Comparative Librarianship*, Chicago, American Library Association, 1973.

Davis, Trisha: *Serials Control Systems for Libraries*. Westport, Meckler, 1994.

DePew, John N.: *A Library, Media, and Archival Preservation Handbook*, Santa Barbara, Calif., ABC-CLIO, 1991.

Dorothy Grant Cunha: *Library and Archives Conservation: 1980s and Beyond,* Metuchen, N.J.: Scarecrow Press, 1983.

Fox, Lisa L.: *A Core Collection in Preservation*, Chicago, American Library Association, 1992.

Greenfield, Jane: *Books: Their Care and Repair,* New York, Wilson, 1983.

Hamilton, Marsha J.: *Guide to Preservation in Acquisition Processing*, Chicago, American Library Association, 1993.

Johnson, Peggy: *Guide to Technical Services Resources,* Chicago, American Library Association, 1994.

Kahn, Miriam B.: *Disaster Response and Planning for Libraries,* Chicago, American Library Association, 1998.

Khanna, J.K.: *Colon Classification,* New Delhi, Ess Ess Publications, 1986.

Kumar, P.S.G.: *Introduction to Colon Classification,* Nagpur, Dattsons, 1987.

Langridge, D.: *Approach to Classification: for Students of Librarianship*, London, Bingley, 1973.

Middleton, Kent & Chamberlin, Bill: *Law of Public Communication*, Longman, 1994.

Mortimer, Mary: *Learn Descriptive Cataloging*, Lanham, Scarecrow Press, 2000.

Nisonger, Thomas E.: *Management of Serials in Libraries*, Englewood, Libraries Unlimited, 1998.

Parkhi, R.S.: *Decimal Classification and Colon Classification in Perspective,* New York, Asia Publishing House, 1964.

Ranganathan, S.R.: *The Five Laws of Library Science,* Bangalore, Sarada Ranganathan Endowment for Library Science, 1988.

Ritzenthaler, Mary Lynn: *Preserving Archives and Manuscripts*, Chicago, Society of American Archivists, 1993.

Taylor, Arlene G.: *The Organization of Information,* Englewood, Libraries Unlimited, 1999.

Tuttle, Marcia: *Introduction to Serials Management.* Greenwich, JAI Press, 1983.

Vatuk, Sylvia: *American Studies in the Anthropology of India*, New Delhi, Manohar, 1978.

Wynar, B.S.: *Introduction to Cataloguing and Classification*, Englewood, Libraries Unlimited, 1992.

Index

□□□